UNSUCCESSFUL LADIES

Maria Fitzherbert
Morganatic wife of George, Prince of Wales (George IV)
From the portrait by George Romney

UNSUCCESSFUL LADIES

*An intimate Account of the
Aunts (official and unofficial)
of the late Queen Victoria*

JANE-ELIZA HASTED

Biography Index Reprint Series

BOOKS FOR LIBRARIES PRESS
FREEPORT, NEW YORK

INTERNATIONAL STANDARD BOOK NUMBER:
0-8369-8063-8

LIBRARY OF CONGRESS CATALOG CARD NUMBER:
73-148216

PRINTED IN THE UNITED STATES OF AMERICA

FOR MARY

Although the fortunes of war made it impossible for me to have access to all the material I wished to see, I was able to study a great deal and should like to thank all those who made it available to me. My gratitude is due especially to the officials of the British Museum and Carnegie Libraries.

Jane-Eliza Hasted

Parham
Suffolk

1950

Johannesburg
South Africa

GENEALOGICAL TABLE

GEORGE III

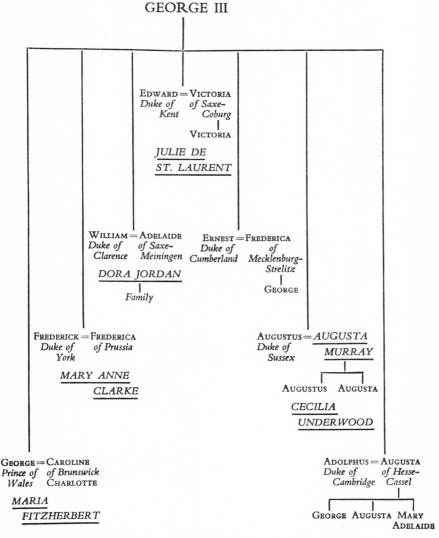

EDWARD = VICTORIA
Duke of   of Saxe-
Kent   Coburg

VICTORIA

JULIE DE
ST. LAURENT

WILLIAM = ADELAIDE   ERNEST = FREDERICA
Duke of   of Saxe-   *Duke of   of*
Clarence Meiningen   *Cumberland Mecklenburg-*
Strelitz

DORA JORDAN

GEORGE

Family

FREDERICK = FREDERICA   AUGUSTUS = AUGUSTA
Duke of   of Prussia   *Duke of*
York   *Sussex*   MURRAY

MARY ANNE
CLARKE

AUGUSTUS   AUGUSTA

CECILIA
UNDERWOOD

GEORGE = CAROLINE   ADOLPHUS = AUGUSTA
Prince of   of Brunswick   *Duke of   of Hesse-*
Wales   CHARLOTTE   *Cambridge   Cassel*

MARIA
FITZHERBERT

GEORGE AUGUSTA MARY
ADELAIDE

NOTE :   Italic underlined names are those of mistresses or wives not officially recognised.

CONTENTS

CONTENTS

ILLUSTRATIONS

ACKNOWLEDGMENTS

The illustrations are reproduced by kind permission of Colonel F. J. M. Gore and Miss I. Gore; Mr. Terence Dennis; Victoria and Albert Museum; British Museum, and Edward H. Gooch Ltd.

INTRODUCTION

BECAUSE OF the vulgarity of its ostentation and the ostentation of its vulgarity, the Regency period is well able to maintain its position as the pet of the smart set. In its unattractive heyday it had a *succès fou* with the world of fashion; never since has it entirely lost its fascination. In art, sport, politics, domestic life, the generation agreed to set aside sincerity, continence and commonsense, as later generations were to do in their turn.

As a comedy set-piece, the stout German gentlemen who were the royal princes of England could hardly have been bettered. Their graceless dives into matrimony when the death of the one and only legitimate member of the rising generation sent them scurrying for an heir to the throne were, and are, entertaining to the cynical or shocking to the simple.

The lay-out is as simple as that. Of the sons born to King George III, seven lived to manhood. By the time the youngest of them was over forty, there was still but one grandchild born in wedlock, and a girl at that, Princess Charlotte.

George III was a man who lived respectably at Kew and suffered from mental instability. His mind lapsed, at first for brief periods, and finally into lasting darkness. His eldest son, the Prince of Wales, later Prince Regent and, eventually, George IV, married in 1795 the Princess Caroline of Brunswick. She was a harmless, stout, vulgar woman who, in the brutal malice of the handling she got in England, appears to have lost most of her virtues but good nature.

Their daughter, the Princess Charlotte, was born nine months after the wedding and her existence came to her father as a welcome reprieve from his wife's society; she had a dismal childhood, an oppressed girlhood, and a happy marriage to Prince Leopold of Coburg. In less than a year she was dead. "They have made me tipsy!" she complained to Baron Stockmar, called to her bedside by the frightened accoucheur, too late to save Charlotte or her son. In labour of her first child, she had been painstakingly bled to death by a medical man of standing and repute. His next service to his country took the form of suicide, but meantime the Princess Charlotte, heiress of England, lay dead at Claremont. It was the home of her marriage, the only house wherein she had ever been really happy. She died very early in the morning of November 6th, 1817. Her baby boy had passed before her only a few hours earlier.

It would be easy here to give one of those relentlessly unforgettable pen-pictures of the European scene, setting out in an industriously intricate pattern of words the usual European jumble as it appeared just after the Napoleonic era. Mercifully, no purpose whatsoever is served by doing so. This is no chronicle of nations, but a tale of certain of the women whose lives were drawn towards one facet or another of that seven-sided figure, the princes of England. We can picture a solid wax candle of seven sleek sides and, drawn to each side, moths of varying degree. Some, it will be noted, more mothlike than others. Variety is also to be noticed in the brothers. Hanoverians as a type appear to be stout, greedy, courageous, inclined to fuss and expensive to keep as pets or hobbies. But they had their individualities, preserved at we know not what cost through the routine rigours of their upbringing at Kew.

George, Prince of Wales, was charming and timorous; Frederick, Duke of York, was an excellent quartermaster; William, Duke of Clarence, was domesticated and had a predisposition to his father's lack of definite mental outline; Edward of Kent was a sadist on the barrack square, a Radical and a born organiser; Ernest of Cumberland was a High Tory, had a life chequered with scandal, and ultimately made an exemplary King of Hanover; Sussex and Cambridge have a tendency to run together in the mind, but Cambridge was the more able and had a kindlier disposition.

As a normal rule, the family enjoyed excellent health and could survive a great deal of Georgian medical treatment, but the Princess Charlotte was having her first child and was in no fit state to receive her doctor's ministrations. She threw down the crown of England as a challenge to her uncles, for as yet not one of those middle-aged, Anglo-Teutonic pseudo-gentlemen was the father of legitimate offspring.

Much of their time was spent out of England, but London was their focus and their playground. In London they scattered their money and piled up their debts.

Vulliamy, the Court clockmaker, made for the Prince of Wales a large French clock, a round temple on whose altar the hours were marked out, the figure of Time sitting, dipping Cupid's wings upon the steps. It is a not unsuitable comment. Sedden, the cabinet-maker, employed four hundred men, for it was a spending period, when showy results had their applause. Good taste was not necessarily inconspicuous, and the florid German style of the brothers was excessively good for trade.

Boydell, the celebrated print seller, had a stock of drawings worth twenty thousand guineas, for engraving purposes. To this trade the brothers were as good as an endowment, for they were a constant target for the caricaturists apart from any polite portraiture.

The London of 1786 has been well described by Sophie van de Roche. Oxford Street was a dazzling thoroughfare, down which it took half an hour to walk. The double row of bright lamps lit the six-deep flagged pavements, shone on the long row of lacquered coaches standing down the middle of the road, and on the handsome glass windows of the shops, in which were displayed luxuries from every quarter of the globe. The spirit booths were spectacular and well-stocked. Hatchett, the saddler, employed hundreds in an organisation unknown on the Continent. He had premises for cartwrights, smiths, harness-makers, sculptors, painters, upholsterers, gilders, girdlers.

Figs were for sale, and grapes and oranges; pineapples cost six shillings apiece. Lamps were many and various, richly ornamented, decorations as well as sources of light. The wick was packed separately in a dainty box, the oil could be carried home in a beautiful glass flask. Oxford Street was a promenade up to eleven at night, coaches dashing up and down it to even later hours. Foot passengers took their own risks, "nearly all the women wear black shoes with very low heels when walking, and get across the road very rapidly." The joke about "the quick and the dead" may be older than we know. The same writer also observed the houses, very much as we know them now in older London. They were "mostly of brick, and have no decorations other than big, well-kept windows, whose panes are framed in fine, white-painted wood." She comments on the tall and elegant front doors, and on the fact that staircases were lit, cleaned and carpeted. Another feature that struck her was that, in the better streets, an iron railing, "erected some few paces from the houses, runs up to the front doors, dividing the road from the basement."

But it is the dress materials about which she is really excited, the silks and chintzes, and the muslins in all colours. For they were displayed to the public in a new and elaborate way, not merely as rolls stacked on deep shelves, but craftily hung in folds, behind fine, high windows. The fall of the drapery could be studied and admired. Temptation was lavishly laid on.

For England, so plaintively and barbarously lagging behind the high civilisation of France, had come up in the world of wealth. Her overseas contacts were growing, if war had cut her off from the Continent. England was very conscious of being English, and only the royal couple at Kew remained uncompromisingly German.

By now, their sons were out of their control in the daily matters of life, but, when it came to marriage, the parents not only held the purse strings to a great extent, but the Royal Marriage Act gave them even greater powers. The King's consent was necessary to ensure validity, and German royalty, great or petty, was bound by an article of faith which decreed that the only parties suitable for a marriage alliance should be of royal, and preferably German, blood.

It was a case of marrying, as Victorians would say, "in one's own class." Even young Charlotte had no English peers or German noblemen presented for her approval. A Prince of Orange came, and departed. In the end Prince Leopold of Coburg, whom she married, took her fancy as strongly as his Coburg relative, Albert, was to take that of her little, unborn cousin, Victoria. Indeed, if Charlotte had not died in bearing

B

Leopold's child, and if the child had not died with her, it is rather doubtful if Victoria would have been born at all.

Had Charlotte survived, produced a family at Claremont, and come ultimately to the throne, she might have given her name to an age as great as the Victorian, and as strongly defined in character. But she died too young even for very much promise, let alone its fulfilment.

We know something of her character.

Unlike her father, she was spirited, but without malice. She had her mother's good humour. Even Lord Chancellor Eldon, who spoiled her one adventure, the hackney carriage rally of her runaway escape to her mother, in refuge from her father's browbeating, became her friend in the end. He was at Claremont when she died.

Baron Stockmar was there too, and he also had become one of her friends. It was to the credit of them both, for she could well have been jealous of his influence over her adored Leopold. It is true that she met him for the first time on the third day of a happy marriage, a time when anyone may take a rosy view of mankind. Stockmar has left a record of that meeting.

"'Aha, docteur!' she said, 'Entrez!' She was handsomer than I had expected, with most peculiar manners, her hands generally folded behind her, her body always pushed forward, never standing quiet, from time to time stamping her foot, laughing a great deal and talking still more. . . . In the evening she pleased me more. Her dress was simple and in good taste."

It was his ideal and he approved it in her.

Four months later he writes of her with decision, on the subject of her wardrobe. "I have never yet seen her in any dress which was not both simple and in good taste." He goes on to say that on that occasion she took his eye in a short,

light blue dress, sleeveless, but with a round collar, and a
puffed-out white blouse with lace sleeves; she wore dark roses
in her hair. We have Stockmar's word for it that the effect was
admirable.

In August of 1817, he is even more complacent. "The
married life of this couple affords a rare picture of love and
fidelity, and never fails to impress all spectators who have
managed to preserve a spark of feeling." And yet early in
November, before the autumn gales had whirled the last
brown leaves from the oaks at Claremont, Charlotte was dead.

So, in the Christmas season of 1817, England's eyes turned
to the King and his six stalwart brothers, and England began to
tick off their matrimonial achievements on censorious fingers.

The succession at Charlotte's death is made clear by the
following table, extracted from Brodrick's *History of England*.

The Regent.
The Duke of York.
The Duke of Clarence.
The Duke of Kent.
The Duke of Cumberland.
The Duke of Sussex.
The Duke of Cambridge.
Charlotte, Queen Dowager of Württemberg.
The Princess Augusta.
The Princess Elizabeth.
Princess Mary, Duchess of Gloucester.
The Princess Sophia.

All these were of the same generation, and the youngest of
the royal brothers was forty-three.

Under pressure of events the bachelor brothers, Clarence,

Kent, and Cambridge, hastily married German princesses likely to provide them with an heir, the two former gentlemen at the sacrifice of their existing partners.

That is the comedy set-piece. The tragedy, the human story beneath, is that the women involved were flesh and blood creatures of desire and affection, ambition, stupidity, principle and greed. It appeared, as they one by one came alive under the leaves of long ago, that there was a good deal of variety and interest in them, and that some of them had made a fairly good job of a not attractive lot in life. And yet, not one of them achieved fully and entirely what she set out to do. Even the Duchess of Kent, Victoria's mother, and so nearly successful that she has been left out of the gallery, was never Queen Mother, merely the Queen's mother. She never reigned, since she could not nurse her Edward through a winter chest cold as well as his Julie had done before.

Not all the ladies were unsuccessful in the same degree, or in the same direction. Some failed to reign; some failed to achieve heirs; some failed in being ladies at all. Some were born to failure and some fell by the wayside.

Augusta of Cambridge had the greatest success among the ladies, since her grand-daughter, Mary, became Queen of England and mother of King George VI. Those ladies who were not duchesses, or who were married by illegal or illicit rites, are included because the association had a repercussion on matters extra-domestic. The list could quite easily be lengthened.

In fairness to the seven sons of George III, it should be remembered that much of the responsibility for the irregular unions to which all but Adolphus of Cambridge were forced to resort, should be placed upon that absurd and tyrannical piece of legislation—The Royal Marriage Act.

UNSUCCESSFUL LADIES

I

MARIA FITZHERBERT

MARIA FITZHERBERT

THE GIRLHOOD of Maria Smythe was as quiet and regulated as that of any young Protestant German Princess. She was, however, neither Protestant nor royal. Her father, Walter Smythe, was one of the great group of well-connected Roman Catholic families who were at that time so treated by the laws of England that they had to marry before, to them, unhallowed altars and to seek service in a foreign army if tradition or inclination indicated a military career. Both her father and her elder brother chose the Austrian army.

The same legislation, only slowly modified, which had sent martyrs to the stake, made the life of the Catholic families a close circle, beyond which, in some cases, they never even entertained. It was as narrowly circumscribed as the life of the smallest German principality. Maria was born into such a setting on July 26th, 1756.

This is the keynote of her life; that she was a devout Catholic, and in that age. That she was also a virtuous and respectable woman is not so important. The point is that she was a virtuous and respectable Catholic gentlewoman. She had enough of the martyr spirit in her to be willing to put herself for the sake of her true love into a difficult position, a position in which she appeared to possess neither of these admirable qualities. But from the moral standard enjoined on her by her Church, she never wavered. Since the law itself treated her Church, professedly her highest authority in the great crises of life, in a way which she must have regarded as worse than cruel, as blasphemously wicked, she could scarcely be expected to have very much respect for its opposing point of view.

She was sent to Paris to be educated, to the "Blew Nuns," whose convent was the recognised school for girls in her position. This is the first important fact that we know about her, for even the place of her birth is given variously by different authorities. Poetically, it is appropriate to believe the one which makes it Tong Castle, in Shropshire, for she was born for castles, not to say Pavilions.

What we know of her, we know very largely through Lord Stourton, her uncle and her confidant, and her latest and charming biographer, Shane Leslie. That is not to say that she was a secret or mysterious figure. The world knew of her existence, and many of its best citizens approved of her in every way. But, like most reasonable people, she kept the crises of her life few and far between and made no parade of them. The fact of her religion forced her to invest her marriage in mystery, but she was not mysterious.

It was at school that she saw her first King. The "Blew" Sister who fastened on her wrap may have had considerable trouble in making little Mary Anne stand still. For one thing, her mother was in Paris and her father too. Even the best school is improved when your people come to take you out. Some of the elder girls had doubtless been to see Louis XV at his queer, silent, solitary public dinner, for it was no unusual distraction, but for Mary Anne, Versailles was a new and glittering world.

She went, she saw a King, and her reaction was to burst out laughing. It was a horrifying breach of etiquette. Someone must have jerked her arm, hissed in her ear and looked round to see whether the royal disapproval appeared alarming.

Mary Anne restrained her mirth. But it was funny, for he had pulled a chicken to pieces with his fingers, and only think what Sister would say if she—Mary Anne gave her attention again to what went forward. The King had summoned a gentleman, and the gentleman was approaching her. The Duc de Soubise bore a dish of sugar-plums in his hands, so either Louis was being royally gracious, or he had a taste for little maidens with very pink cheeks and masses of goldy hair.

He was not the only person with such tastes. We are told by Lord Stourton that she was no great beauty, and Heneage Jesse says the same, perhaps only echoing the noble uncle. On the other hand, she was dowered, in addition to the glory of hair, with a wonderful complexion, which remained when she was sixty as perfect as a child of six, hazel-brown eyes, attractive features and a very charming figure. Lord Stourton, one feels, had exigeant tastes.

Other testimony, from casual inhabitants of Brighton, from people who met her, worked for her, all go to show that at least she knew how to leave the impression of charm.

Certainly when she was eighteen she married well, or was married well, to a Mr. Edward Weld, considerably her senior, who made her mistress of Lulworth Castle. He died suddenly before the year was out, not having signed the Will which was to leave her everything of which he could dispose.

Mrs. Weld did not return to her maiden home. Besides being beautiful, she was quick-witted and independent, this widow of nineteen, with rapid little slangy turns of phrase. Her father was alive at the time, although he died before her second marriage, but she clearly intended to live her own life. A young widow was then in the same position as a girl of to-day with a little money of her own. She took a cottage.

Knowing her, it must have been cousin in cottages to that with which Meredith endowed Diana, and she left it in a few years for the same reason as the Irish beauty—to make a good marriage of affection to a man occupying a recognised position.

Thomas Fitzherbert of Swynnerton in Staffordshire and Norbury in Devonshire occupied a town house off Park Lane and entertained in a wider circle than most Catholic families. Here she first moved out of the little circle of allied Catholic families and met people who mixed easily across the frontiers of sect. It must have been surprising at first, not always easy, and yet a relief. As Thomas was wealthy, she cannot have regretted the cottage.

The respite from the incessant consciousness of religious persecution did not last for very long. She married for the second time in 1778. In 1780 London was in the throes of the Lord George Gordon riots, and that intolerant imbecile was inciting the mob to every kind of violence. All Catholics of any position were out to offer rescue and shelter to the persecuted, to priests in particular and Thomas Fitzherbert was to the fore. There was a good deal to be done. It was hot work as well as dangerous, dirty as well as risky. When he came in, with the sweat running down his forehead, Maria (she preferred it to Mary Anne) was so injudicious as to permit a bath. It did him no good. He took a chill at once. She carried him off to the South of France, to Nice, but in spite of the change, she lost him in the following year, 1781.

At twenty-five she was a widow for the second time, but now she had an income of £2,000 a year, and the remainder of the lease of the Park Street house. She did not live there, she retired to Richmond, and from there her story begins.

She was the "sweet lass of Richmond Hill," for whose sake His Royal Highness, the Prince of Wales, would "crowns resign." The tale says that he saw her first in 1783 on the banks of the river. It is too appropriate a tale not to be true. She had pale gold hair and a perfect form; he was the Adonis *de ses jours*; the banks of most rivers are sentimentally seductive, and the banks of the Thames traditionally so.

In 1784 she came out of her rusticity and returned to London. She began to entertain again.

Events show clearly enough that Mrs. Fitzherbert desired no relationship, seeing no comfortable and honourable one, with the Prince. But fitting in the pattern of the days and places one can see that Maria returned to the world of fashion the season immediately after she met His Royal Highness. It looks as though the singing bird in the heart of the lady had been re-awakened. She had not the smallest intention of becoming her admirer's mistress, or hope, even if she had the wish, of becoming his lawful wife. She merely came alive again.

The roses passed and the last summer fête died as a chill-winded penance, as the last summer fête is apt to do. The further south the sun rose, the warmer grew the Prince's passion for Maria. He pursued her incessantly.

It was no good asking him not to call. She tried. First she beseeched His Royal Highness, and from thence she grew to ordering her persistent slave to leave her. He swore all the resounding and minutely detailed vows of fidelity which men can by regular practice acquire skill in phrasing.

She entirely declined to become his mistress. The Prince thought of marriage. Probably he first thought of "marriage," some formality with a ring and a signed document, which should overcome her scruples. But "marriage" had no attractions for her.

As love nibbled hungrily through the stay ropes of reason, the Prince thought of marriage in due form. The trouble lay very greatly in the fact of the lady's religion. Any marriage that he contracted without the King's consent would be null and void under the Royal Marriage Act of 1772. But marriage with a Catholic, if legal, would exclude him from the succession to the throne, according to the statute known as the Bill of Rights or Act of Settlement.

Maria refused to change her religion.

The first frosts did nothing to cool the Prince's ardour. His associates, including Fox and the lady who was still Mrs. Armistead in name, heard nothing but the ditty of love scorned. They also saw in its frenzy something of the nervous excitability which ran in the family, a sign that made them all instantly apprehensive.

In November, Maria thought that matters had gone far enough. She knew the Continent, she had friends abroad, and a position which ensured her a reception anywhere. She resolved to get away at once, in spite of the season.

All the business of packing, storing, making financial arrangements, began immediately. She was engaged on them when four gentlemen arrived in a coach—Lord Onslow, Lord Southampton, Mr. Edward Bouverie, and Keate, the surgeon. The first three names showed her from whom the delegation came, they were among her lover's intimates. To find the surgeon in their company was enough to make any woman anxious about a man who at least had the good taste to be fond of her.

The Prince had stabbed himself. Keate confirmed it. He had stabbed himself in the despair of a hopeless love. Nothing but her presence could save him. He was not dead, not even fatally injured, then? They confirmed it. But he was seriously injured, the consequences might be fatal. They repeated the assurance that her presence was immediately necessary at Carlton House.

Maria hesitated. Too many humbler flies had been lured into the spider's unsavoury parlour. The delegation urged her. She made it clear that she hesitated because of the proprieties. Prince or no Prince, these proprieties must be observed! She demanded a chaperon.

Quickly they suggested Georgiana, Duchess of Devonshire. She was in the Prince's set but she was also a great lady, her presence was sufficient. Maria allowed herself to yield. They rushed her into the coach and straight to the duchess. That spirited lady was only too delighted at the thrilling situation and at being offered a share in it. She joined the party.

In a mixture of suspicion and anxiety, Maria hurried to Carlton House, across the threshold and to where the Prince lay. He was pale, he was blood-stained, at his side stood brandy-and-water.

She was overcome, and swept for the moment off her feet. She allowed him to put a ring on her finger, one of the duchess's. But she would not stay under his roof. Once she had allowed so much, it seemed even less safe to remain. They went instead back to Devonshire House, where one of the gentlemen drew up a document attesting the marriage. She may have regained her wits still more by that time, for she did not trouble to take the paper with her, she left it behind when she returned to her half-dismantled home.

Her uncle, Lord Stourton, when she told him the history many years later, sceptically demanded whether she was sure that the Prince was really stabbed, and stabbed by his own impassioned hand. She asserted solemnly that she had frequently seen the scar in later days. And, besides, there was the brandy-and-water!

However, when she had taken still more time to think, she saw one thing clearly. That was that the crisis had given him the opportunity to rush her into the very arrangement which she had firmly refused, a mock-marriage. November evenings are long and she had time in the candle-light to write to the four gentlemen who had acted as accomplices. She told them firmly that she did not consider herself bound by a ceremony that was neither marriage nor anything else. She put down the pen, folded the note, and went back to decide with her maid what she should take and what she should leave behind. Her purpose held.

Next morning she left England.

She went to Aix, and then on to The Hague. There she tumbled into an odd situation. The Stadtholder had a daughter. There were discreet preliminary enquiries in progress with the object of marrying her to the Prince of Wales. The father knew that Maria was a lady of the world, received in London society wherein the Prince circulated so fast and freely. He was anxious, as was his daughter, to question her minutely about town, the Prince, the Court, ten thousand details.

Maria behaved admirably. She may have thought that a sound marriage would be the one thing that would put an end to the Prince's unwelcome pursuit of her. At any rate, she spoke calmly, gave no hint of the present situation, and made a friend of her young rival. The situation was embarrassing enough, but it became much more so when she learned that Sir James Harris was expected.

He was Cupid's semi-professional messenger. It was he who, as Lord Malmesbury, approved the Duchess of York and brought home the bouncing Caroline. He was also a friend of the Prince, and he knew very well that Maria was the object of at least the moment's adoration. It seemed a needless complication. She repacked her trunks and, in the dignity of the royal barge, left Holland.

She toured Europe.

It was only a matter of time before the Prince ceased rolling on the floor at the feet of Fox and Mrs. Armistead, and began to show his passion more practically. The Dutch marriage was dropped. He had Maria traced and, when he found her, flung across Europe a series of couriers who wrecked diplomatic peace of mind by their number and their speed. Was it war? Was it peace? It was love! Europe was hushed again, and the perspiring cavaliers delivered letters sometimes thirty pages long. These fine poetic flowerings of the eighteenth century were to go up in smoke under the grimly appropriate nose of the Duke of Wellington, himself that century's last fling in the teeth of democracy.

Somewhere, somehow, in the long months of 1785, the moment came which was to decide so much. Now, Maria did not love; now, she did. January, February, March, May to September, October—we can tick them off on our fingers and wonder in which month the first change came, and for how long she "fought it off." That was her own phrase, the one she used when she spoke of this period later to her uncle. She was trying to fight off her marriage, for marriage it had become.

Of course, she must at times have been lonely, and loneliness is great guns on the side of an absent, importunate lover. Then she found herself in the position most infuriating to the person whose motives for resistance remain private, she was being pursued on the spot by one of the most notorious libertines in France.

She decided. In December she returned to England, thirteen months after she had left. The dove returned to the dovecote and the political hawks were considerably put about. They only hoped that she had decided finally, would yield sensibly, and stop any scandal that the Prince's proclaimed desire might cause, by accepting him as a lover. In view of her religion, his openly declared love held a hint of danger, and a real fear of marriage had begun to grow. Fox, in particular, was worried, writing at length to the Prince, begging him not to consider marrying Maria, stressing that any other connection would be preferable for both their sakes. It was a most commonsense epistle, and, of course, he spoke from experience.

The Prince gave what is politely called an ambiguous reply. He wrote and said that he "had not the faintest intention of marrying her, my dear Charles," and on December 21st he married her.

It was a difficult ceremony to arrange. The witnesses and the clergyman had to be carefully chosen. Maria produced an uncle, Henry Errington, and a brother, Jack Smythe. Secret her third marriage might be, mysterious or doubtful it was not. The Prince produced Orlando Bridgeman.

For officiating clergyman, they needed a man of some courage, either extremely weak and perhaps buyable, or extremely strong. He must keep his mouth shut. And as there were two Acts of Parliament to be ignored, a resilient conscience so far as the law was concerned was required.

They approached Johnes Knight, father of the kittenish Lady Shelley, but he rebuffed them. A young curate, Robert Burt, was more willing, and was paid a fee of £500 with the promise of later preferment—a promise which was kept. Orlando Bridgeman kept *cave*, while, in her own drawing-room, Maria took the Prince as her husband in a manner acceptable to the canons of her Church, to his, and to the law of the land, except in so far as the marriage was an offence in itself.

People have asked why there was no Catholic priest present. True, the Pope himself must have owned them man and wife without it, but still, why? She was faithful and devout, it would have given her added satisfaction.

Almost certainly Maria made this sacrifice on the altar of the Bill of Rights to protect her husband. She could not prevent the possibility of the whole marriage being annulled, but she could not forget that marriage with a Catholic forfeited the Prince's right to the throne.

For his further protection in that dramatic December, she made another promise, which she held as binding as her marriage vow. Never during his lifetime, without his consent, would she publish the fact of their marriage. She locked away her lines, and kept her word. Later, during the Catholic relief troubles, she even snipped the witnesses' names from the certificate, lest they should suffer in the unlikely event of the document coming to light.

When the ceremony was over, he did not lead her back to Carlton House. Never through all their married life did he make a home there for her. Neither, when Uncle Henry and Brother Jack and Orlando and the Reverend Robert Burt had all departed, did they stay in London. It was December, it was snowing, that festive pre-Christmas snow of our

c

ancestors, but tradition says that they set out together at once for Richmond.

Maria was as light-hearted as a lark, the husband the gayest of the King's sons. They bundled on westward through Knightsbridge and Kensington, growing later and later as the roads delayed them. They broke the journey half-way, at Hammersmith, and supped merrily at an inn.

It was only a bird-flight of a night or two, down on the leafless river bank, for before Christmas they were back among the lights of town. They found the whole of Society in a buzz of gossip and speculation. Given her known devotion, given the Prince's passion, given their present connection—was it marriage? Surely it could not be? Maria said nothing.

Although later she was to be treated with much kindness by the King and Queen—for she did a lot to civilise their heir—she was not now received at Court.

The old house would not do. She moved to St. James's Square, to be near Carlton House. She refused to take more than £3,000 a year from the Prince, and that she needed for the establishment. However, he increased his debts by lavish presents of silver, jewellery and other gifts. His debts were so enormous that what could be spent on a wife and her house plenishings would not make much difference.

He was a young man then, as one forgets, debauched but not yet coarsened, and the possessor of the most polished manners in the world. His behaviour to her was respectful and correct in the extreme. All the deference which Sir Percy Blakeney paid to his lady could not have exceeded that which Maria received from the Prince. He insisted on her being honoured where he was invited. Rumour buzzed incessantly. In Catholic families, it buzzed with the knowledge that she continued to go to Mass, and belief in the marriage gained ground.

Great Catholic doors were open to her and Society rallied to her. The Duchess of Devonshire stood behind her, in spite of an earlier decision to the contrary, only to receive her at big assemblies. Even the die-hard generation of elder hostesses, Lady Salisbury and Lady Clermont, received her openly.

But public credence of the marriage had another side. Combined with the Prince's Whig politics, it was sufficient to fan the flame of another No-Popery scare.

The Prince's real friends might be glad that he had found so good a wife, one whose influence was so obviously for the better, but the world and the caricaturists saw all the ancient threats revived. And meanwhile the Prince became more and more entangled in the wreck of his finances. His father had recently persuaded the country to settle his own debts, but he firmly refused to help with his son's. Fox and Sheridan, the Prince's friends, brought the matter before Parliament in April of 1786, but Pitt firmly opposed relief. Maria, so capable a manageress of her own affairs, moving so calmly from castle to cottage or to villa as circumstances dictated, must have been more than anxious at Pitt's antagonism. A little help, relatively speaking, and her husband's position could be retrieved—and this man refused it. They were never to be friends, largely because of the events of these two years.

The result of Pitt's refusal, and the loss of popularity caused by rumours of a Catholic marriage, was that Maria found the Prince busily circulating counter-rumours that he was not married at all.

However, his public and private behaviour towards her in no way changed. The 1786 season was a brilliant one; London was not to see such another until the Waterloo era. Maria was, in a sense, its heroine. The Duchess of Cumberland received her at her weekly assemblies, treated her as though she were the Prince's wife in every legal aspect. She acted as hostess at Carlton House whenever the presence of ladies made it necessary. The level of Carlton House entertaining at that time was not low. Fox was there, friend to both for the season, Sheridan, Burke whom she knew and liked; North, Grey and Windham were in the set.

It was a brilliant year, but when it ended the debt question had to come to a head.

It was natural that her advice should be asked, and even more natural that it should be given. Here was a question, as Maria would see it, of commonsense, solvency and honesty. She had run her own income capably, and she disliked and disapproved of her husband's position.

A meeting of the main creditors was held. She discussed the problem with her husband, and her considered advice was that the debts must be paid. If necessary, he must somehow save money and pay them himself. But they must take all the facts together. For instance, the King had intervened in the matter of the Prince's allowance, and had caused the amount originally suggested to be reduced by one half. The Prince might therefore make one last appeal, first to his father and then to Parliament, before he took any other steps.

It was good advice, but in every item it was to make trouble for her.

First, then, the Prince asked his father for the money. The King asked for a list of the debts. This was supplied, and he kept it, but nothing was done about the money.

On reconsideration, nothing further was said in the House.

Pitt had already proved unhelpful. To bring it up again might create more anti-Catholic feeling, and the one thing which the Prince could not stand was unpopularity. The threat of it was sufficient to make him turn on his dearest friend. He had received adulation from his birth and he meant to go on receiving it until his death. When public feeling turned for a while against him, Maria had seen him anxious that their marriage should not be credited, not for fear of losing the throne but for fear of criticism. She may have been glad when he decided to try at once the more practical part of her plan.

He sold his horses and carriages, shut his state apartments and generally reduced his establishment to the standard of that of a private gentleman. The realisation of palatial dreams was his hobby, but he stopped the work in progress at Carlton House; however, the Brighton Pavilion, in its first form, was almost completed, and they decided that seaside distractions need not necessarily be extravagant. He hired a post-chaise and drove down. A fortnight later she followed him. Behind green shutters, separated from the Pavilion by only a strip of grass, she unpacked and arranged, with her usual gaiety and a good deal of hope.

She may have agreed secretly with the King that to settle the volatile Prince's debts too quickly was to incite him to amass more. She hoped that her husband would prove the honesty of his present intentions, thus regaining his father's favour and eventually be reunited with his family. That was a state of affairs which she regarded as suitable, comfortable and desirable.

Yet the sudden economy and rustication at her favourite Brighton had a very bad effect in many quarters. The Prince himself was doubtful of the wisdom of his step. It was looked upon as an insult to the King. Maria might regard matters from the point of view of a gentlewoman; he was a courtier by birth and training. However, he followed her advice, and when Egalité Orleans, one of the richest men in Europe, pressed a generous loan, he did as she wished and refused.

They treated Brighton as their headquarters. Maria had given up her town house and neither of them took another. They borrowed residences for a few weeks here and there, paid a round of visits, and made merry. In six months Maria could begin to count up receipts instead of bills. The small debts were paid, they braced themselves to tackle the larger ones. By 1787, nine per cent. had been cleared, and she breathed a sigh of relief. Daylight, although still a trifle distant, could be glimpsed through the fog.

But the distance was the difficulty. Perhaps she, like other people, began to see that at this rate it would be the best part of another five years before the heir to the throne could emerge from obscurity. The position was undignified both for him and the country. Something had been done, the Prince had shown goodwill, perhaps there was another way out.

There were further meetings to discuss the debts and Maria was present, although her presence must sometimes have prevented complete freedom of speech. The one thing to which it was impossible to refer in her presence was the possibility of marriage. That they were man and wife they had not definitely avowed even to their intimate circle. Once or twice in his life the Prince admitted it, but his reliability on points of fact was not great. Maria herself said nothing at all.

Now she agreed that they might well go back to the omitted part of the programme and ask Parliament for the money. Pitt,

as before, was against it. An independent member was induced
to bring up the question of settlement of the Prince's debts.
Fox, strong in the fact that the Prince had once written to him
flatly denying that he intended to marry Maria, got to his feet.
The discussion grew warm. A great deal was to depend on
that question of the marriage. Maria sat at home and waited
for news. It was Sheridan who appeared first, suddenly. Of all
things, he had come to sound her about the marriage. She
could tell him nothing. She was, she said, "like a dog with a
log tied to its tail!" Even in crises her coloured phrases had
their way. She depended upon her friends, she told him, and
Sheridan bowed himself out.

The next thing that happened was that Fox came out with a
round and unflattering denial that any marriage had ever taken
place.

Maria had taken no town house again, she was staying with
the Hon. Mrs. Butler, and as she waited for news, her husband
called. He strode in, took her hands, "Only conceive, Maria,
what Fox did yesterday!" A pause. "He went down to the
House," one can hear the indignation mounting, "to the
House, and denied that you and I were man and wife! Did you
ever hear of such a thing?"

She had. She had heard him spreading rumours to that
effect, a different matter from merely keeping silence. Now
she turned pale.

A torrent of her husband's familiar eloquence descended on
her. Fox had behaved impossibly. Fox had no right, Fox was
a conscienceless scoundrel . . . she listened quietly. Later in the
day she learned the actual phrases which her husband's dear
Charles had used, and she expressed herself with more than her
usual vehemence and a quite unusual venom. Never again,

although once he offered to make her a duchess, were she and Fox to be friends.

The Prince could have ignored her quarrel, as he usually ignored feminine differences, but she extended her coolness to him too. She sat at home, mortified and angry, and icily returned his messages and letters. This was unfortunate, because financial relief was forthcoming and the Prince felt that his prospects were uncommonly bright. The next thing Maria heard was that Sheridan had risen, *à propos* of the accommodation arranged on the basis of Fox's denial, and paid her some nebulous compliments which the House received in kindly fashion. The Prince was now solvent, reconciled with his family, popular once more; he wanted to persuade her out of this tiresome mood as soon as he could.

Maria refused to see him. His old excitability flared up, he fell back on his old trick of pretending sickness and threatening to kill himself.

She gave in. After all, the major point was settled, she was his wife, and the nebulous line dividing the possible from the impossible in the means of keeping it secret was exceedingly hard to find. He was faithful to her, at least.

May 25th seems to have been a busy and happy day for him. He had a three-hour interview with the King, saw his mother and sisters, and then took Maria to the Epsom races and to a ball in the evening.

If she had been hurt, she was repaid. The Duchess of Portland, Lady Sefton, and others who still held out against her, now came round. The masses could gossip in their ignorance, Maria was respected and the Prince was more than ever anxious that this should be so. In June, the romantic Lady Sarah Napier was writing that "there is no truth in his acting contrary to Mrs. Fitzherbert's wishes, for he likes her better than ever, and makes more fuss with her." So the gay and charming Maria wore the white roses of lawful love, and kept her head out of powder, for one part of her good sense was to prefer pale gold curls to flour-caked ringlets.

The malicious dislike for her felt by the nation at large was based on religious grounds. Everything had been pardoned in the adorable Nell because she was Protestant, everything was reviled in the balanced and humorous Maria because she was a Catholic. The Tudors began a spiritual bitterness of feeling that survives here and there to this day.

However, in 1787 she was happy enough. It had been an eventful three years, the stabbing incident, the "fighting off," the marriage, the brilliant season, the merry impecuniosity of their Brighton stay and their round of visits. Now they returned to Brighton, but they were no longer rigidly economising.

Always attended by her husband, himself the centre of a swarm, Maria went to the play, walked, talked, sang, and bathed in the charge of Martha Gunn. Brighton adored her. "She was a woman who needed nothing but a diadem to make her a queen!" Mrs. Gunn addressed her as "Mrs. Prince," and dipped her with loyal jollity. Maria dried the golden curls, and most probably complained of the sea air's effect on them. Her drawing-room accumulated more of its knick-knacks.

In August, she acquired one of her greatest and most loyal friends, a man who, holding the secret which might have meant a crown for him if he had taken advantage of it, nevertheless kept silence all his life. Frederick, Duke of York, returned to England. The news came to her husband as he sat at dinner by her side.

Quickly he explained. Certainly he had her permission to leave the table that instant. Certainly she was all eagerness to meet the favourite brother, but George must go straight home first and join the family celebrations. She did not have to wait long for them both to come to her, and in the meantime her mind was set at rest by reports of the reception. The whole family gave a joyful welcome to the returned Frederick, and the rejoicings included the Prince, now returned to favour. In fact, so far as his mother was concerned, he was once more established favourite.

Maria welcomed the Duke, and from then on they were friends, and this friendship was maintained all their lives. Sometimes his visits were almost daily, sometimes circumstances prevented them from meeting. The Duchess of York was never to be an intimate; at one time she was hardly courteous, but the Prince's favourite brother became Maria's favourite brother-in-law, which in the peculiar circumstances speaks well for the Duke of York.

She finished the gay Brighton season and returned to town. Trouble was beginning to brew up for her once again. For one thing, the Duke and her husband open-heartedly introduced each other to any type of dissipation which happened to have escaped the other's attention. It included very high play. The Prince began to pile up another series of debts. She was worried. She tried hard to keep them both within bounds. When the Duke took up with the Countess of Tyrconnel, she begged to be excused from receiving the lady on account of her character, and the brothers had words on the matter.

The Prince's entertaining became rowdier, losing elegance and wit in noise and nastiness. It may have been the Duke of York's influence, for Lord Bulkeley writes that his conduct "is as bad as possible . . . and his company is thought *mauvais ton*." However, she made the best of a bad job and was gay and charming. Personally she was at her zenith and had her husband's love and every one else's admiration. In 1788 they went down again to Brighton, where she resumed her position of local deity, and where the entertaining was more brilliant than ever. It was also faster, and the ladies invited by the Prince's cronies were such as she could not approve.

They were still there in November when the news came of George III's insanity, and the Prince dashed back to London.

He found his father's life despaired of, and when she heard the news, Maria must have realised that on her, more than on anyone else, devolved the duty of advising the Prince, for he would almost certainly listen to what she said. He held a secret meeting of his supporters, at Bagshot, and she came up to it. It was very likely upon her advice that he sent off post haste for Pitt, telling him to abandon his Italian tour and come home.

She had seen one thing before, the effect on the Prince of unpopularity with the country. It had even goaded him into unkindness towards her. Her unpopularity, on religious grounds, might flare up and be reflected on her husband. Pitt had not proved very co-operative over the debts, but that had to be forgotten. Without deserting his old friends, the Prince must still stand well with Pitt. Pitt would have to propose the Regency, he must be encouraged to offer it in its most un-trammelled form, and the Prince must be able to accept it with good grace.

She was even ready in this emergency to allow rumours to be broadcast that the Prince was tired of her, in order to prevent their alliance from being again discussed in Parliament. All courses were difficult in their position. She may have felt that if her husband became Regent, with full regal powers, their position might in some way be officially recognised. Certainly the Royal Marriage Act could then be repealed. She still refused to be reconciled with Fox, even when he offered to create her duchess, but she threw herself into the Prince's intrigues.

The newly manufactured rumours did not entirely serve their purpose. Rolle, who had made the first Parliamentary trouble, was not to be prevented from making more. This time Grey came out with a downright denial of any marriage. "Save me from my friends!" exclaimed Maria.

In other ways she was worried. That she, with her open desire for good feeling in the royal family, and her known kindness and humanity, can have approved of her husband's behaviour towards his father, is impossible. But in one or two particulars he acted, at the least, without unkindness. It is very probable that she may have inspired these semi-filial flashes.

Then the King recovered. In some ways, it was not a matter at which she could rejoice; some of her hopes were never to revive. The first and last chance of openly regularising her position was gone, for when the Prince did become Regent, he no longer desired to do so. Secondly, in his disappointment, the Prince's conduct went rapidly down a steep place and, by the time he got to the sea again, at Brighton, it was realistically swinish. His cronies there, in the 1790 season, were the notorious Barrymore brother, Old Q., and others of the same kidney. Maria's own family contributed two wild brothers. The pace was too hot for her. Much as she liked gaiety and appreciated amusement, she did not care for the Prince to come to her at night, drunk and with a drunken party, and "in fun" rout her with his sword from a refuge under the sofa.

Then, she was plagued by a deluge of public and scurrilous libel. The press exceeded even its then limit of scandalous speech, and was checked only when one enterprising article-writer got a fine of fifty pounds and a year in Newgate.

What she had to suffer, she took with calmness. It was a very great consolation that the King and Queen now received her and treated her with kindness. If she owed something to her own qualities, she was also indebted to the Duke of York, her constant go-between with his parents, and her constant ally. Clarence was her friend, Edward of Kent would be too, when they knew each other. Through them, and through her own power over the Prince, she worked hard for a reconcilia-tion again with his family. If the Queen wished to use Lady Jersey to weaken Maria's position, it was only because she ardently wished to arrange a marriage for her son.

The present bone of contention was the Prince's outspoken opposition to his father over the India Bill, and his violent Whig partisanship. It is true that the Heir-Apparent is as a rule the property of the Opposition, but to pay for the resumption of at least his mother's favour, the Prince had to stop his controversial political activities. Whether on Maria's advice or not, he also tried to get his debts paid once again.

For the first time a bargain was suggested. His debts would be settled if he consented to a royal and Protestant marriage. His mother already had her eye on a suitable princess. Marriages were in the air, for in the October of 1791 the Duke of York married Princess Frederica of Prussia.

One of Maria's difficulties arose from the manner in which this lady met her. Being quite accustomed to the morganatic marriages of German Courts, Frederica saw her as on that footing. Maria, herself, had been known to refuse to receive ladies whose character she deplored, but the new duchess's condescending attitude was a sharp contrast to that of the English great ladies, who knew her and guessed more than they declared. The duke at that time was still in love with his wife. As a consequence of the coldness between the ladies, there was a rift between the brothers. The Prince mentioned it to Lord Malmesbury when he had a series of interviews with that harbinger of Hymen. The discussions made her nervous.

Not only was Maria so much involved in her husband's money troubles that on one occasion only his prompt action saved her from the broker's man, but she had difficulties with him over an actress, Mrs. Crouch, whom he pursued with ardour. Maria chose the wisest course and laughed him out of it. She started a flirtation of her own. The Prince came back to her.

It was almost like the old story of the first years of their marriage. Debts piled up. Carlton House was shut down. They retired again to Brighton. It was not the happy Arcady it had been before; the Prince was straying. But Maria stuck to him loyally, and they remained on good terms.

With him she attended race meetings, particularly, one supposes, when his own horses were competing, and on one occasion she had to borrow five pounds to get them home from Newmarket.

Their money affairs became more involved than ever. There was another appeal to the royal family, and the King laid down the same condition of marriage with a Protestant Princess. Again the Prince refused.

If that made Maria happier, and turned her thoughts again to housewifely courses of retrenchment and economy, the relief was short-lived.

In 1794 the Duke of Sussex's private marriage with Lady Augusta Murray was annulled in the face of two protesting parties. One summer day not long after, as Maria was dining with the Duke of Clarence, she received a letter from her devoted husband. It intimated that he did not in future propose to do himself the honour of crossing her threshold. An annulment he apparently did not seek—it was perhaps too dangerous to acknowledge that the marriage had ever taken place—he would behave as though he had, in fact, never been married at all.

Maria did not acknowledge the letter. She went first to Richmond and then, as she had done once before, she packed quickly and left England. This time she went to Switzerland. The Prince had been tempted, the path seemed easy. In November she learned of his engagement to the Princess Caroline of Brunswick.

It was a very hard time for her. True, the Prince continued her allowance and took pains that she should receive a letter through the hands of her companion, Miss Pigot, to the effect that he had asked and received the King's promise to continue this should the Prince die before his father. He was not unthoughtful, and he was not mean. But where generosity merely meant the accumulation of more debts which he would expect to have paid for him, it is difficult to see absence of meanness as a positive virtue. But Maria was not penniless, and she did not wish to be what women in her position tersely describe as "beholden to him." She wanted to refuse the money. Only her uncle's persuasion made her change her mind. Perhaps that alone would not have been enough, for even now she knew that if she cared to call, her husband would come back.

But she made no move, except back to England, to Richmond, and seclusion at Marble Hill, almost a widow again.

The day of the wedding came nearer. Through the curtains one day she saw a rider on a galloping horse approaching the house. It was a figure she knew. In silence, and behind the curtains, she waited. Twice the Prince galloped past, and then he rode away. Still she made no sign.

Lord Bradford, as Orlando Bridgeman, had kept *cave* during her own wedding. It was he who came down in December— a very different December!—to tell her of the Prince's second marriage.

Maria would not believe him, she could not. Again he told her. It was national news, easy to confirm. She fainted.

It seemed that everything had ended. For over a year she lived in retirement, and what comfort she had came from within herself. The brief fiasco of the Prince's wedding was over. Maria remained hidden as the months went past.

Then Lady Clermont advised her to come out again and face her world. Lady Clermont was old, *doyenne* among great hostesses, a woman who had lived long and always at the hub of the wheel. Whatever words she uses, the wisdom of an old woman is quiet certainty. Backed by her, by the other great ladies, and by the never-failing Duke of York, Maria emerged again and took a Park Lane house in 1796. She still saw the other brothers. With Edward's Julie, she had so much in common, except this open stroke of betrayal.

And in that same year the Prince begged Maria to return to him. His daughter Charlotte had been born and he was already separated from Caroline. Other women could hold him only for a short time in the sunshine of new flattery. He implored but Maria refused. "The link once broke," she said, "could never be rejoined!" Love might hold, but security and sanction were gone. For three years she stuck to this second refusal. At the end of that time the desperate Prince sent her an ultimatum that he would at whatever cost to himself publish the fact of their marriage if she could not be brought back to him otherwise. Even the princesses came to beg her to return to their brother; she was told the Queen desired it.

She showed again the ruling spirit of her life. At Kemshott, which she and her husband had borrowed once for a temporary residence, they met again, at dinner. Very quietly she made her condition, and he agreed, since he had no other choice.

It had nothing to do with money, prestige, security, his fidelity. Only she must have the sanction of her faith before she could come back, she must know that they were still man and wife.

She departed quietly for Wales. There she waited while Father Nassau went to Rome to state her case. He returned with a brief which she later destroyed, in obedience to that vow of secrecy made long ago. Its ruling was definite. She and the Prince were husband and wife, and she could go back to him on those terms.

There was nothing hole-and-corner about Maria.

She returned openly to the Prince. In her own house, in which so far only the other royal brothers had set foot, she gave a huge breakfast party, "to meet the Prince of Wales." It was June, her white roses were flowering again, and they blossomed out over the rooms, the tables, herself. Her position was more difficult than before, even more ambiguous, now that there was a Princess of Wales, but she was happy nevertheless.

Once more the Prince treated her with respect as well as affection, once more the old money troubles ebbed and flowed

D

as the months went by. For eight years they found happiness without very much history. In her own gay words to Lord Stourton, they "were extremely poor but as merry as crickets!" They were once even reduced to refusing the life savings offered them by an old servant, and one feels that it was Maria who did the refusing.

With the existence of the Princess Charlotte the succession was now secure. The royal family liked Maria, and could and did treat her with affection. With the little Princess herself Maria was on affectionate terms, and remained so until there was a public outcry on the old religious grounds.

Brighton remained the couple's headquarters, and the new town rejoiced in them. Maria built herself a house, which is supposed to have been connected with the Pavilion by an underground way, filled up later, during the reign of one of her husband's mistresses.

Three times married, and without a family, she was still very fond of children. So was the Prince, and between them they adopted a daughter. Lord Hugh Seymour had been one of the Prince's great friends. He and his wife had to go abroad, leaving a baby daughter. Maria undertook the charge. When the parents returned, she was unwillingly prepared to relinquish her charge, the little Mary—Minney—but the mother's untimely and sad death left the little one still in her care. There Maria wished her to remain. The Prince agreed. The Seymour relations staked claims. Lord Hertford was the head of the family.

Herein lay the seeds of the end of Maria's happiness. One of the ostensible arguments against her adoption of the baby was the difference in Church, but there was more to it than that. A long lawsuit had to be fought before she could become

Minney's guardian, and Lord Hertford was opposed to the plan. The Prince thought that Lady Hertford could be persuaded, if his charm were brought to bear on her, to exert her influence over her husband. He unleashed his charm with this end in view, and began to seek her society.

Maria may at first have thought of nothing but the object they both wished to attain. Then she may have been ruefully amused at this new infatuation. She herself was occupied, for Minney was not the only "little animal" in her heart. There was Marianne too, some years the younger, and known as her niece. It has been said that this younger child was indeed her own, and she was sent to her own school, to the "Blew Nuns," in Paris, to be educated.

But they were still small girl and baby when Lady Hertford's power over the Prince was waxing. It was a power that was not altogether desirable, and, for Maria, it was a humiliation. She would insist upon Maria lending her presence to entertainments at which she would be openly slighted. This was bad. It was worse when the Prince, after passing the morning with Maria as of old, would subject her to indignities in the publicity of the evening in order, as she learned, that reports of these indignities might be borne back to Lady Hertford. The charmer was in his turn charmed.

It was winter and frost on the warmth of her love. Little by little, Maria ceased to see the Prince.

For a long time, so gradual was the cooling, so great her fortitude, their acquaintances did not know how matters stood between them. He could have won her back at any time, if he had wished, but something happened which made his Roman Catholic wife an extremely dangerous property. His father's reason collapsed, never to recover, and the Prince of Wales became the Prince Regent. He made no move to substantiate his marriage. In fact he took very opposite steps.

In honour of the exiled royal family of France, the Prince arranged a fête at Carlton House. Maria went to see him to ask where she was to sit. It would be too marked if she merely received an invitation card and was herded amongst his guests. Would he preserve the traditional informality of his entertaining and give her the traditional place at his side?

"You know, Madam," the Prince Regent had a courtly form of address, "you know, Madam, you have no place!"

"None, sir," his wife answered, "but such as you choose to give me!"

She was to see him only once more, and then, in self-respect, she asked for a separation. It was to be absolute, and also final, although he did once demand her presence as his wife, to ask advice which he did not take.

Maria went back alone to Brighton. That was her home now, and Tilney Street the town house. She had to be a little firm with the Prince, but he was just and generous financially, and remained very fond of the girls.

Certainly Maria did not retire into the mists. She remained fond of cards, parties, dinners, music. It was a cheerful house still, with the children describing her fine-cut profile as a "Roman Catholic nose!"

The peace was stirred once, and deeply. The Regent became King; time passed and the King lay dying. She wrote to him, and waited through the days that followed, but no word came. Only later did she learn that her portrait was buried with him.

Quietness closed again. The other brothers remained her friends, among them the Duke of Clarence, now King William IV.

Then, quite suddenly, the Pavilion was opened to her again, and, treading on memory, she entered.

William communicated with her. She asked permission to lay her papers before him. They included her marriage certificate, and the new King, it is reported, wept. Whatever could be done now to make amends, he would do. The Prince was dead, Charlotte too, and the Duke of York had gone. It was many years since Dora Jordan had died in exile. He and Maria were old friends.

He immediately ordered her servants into mourning for his late brother, at least she should be allowed to pay a widow's or a relative's respect. When mourning was over, her servants were to wear his liveries, in honour of the lady who could not be Queen. He introduced her to Adelaide, his young wife. He sent presents, wrote to her.

One point which had to be settled was the disposal of all the documentary evidence of her life. She and William and the Duke of Wellington arrived at a satisfactory arrangement. The Duke, as George IV's executor, had found countless letters and papers in the late King's possession. Something had to be done. Maria had other papers herself, which Greville tells us that George IV had tried to get into his own hands. He reports that as she once lay ill, the King sent a friend to her house to fetch them. Maria might love, but by now she knew better than to trust, and from then on, documents of value were placed away in safety.

Now they were all out. With the exception of such as safeguarded her reputation and her financial position, she and the Duke burned them. Some were notes, some were letters, some were effusions running to thirty pages. Like their writer's devotion, they vanished in smoke and ashes.

Still life went on kindly for her. The eldest FitzClarence, the Earl of Munster, loved Minney dearly and wished to marry her. Minney herself chose someone more stable, and, after a long courtship which every one had tried to persuade her to break off, married George Dawson, afterwards Dawson-Damer, in 1825. He made her as happy as she hoped, and the King stood godfather to the infant Georgiana. Maria herself grew to love George Dawson-Damer, and the children were a delight to her. She could forget that she had paid a round of country-house visits to distract her grief at the marriage.

Only a few years later, Marianne became Mrs. Jerningham, with her entire approval, and Maria was writing of her "pleasure and delight to hear my little girl has been received in the manner you mention. It really affected me so much that I have shed abundance of tears. . . . You would laugh at me if at this moment you could witness the large drops that trickle down my cheeks . . ." For Maria was quickly moved; she would say of herself with humour, "I am a great alarmist upon all occasions!"

In these last years she surmounted her dislike of the sea sufficiently to spend much time on the Continent, at Aix, in Paris, at Spa, until time came when this was not possible.

In March of 1837 she died quietly at Brighton, Minney and the children with her, Marianne hurrying towards her.

Maria was hardly buried, and wholly unforgotten, when the Victorian age began.

THE DUCHESS OF YORK

FREDERICA, PRINCESS ROYAL, niece to Frederick the Great, was the eldest daughter of the King of Prussia and one of those several royal ladies of Germany who suffered chilly and sometimes hungry incarceration for failing to see eye to eye with their husbands on questions of wifely duty.

Her education was uncommonly good, because it was suited to her intelligence. She enjoyed reading and study, liked to pursue a subject once her interest was aroused, and she was fond of animals. She showed early a taste for puppies and a dislike for shooting. She was before her time in revolting at the inhumanity of blood sports.

But the King of Prussia had no such feminine weakness, and he did not encourage it in his eldest daughter. Observing her aversion, he insisted firmly that she must learn to shoot and attend his shooting parties. There, with a horror of seeing the sufferings of wounded animals, she always shut her blue eyes before she pulled the trigger. Then, to her dismay, huntsmen told her that thus she was more likely to cause than avert pain —the marksman shot dead, his game dropped.

Frederica considered the matter, and then, small and determined, went to her father. Would he let her off for ever if she could once shoot a stag dead? It was too easy a bargain, one is bound to kill something some day or other. The King would release her only if she would kill two deer, one after the other, without missing. Those were the terms, and she fulfilled them. The beasts dropped, and the princess was excused future hunting parties.

She was short, tiny beside the height of her future husband, and light-footed. Her eyes were the genuine china blue, her hair the genuine flaxen, of the Prussian ideal. It was a pity that the smallpox had marked her, for she had no beauty to spare, and her teeth were born too early for the dentistry they needed.

In white, with her hair not disproportionately highly dressed, she made a more than passable show, with her figure and her bubbling vivacity. It was the outward show of a strong vitality, that quick animation. Within, the stream ran deeper, the current was steadfast and powerful. The scope of her interests widened her knowledge, and stimulated her to make it even wider; she was a provocative talker. The vivacity was almost clever enough to be called wit. Like many German royalties, she wrote her letters in French. Up to a day or so before she died, it was quick, alert, mocking French.

The stream ran deeper still. She had two quite surprising qualities, sincerity and loyalty, both of which were to abide in her, and she had excellent "manners."

Her uncle, Frederick the Great, had a penchant for Frederick, Duke of York. He was, after all, England's heir presumptive, and well worth a little civility. The English prince was ready to respond; young, Hanoverian in courage, flattered, both envious and ambitious of military reputation. Frederick, Duke of York, takes a high place among England's quartermasters, and it is not entirely his own fault that he does not appear on our list of reasonably efficient generals.

There were balls at Berlin, in the Prussian tradition of glitter and jingle. The thick uniforms stank of their sweating wearers, hair dressed high swayed above shoulders dressed low, servants with step-ladders incessantly changed the wilting candles. The ballroom was filled with the rhythm of the *waltz*. Frederick danced with the young Frederica. Frederick was attracted.

The attraction of princes involves long and stately diplomatic correspondence, but love was supported by a *dot* of thirty thousand pounds and the promise of twenty thousand more towards the young husband's debts—a family characteristic. Frederica's father was pleased with the match and he was willing to put down the money. *"Ma fille,"* he said, *"vous avez attendu longtemps"*—she was twenty-three—*"mais vous avez tiré le gros lot!"* They were married on September 29th, 1791, in Berlin, and the Duke of York immediately set out for England with his bride for the second wedding in the presence of his family.

But if Germany was quiet enough, France was not. It was October of 1791 and royalty was notably unpopular. At Lisle their carriage was surrounded by a mob, and a mob in a very bad temper. Servants and attendants went green in their elaborate liveries. Fright is contagious; the horses' hooves beat out a terrified tattoo. We do not know how Frederica took it, but the duke was quick and courageous. Every trace of royalty emblazoned arms and other pomps—was removed, and he deposed the coachman to drive himself. If it was a desperate sortie, he would lead it. Frederica kept her seat and they came through unharmed. They arrived in London on November 18th.

Lord Malmesbury, well embarked on a long career of

marriage-mongering, had thought well of Frederica in Berlin, and his diary has a neat and conclusive little entry. Most properly, he believed and hoped that "she" would make "him" happy, and that she would be liked in England. "She is far from handsome, but lively, sensible and very tractable; and if one tenth of the attachment they now show for each other remains, it will be very sufficient to make an excellent *ménage*."

Frederica's dowry was of a magnificence most acceptable. Gilray caricatures the old Queen with her apron held wide for the money-bags. This dominant mother-in-law had been placated by a request that she should choose the ladies for the new duchess. Besides pleasing the bridegroom's parents, the request let the bride's out of a task which might have had its embarrassments and certainly would have had its difficulties.

As soon as the Duke and Duchess of York arrived in England, they were married again, and she made her first public Court appearance.

Her hair was dressed too high for her stature, and too elaborately, with a large toupee, large chignon, and carefully pinned curls. It was decorated generously with gauze, crêpe blond and white feathers. On the left side there was "a very large double sprig of brilliants of uncommon lustre." However, as Mrs. Elton observed a year or so later, people expect a bride to be fine.

The rest of her attire was on a more moderate scale. Robe and train were of white tissue, spotted generously with silver and trimmed with broad silver fringes. It must have been hot as well as heavy, for there was more silver fringe half way down the arm, and the white satin sleeves were decorated with silver foil, ending at the wrist with an edging of diamonds, whose settings may have been uncomfortably scratchy.

Their glitter was repeated. The stomacher was of white satin, topped with a bow of brilliants, very large. It was splendidly laced with more of these baubles to the almost complete concealment of the white satin. The petticoat was "of white satin, covered with crêpe, richly spotted and sprigged with silver, tied in festoons with silver flowers and tastefully trimmed and decorated with silver fringe." So, as a blonde and silver Christmas-tree fairy she made her official entrance.

At first, Frederica behaved with the reserve which she generally showed towards strangers, and her natural sparkle was not much in evidence. At the same time, she began resolutely in the way in which she meant to go on. First, no embroilment in family quarrels which, mainly financial or matrimonial, were to be numerous. In her immediate circle she was a councillor wise enough to be also a peacemaker, but throughout her life she saw as little as possible of the family protagonists. She interfered with no one and expected no one to interfere with her. She soon acquired a reputation for eccentricity. In Germany, she probably would have gone the same way as her mother, a number of her aunts and great-aunts, and various other ladies who were imprisoned and under-nourished in chilly keeps or isolated corners of their husbands' palaces. There was a degenerate softness even then in the English air, which must have made it considerably easier to breathe.

The first contretemps was over a question on which her opinions can be understood. She was immediately introduced into the society of the Prince of Wales, for he was her husband's favourite brother. He was just now at the height of his adoration for Mrs. Fitzherbert. Frederica met Maria perhaps for the first time at a Court ball (at which the duchess wore a gauze petticoat and blue bodice, but no jewels, feathers or flowers). Frederica's charming manner bore the best, self-deprecating tone of Berlin polish, and it was particularly observed. It was also noticed that both she and Maria braced themselves a trifle for the meeting. They followed it by only a few moments of desultory chat.

So far as Maria's position was that of *maîtresse en titre* Frederica could appreciate it and respect its confines. But Maria regarded herself as a friend and a wife. Neither the English tradition nor the Catholic Church encouraged her to think that an English gentlewoman of aristocratic connection could stand in no other amatory relation to a royal prince than that of mistress. Frederica was trained as a princess, but Maria had been respectably brought up. The Prince of Wales was devoted, the Duke was still ardent, so for a while feminine differences separated them.

At first London saw a good deal of Frederica. She was a bride. Frederick was "one of the boys." His companions were the wits of folly and the fools of wit of his generation, the level perhaps a little higher after his marriage than it had been before. Frederica was too much of her own world for discomposure, but she could only tolerate coarseness, she could not copy it. However, in time she found some quick spirits—Lord Alvanley, Lord Lauderdale, Raikes and a few others—and made them her friends.

But London, from the family point of view, meant a whirlpool of scenes and scandals. The best way to avoid each successive wrangle or disclosure was to keep out of town, since Providence still graciously withheld the age of science; one can only faintly imagine what George III's family would have been like on the telephone. In 1790 the Duke had bought Oatlands in Surrey. The place was destroyed by fire and he gave way to the family weakness of expensive rebuilding. He also bought the manors of Byfleet and Brooklands to round off the property. His wife surveyed it all calmly and installed herself and her dogs.

But the marriage of which Lord Malmesbury had hoped so much did not come up to expectations and Frederica recognised the fact. She had the power of withdrawing into herself, not *pour mieux sauter*, but to rationalise, to consider how to make the best of her life as she found it.

She had no children. Dynastically, this was a disaster. Year after year saw the Prince of Wales childless. Possibly this very childlessness increased her love for animals, for the nuzzle of a cold, damp nose, the whine at a door, the flopping sprawls of blind-eyed puppies. She would sit until late at night with her company and her dogs, her attention now for one, now for the other, her mind racing at top speed, slackening, racing again. Sometimes she sewed, and the upthrust muzzles stained the work in her hands.

Soon she was forced to realise that the Frederick of Berlin was not the Frederick of home life. There were moments when tempers might have flared, typical family scenes ended in typical family abuse, but her intelligence ruled and dignity was preserved.

In 1793 the Duke was sent to command in Flanders. It was a respite, and he may have regained some sentimental value in the shadow of imagined danger. He commanded in the field again in 1794, but in the following year he was recalled, and domestic difficulties again became urgent.

Troubles of other kinds crowded upon Frederica. Lord Malmesbury records that on June 4th, 1793, he saw both Duke and Duchess in their own house, and learned from the Duke that the King of Prussia had been ignoring not only his, the Duke's, letters, but also those of his daughter Frederica. Neither of them could think of any explanation. Possibly he had begun to regret the dowry.

Four days later Malmesbury learned from Colonel St. Leger, and confided to his diary, that the relations—or rather lack of relations—between Frederica and Maria had caused a cleavage between the two brothers.

In 1795 the Prince of Wales had married and in 1796 his only legitimate child, Princess Charlotte, was born. Frederica, still childless, was not jealous. She genuinely welcomed the baby. There was to be something a little tragic in this affection, continuing until Charlotte's own death in childbirth not twenty years later, for in the year the little Princess was born, and the succession was assured, Frederica and Frederick parted.

With her usual dignity and discretion, she saw that it was done as unobtrusively as possible. No baskets of dirty linen were carried from her door. For a while the Duke and Duchess remained under the same roof. Even when she left London and withdrew permanently to Oatlands, he was frequently her guest. They were one day to be friends.

For all that, she showed herself the fiery niece of Frederick the Great when, on the occasion of a June 1st ball, given by the Knights of the Bath, she and her husband were invited to share a table with the Prince, accompanied once more by Maria Fitzherbert. She refused point blank. Hurried and worried gentlemen muttered, stewards conferred, and the issue was neatly avoided by a little judicious staff work. Two tables were arranged, one for each brother.

It was a weary year. Her health broke under the strain of

the Duke's infidelities. After all, she had loved him. She withdrew in silence to Oatlands and busied herself with her dogs, her ever-increasing charities and her needlework. Her friends cared sufficiently for her company to follow her. The little town of Weybridge was poor, the villagers and estate labourers even poorer, and there Frederica laid the foundations of the charity which was to be her life's work.

Rumour buzzed round the family. Frederica . . . separation . . . quarrel . . . scandal . . . so presently she returned to town, made a few appearances at her husband's side, and then went back to Weybridge.

Soon Frederick followed, on a flying visit. Their long friendship had begun. He enquired after her health. In one way, at least, he had missed her, for she had been the Chancellor of their increasingly hollow exchequer, and his finances were, as usual, hopelessly involved.

Mr. Raikes visited at Oatlands, and he has left some account of Frederica. The country house became a social centre, the focal point of many lights, but the establishment was fast becoming penniless. It was not merely a matter of running out of money, they ran out of credit; at times they even exhausted their credit for ordinary household supplies.

At twenty-nine Frederica started to build her own life. At fifty-two she died. Two quite surprising facts stand out. One is the enormous and widespread affection for her which showed itself when she died, and the other is the silent inconspicuous manner in which she created that regard.

It is easy to find little references to her and to the parties down at Oatlands. It is testimony to her to notice how often these references are in the letters and journals of the foremost men of the day. They all travelled down and, if they wished to pay tribute, added to her menagerie. Apart from monkeys, and eccentric variations on the white-mice theme, there were the dogs, English, French, Dutch, any and every breed, lapdogs, pugs, barbettes and outsize hounds of uncouth manner and untidy habit. They went where she did, and their progeny, many and varied, were boarded out among the grateful occupants of Frederica's model cottages.

She systematised her charities and established her own pension list. All her reorganising was made the more involved by the scantiness of her resources. Slim as they were, however, she had them under control.

As youth receded she acquired a precision of habit. All the summer, sitting in Oatlands garden, she gave her orders over her needlework. Every Sunday she laid it aside and attended Weybridge Church.

As time went on, autocracy became eccentricity, as often happens with ladies living alone. She had never liked retiring before the small and witty hours, and bedtime retreated further and further into to-morrow. She always had loved animals and indeed all nature. Now, if she chose to wander alone on dewy grass, no one could stop her. The dogs were sufficient company when she walked alone at night.

The century turned. Frederick was by now Commander-in-Chief of the Army. In private life he was the lover, or one of the lovers, of Mary Anne Clarke. In 1809 both roles were publicly combined in the Mary Anne Clarke Commissions affair. The lady had used her influence to gain commission or promotion from her lover for those who paid her sufficiently well. It was asked if the duke had known of these transactions.

It was never difficult to stir up scandal about one of the brothers. Frederick not only had the reputation of a libertine,

Frederica, Duchess of York. Eldest daughter of William II
of Prussia, and niece of Frederick the Great

Oatlands Park, Surrey, residence of the Duke and Duchess of York.
A view from the gardens, *circa* 1818

From a contemporary engraving in the possession of Terence Dennis

but he also was recognised as a zealous and efficient officer. The latter distinction he was anxious to keep.

Frederica went up to London to his aid. It is one of those actions from which it is unnecessary to deduce character; they mirror it too brilliantly. She slept under his roof, she appeared with him day by day. She could and she did advise at a difficult time, for Mary Anne held the House in fascinated admiration. She had great charm, a quick wit, and the Duke's love-letters. They were read aloud, the epistles of a stout, adoring, and not over-educated rake.

Through it all, and it was a rich sensation, Frederica showed herself with her husband. When he had been suitably acquitted, he resigned his army appointment, a move which gained general approval and paved the way for his reappointment in 1811. It is more than likely that Frederica prompted this judicious step. At any rate, after the resignation, he returned with her to Oatlands.

She did not intend the retreat to look like either sulks or shame. In 1810 she entertained the King, and extended the hospitality to the entire neighbourhood at a celebration banquet. It was a magnificently catholic affair. She invited every one, regardless of rank, and set them down to mountains of beef and ham, fowls of every kind, ale and bowls of punch.

She liked entertainment on that scale. She kindled to the blend of feudalism and democracy. Once, on the Duke's birthday, she feasted all his tradesmen. Birthdays had been celebrated with splendour in her Berlin days, but this must have appealed to her sense of humour, for she sent all the guests two guineas apiece for their conveyance down to Oatlands, where they were invited to partake of, or admire, their own legal property.

E

Her humour bubbled up more freely as time put a brake on her vitality, and her life developed a clear and ordered pattern. Out of charity she attended with all her servants the performance of some more than usually indigent barnstormers who asked for her protection. Out of charity she sent the same servants next day to the same barn to swell the congregation of an itinerant Methodist preacher who asked her patronage. When they tried to excuse themselves on the plea that they could not understand English, Frederica was ready for them. "No. You went to the comedy which you understood less, so you must go to this."

The ostrich- and kangaroo-enriched menagerie assumed the proportions of a zoo, and every animal, from the carriage-horses to the most outlandish marsupial, was the object of her jealous regard. As each dog died it was buried in no nameless pit, but under an inscribed tablet in the garden, near the goldfish pond—an old-maidish trick and what a pathetic inversion of the loving instincts which Lord Malmesbury had noted with such satisfaction in the days of her courtship in Berlin.

With time and freedom and loneliness of soul, her habits grew even more eccentric, but the core of her mind stayed keen and sane, the core of her heart kept its loyalties. Her niece, Charlotte, was one of them. In 1811, Frederica gave a ball for her, a ball which illumined a long November evening to such effect that Charlotte's royal papa sprained his ankle during a spirited demonstration of the highland fling. Impulsive Charlotte did not have much disinterested affection in her life. She was very ready to return her aunt's regard, and it was to her she came for help when, in 1814, she met Prince Leopold of Coburg, was attracted and unable to see more of him. She complained that she was being kept out of the summer's festivities, and again Frederica proposed to give a ball for her.

With or without the aunt's assistance, but certainly with her sympathy, Charlotte succeeded in marrying Leopold, and thereafter, during their short married life, Frederica came several times to visit them at Claremont. It was there that she met Baron Stockmar, whom fate so perseveringly intended to be the guardian angel of a prince consort.

"A little animated woman," he describes her, "talks immensely and laughs still more. No beauty, mouth and teeth bad. She disfigures herself still more by distorting her mouth and blinking her eyes. In spite of the Duke's various infidelities their matrimonial relations are good. She is quite aware of her husband's embarrassed circumstances and is his prime minister and truest friend; so that nothing is done without her help. As soon as she entered the room, she looked round for the Banker, Greenwood, who immediately came to her with the confidentially familiar manner which the wealthy go-between assumes towards grand people in embarrassed circumstances."

It is fortunate that most men are not distinguished by cold-blooded intelligence.

Mr. Raikes, her crony from the first English days, laid periodic tribute at her feet as so many did. One of his toys was a musical box, the fashion of the moment. It was in the late spring of 1817 that she wrote to thank him, "*Il me sera difficile de vous exprimer, Monsieur, toute ma reconnaissance pour la plus jolie des boîtes que jai reçu hier au soir de votre part. C'est tous ce que jai vu de plus nouveau, et du meilleur goût; et je me suis amusée toute la journée à en écouter les sons. J'attends avec impatience le moment de vous en réiterer mes remerciment à Londres, et de vous assurer combien je suis sensible à cette obligeante attention de votre part.*" One could pick out anywhere a letter from Frederica by the grace with which she decorated detail with formality.

By the end of the century's second decade life was becoming more hurried, and now and then she would feel that she belonged to a dead generation, one that died to the roll of Napoleon's artillery. But she still had one contact with that spacious age. Periodically she went to Strawberry Hill to visit Mr. Walpole. The visit was always fragrant with ceremony. A carpet lay unrolled from gate to door. Mr. Walpole met her, kissed her hand, escorted her in. She laughed, and he bowed and echoed it. Perhaps he would offer some novelty, a piece chosen from the museum which he called home. After Oatlands, it was strange to drink chocolate with a host who insisted on remaining standing in her presence. Then down the carpet again to the carriage and the Weybridge road.

By 1818, she had almost given up going to London. She had acquired instead the week-end craze, and all through the summer she and the duke kept the house full from Saturday to Monday. He came and went with the guests. She stayed on, eating fruit in the garden, compounding with creditors, and attending to her school and charities, her aged, the animals, and her correspondence.

She had almost given up going to bed at all. What sleep she needed, she took dressed, on some handy couch, with the dogs and monkeys round her. When she left her table of half-crown whist, it was to walk outside, and when she came in she still could not sleep. A maid, shivering by the ever-open window, would read aloud to her, sleep ebbing and flowing in her voice. Then, for a few hours, Frederica would sleep too.

Greville has said that Oatlands was the worst managed establishment in England, for all its magnet attraction for the world of its day. "There are a great many servants," he says, "and nobody waits on you; a vast number of horses, and none to ride or drive." She had even on one occasion sent back to the stables a curricle, ordered round by the duke for the use of two visiting gentlemen. It may have been out of tenderness for the horses, but it is always difficult to run a house smoothly if finances are never in order.

Her great love of animals is commented upon again and again. "Monk" Lewis owned a cat, which came one day with the disdain of cats and sat itself upon her skirt. "No, no!" she protested, "you shall not disturb her now! Poor little thing! I do think she love me, and do not take from me anything that love me!" Her speech retained its German accent to the end. "Ah, *mein Gott*, yes, dey are so dependent on us for kindness and protection, and when dey make dere appeal, in dere innocent language, I think we ought to love them, if only to awake the better part of our nature. Besides, dey are grateful for kindness, dey are sincere, dey are honest!"

"Ah, Master Luvise, we know that the poor animal follow but their nature!" she said of a thieving dog. Then, sadly, "Would *Gott* that man so truly follow his—for *his* nature is *divine*!"

She still remained in many ways the princess who had come from Berlin. The dislike between her and the Prince Regent had crystallised into something definite. She mourned Charlotte too, and Claremont with its affection and simplicity. Both she and the Regent were extremely sensitive to the least sign of antipathy. He wanted the world to worship him, she wanted friends to be cordial; but a desire for popularity is the most sundering of all possible common tastes—except perhaps cannibalism.

Greville outlines everything and underlines one thing. Frederica commanded affection and respect from every one, even her husband. The life she had built was successfully completed now. The substitutes for love had proved, as strangely they sometimes do, even more substantial and lasting.

One of her real dislikes was for hen-headed women. According to Croker, she very seldom indulged in that typical appanage of elderly ladies, a "companion."

Brummell was a friend whom she did not desert in bad times. Even when the Beau had fled from his creditors to Calais she wrote to him and sent him an armchair. Long ago he had sent her a little dog as a birthday gift—"*l'emblèm de la fidélité*," as she said in her letter of thanks. She embroidered him a table-cloth. Always she signed herself "*votre toute affectionée amie et servante*." The anonymous pension which supported him in his dark hours probably came from her.

We have one cause of complaint against her, that she made Brummell promise her that he would not write his memoirs. He kept his promise to the end and posterity is the poorer.

Towards the end of 1818 her health began to fail. Greville was down for one of the last house parties of the year, and she was unwell most of the time. She was in good spirits, though, and her guests were appreciative, for when she wanted to send an unflattering portrait of herself to the Duchess of Orleans, they subscribed for a substitute, to be painted by Lawrence. It was a good thing for the artist that his fees did not depend upon the York purse, which was even emptier than usual.

By the following summer, when she had recovered and gave the largest party of her life, there was such a financial crisis that the festivities had to be cut short. According to Greville, at the beginning of the party there was not even any water in the house. "It came by pipes from St. George's Hill, which were stopped up with sand, and as the workmen were never paid, they would not clear them. She ordered it to be done and the bills brought to her. On Thursday there was trouble as the steward had not money to pay the tradespeople and the duke was made to produce a small sum." He tells us, dramatically, that "the house is in ruins."

It was the last August party. It was the last coat of paint on Frederica's edifice. She dismissed her guests, and she retired.

There was a great deal to do. She gave innumerable Christmas presents and they all had to be prepared. Christmas duly came and went; crocus time came and went; the summer came, and Frederica died.

Her illness began some time in May, but by June she was not expected to recover. Her husband came down to her, and every one discovered with a shock just how much the Duchess of York meant to them. July dragged itself out. Her illness was diagnosed as dropsical, water on the chest. August came again, but there were no more parties. She was unconscious for two days and then, on the 6th, she died. Her husband was with her, and for an hour he sat by the coffin, before he followed it to the Weybridge parish churchyard. Then he burst into tears. "*. . . if one tenth of the attachment they now show for each other remains, it will be sufficient. . . .*"

Victoria later renovated the tombs of her aunt's dogs, but contemporaries can best recall the mistress. One after another they came with tributes, as they had in her lifetime. Lord Holland said truly that she was "distinguished throughout her life from the gentleness and frankness of her disposition, the soundness of her judgment, the constancy and sincerity of her attachments to her family, her friends, her dependants. Her understanding was far superior to the illusions which a situation such as hers generally creates. She made, indeed, no ostentation of her philanthropy, but she silently exerted it, not only in the regulation of her own conduct, but in softening and concealing the political and private errors of those with whom she was connected."

Raikes, who remembered the flaxen-haired little princess in white and silver, said gently that "she was the friend of all who needed her service," and cold-blooded Greville put it on record that she was "extremely regretted, she built cottages for those of her domestics who were married, and had a school which was under her protection." He says with firm factual justice that "probably no person in such a situation was ever more really liked. She left £12,000 to her servants and some children she had educated. Nothing was left unarranged."

For the full and formal farewell, it is pleasant to go back to the good Raikes again, and to quote from Lewis Melville's fascinating *Regency Ladies*. For Frederica "was a person of excellent taste, and a very nice discrimination of good breeding and manners, and the regard which the Princess entertained for Brummell was highly creditable to him." For it was Brummell and his allies in the cause of *ton* who helped to raise the tone of the husband's circle, of the debauched roués who "showed a great want of refinement and courtesy in women's society."

"England had been for many years without a Court, and the limited circle that surrounded the Duke and Duchess of York, though differing scarcely from that of a private family, rendered it the only residence that was the scene of constant hospitality. . . . Here used to assemble, at the end of the week, Brummell and all the most agreeable men of the day, intimately acquainted with each other, and sincerely attached to their royal host and hostess."

He goes on to a noble and sincere summary. "Few characters . . . could be placed in competition with the late Duchess of York. She was not only a *très grande dame* in the highest acceptation of the term, but a woman of the most sound sense and accurate judgment, with a heart full of kindness, beneficence and charity. The former was amply proved by the adroitness with which she avoided all collision with the cabals and *tracasseries* which for so many years unfortunately ruled in various branches of the royal family. . . . Whatever clouds (if, indeed, they ever existed) obscured the earlier part of her marriage were in late times completely dispersed; and nothing could equal the respect and attention with which she was treated by the Duke, who rarely failed to consult her opinion on most questions of real importance to his own interests."

And a little sadly, since love must end, "she was at all times able to take the lead on any subject; her conversation was full of points, blended with great *naïveté*, and devoid of all sarcastic allusions; she had a very refined taste, and a great knowledge of the world; but contrary to all received opinions her study of mankind had never operated to check that feeling of general benevolence which formed the brightest gem of her character."

Such was the niece of Frederick the Great.

MARY ANNE CLARKE

MARY ANNE CLARKE was, strictly speaking, not a lady at all. She was a regrettable, if attractive, young woman born in low circumstances and dying in Boulogne like any fashionable debtor. She earns her place in this book because she had some small effect upon the course of the public affairs of the period. Her lover, Frederick, Duke of York, was on her account removed from his appointment as Commander-in-Chief of the Army. He had been doing good work at the War Office during the progress of the long struggle against Napoleon, and was reinstated when the scandal died down.

It has been suggested that Mary Anne was a daughter of the unfortunate "Colonel Frederick," who served the royal brothers in the raising of some of their numerous and ill-guaranteed loans. He, in his turn, was son to the sad Theodore of Corsica. But it is more probable that Mary Anne was really the child of Thompson, of Ball and Pin Alley, off Chancery Lane, as is reported. In any case, it is not important, for her character seems to have been clearly defined from the beginning, and it is unlikely that parental influence could have had much effect. Mr. Glendenning, a pamphleteer, in writing about her, sets his discriminating finger on the cause of feminine backsliding. *Perfection of principles*—he laments them as lost. "Levity of manners, the frequent result of the gaiety of modern female

54

education, assisted by circulating library readings, is not the least likely to produce any such thing."

Mary Anne herself is emphatic on the lack of attraction of the housewife's lot. "Her superiority of mind aimed at distinction and at the fashionable pleasures of the time, inasmuch as to pay no attention to anything that had a tendency to domestic employment."

She was born in 1776. Thompson *père* died soon after, and her mother married a compositor named Farquhar. Round and about the printing house Mary Anne grew up. She remained petite, with a clear, fair skin, wide and vivid blue eyes; always bubbling with vitality and completely irrepressible. She had enough instruction to read proofs aloud for correction, but she admits that "these readings did not regulate her judgment or mend her manners, she was a romp. . . ." Young Mr. Day, the son of Farquhar's employer, was apparently involved in this proof correction, and decided that the charming pert child with the halo of yellow hair and the engaging ways had the makings of a very suitable Mrs. Day. He is said to have sent her away to boarding school at Ham, presumably to regulate the erring judgment, not to mention mending her manners. But when Mary Anne came home at sixteen, grown into a fine young lady, she would have none of him.

Mary Anne's action in scorning a critical suitor, who must try to make his bride more eligible, in favour of a man who preferred her as she was, arouses some sympathy. At St. Pancras, near London, around the year 1794, she married Joseph Clarke, stonemason's apprentice and son of a working builder and bricklayer. His father's premises were at Angel Court, Snow Hill.

The path to Boulogne had opened before Mary Anne.

Possibly she had one or two of her children by him before they were actually married. This was a period of her life with which later days in Paris played improving tricks. She had tales then of Thompson's having been far above Farquhar in rank, overshadowing that honest Aberdonian, tales of her mother's being widowed during the American wars (do we meet again that piteous orphan, "the daughter of an Army officer?") and forced to marry again to support herself and family. It is even likely, from the vehemence of her disclaimers, that at about this time she obtained a small part in some Shakesperian performance, and rounded those lively blue eyes at fashionable London, for she artlessly protested that not only had she never been on the stage, but that if she had been, it would have been perfectly harmless, just innocent gaiety.

Mary Anne's brothers vanished into the army. Her husband finished his time as apprentice and his father set him up with a stone-yard in Golden Lane. But the family was already in financial difficulties and they moved to Craven Place, Kensington Gravel Pits. Joseph had started drinking heavily. He brought home the pox, failed to provide for his family, and was thankful when his father made him an annuity of a pound a week.

Mary Anne now had two or three small daughters and a son. She began to mend the family finances in the way that came most easily to her. She was extremely attractive, always vivacious and amusing, and it was simple enough to meet people. If Kensington was a squalid mud heap, she was even more familiar with the other end of town, the Inns of Court and the City. When she left Joseph, taking the children with her, it was for a barrister, rejoicing also in a baronetcy and a comfortable income. He bore her away from London to a grand country house in Wiltshire. It was probably the first time since her school-days that Mary Anne had been farther afield than the rural green of Islington. She delighted in bright lights and laughter, music and fine gentlemen applauding her Cockney wit; red wine to drink and silks and laces to wear. Never again, she vowed, would she return to the squalor of the Gravel Pits! Any way of life was preferable to that. She tried her best to induce her kind protector to make a settlement on her, but he was obdurate. True, she was living cleanly and very comfortably and the children were thriving, but she had no certainty of future security. Also, in a short time it became rather dull. Her protector was frequently too busy to give her much time. At the end of six months she decided that she must try her fortune elsewhere. Although it went to her heart to part from her family, she left them behind as a keepsake, in their own best interests, and returned to London. For a while she had a hard time. Her protector was quite willing to have the spirited pretty thing back again. He dutifully cherished the children, and waited patiently for their mother to return!

However, Mary Anne won her way. Sir Charles Milner, a coxcomb of the polite world, found her a merry companion. Sir James Brudenell met her lace bill, an exorbitant trifle at which he protested. She replied, with hauteur, that "she must hereafter despise the ungenerous man who, after *going so far*, abandons me to my folly."

The rank of her admirers rose. One and all found her vivacious, fascinating, amusing; they watched the small lips in the oval face, the delicate arm and the fair, soft skin, and they found her extravagance and artfulness well-matched.

Her husband was now and again her pensioner, but for all practical purposes she was quit of him and he could drink himself addled if he liked, while she reclined with her cheek on her hand, setting off the fair arm, or took riding exercise, ignored by virtuous females and eyed by their envious escorts.

A wild Barrymore found her and she was established in Tavistock Place. Her fourth or fifth admirer set her up in Park Lane. When she left London now, it was for a trip to some fashionable watering resort, and it is said that at one of these she met Frederick, Duke of York.

Her own stories of their encounter tended to get more and more romantic as time went on. She was sixteen, she would say later, and met and loved him, incognito-incognita, on Blackheath, and was taken by him to the theatre, where the audience thought she was the blonde bride he had just brought back from Berlin, and applauded. This according to Captain Gronow, another admirer.

It was in 1803 that she moved to No. 18 Gloucester Place, off Portman Square, in every circumstance of luxury. Eight men-servants were on her establishment. Her entertainments were superb and it seemed to her that now, within ten years of the ill-fated Clarke marriage, she had indeed arrived. The children were catered for, she was safe. Her lover was a royal Duke, and adored the very ground her small feet trod. He only had to be away for a week for her to receive streams of letters, each pouring out, in a style more naïve than the last, the full measure of his affection.

Mary Anne was no fool and she had acquired enough education to know the bathetic and the ridiculous when she met it. However, if Frederick could not inspire her as a lover, as a support in life he seemed admirable. She was to draw a thousand a year from him, and a retiring pension later on of £400. Her position seemed fairly secure.

Gossip was swift to seize on her connection with the Duke. He was living wildly then, his company not considered to be in good taste, and in Mary Anne he had found a companion whose ability to make money fly was truly remarkable. For, much as she wished to be firmly established, nothing clung to her fingers.

Now she was mistress of the King's second son, who had set her up in the first style, even if she might have to share his favours with other gay and delightful friends. He, it is said, had to submit to the same condition where she was concerned. For the moment Frederick was completely enslaved. Not only did he supply her with every luxury to astonish the London world, he also took a house for her at Weybridge. This was near Oatlands, his country residence, and his wife, Frederica, had to complain to Pitt that, on one occasion, Mary Anne had had the temerity to attend church when she and Frederick were there together. Matters were a little more difficult to arrange at Weybridge. A discreet screening wall had to be built to conceal her love's comings and goings, and when some work had to be done on the stabling, Mary Anne had to find ready cash as Frederick's credit in the neighbourhood was utterly overstrained.

How all this was to be managed on Frederick's scanty resources is hard to imagine. Mary Anne brought nothing to the pool. There was a sponging family behind her, as is usual in these cases, and it appears that she was on occasion glad to rent a room from a Mr. Nichols, baker of Hampstead. It was even necessary to wrangle with Nichols over the few shillings' rent, trying to threaten him with her knowledge of some peccadillo of his in connection with a Will. It was also necessary for her to "marry" a frequent visitor, a Mr. Dowler, for she had posed as a widow in the first place. Certainly she was not a woman of property.

Her wild extravagance, when she was with Frederick, was not sated with possession of ten horses and the service of a staff of twenty. She ate off plate that had belonged to the Duc de Berri. Her wineglasses cost two guineas each. She entertained as much as she liked. Her pier-glasses cost between four and five hundred pounds apiece. The children had all that they required, and Frederick had promised to get the boy into Charterhouse.

In the summer of 1805 they visited Worthing, and it was while there that he said that she had more influence than the Queen. That was the secret of it. She was mistress of an adoring lover, who in his turn was a royal Duke, was Commander-in-Chief, and had enormous patronage. Mary Anne needed money as she needed nothing else, and here was a source of it to her hand, as vast as the wide Atlantic. She had but to dip her bucket and fill.

All the more raffish members of London society were her companions, but now army men with an eye to promotion thought well of her good graces. Captain Huxley Sanden, determined on a career, introduced Colonel French of the Houseguards, who had been appointed to the commission for raising new levies. Napoleon was only just across the Channel, fresh defences had to be made and new armies trained. There was a vast number of commissions to be sold.

At that time, commissions were honestly and as a regular form sold by the Commander-in-Chief on behalf of the Half-Pay Fund, which also benefited army widows and orphans. There were regular rates: £400 for an Ensigncy, £550 for a Lieutenancy, to be made a Captain cost £1,500, and a Majority a substantial £2,600.

Mary Anne Clarke (1776-1852)
Mistress of Frederick, Duke of York

Prospect of Berlin during the latter half of the eighteenth century

Colonel French certainly knew of Frederick's constant money difficulties. He was a friend of the Duke's and had been involved in raising a loan for him. This new opportunity was one that Mary Anne could use, and she was very soon a pedlar of influence on an amazing scale. She and Mrs. Carey, another of Frederick's friends, even rented an office in the city, where civil clerks openly said that they were employed by the reigning mistresses of the Commander-in-Chief, and were empowered to sell offices in every department of Church and State. These offices were going cheap, too, for this was a black market with a difference. It was very much less expensive to buy here than through the regular channels. It was also easier, in that cash, and cash only, was the qualification.

Exchanges from one regiment to another were now, with active service afoot, hard to get. Approach Mrs. Clarke, as did the worthy Colonel Brooks in July of 1805, and for a couple of hundred pounds the whole matter could be fixed in a day or two. Captain Maling of the Royal Africa Corps secured a rise in rank from the same quarter, having seen no service. Major Shaw wished to be Deputy Barrack Master in the sunshine of the Cape, and was ready to pay £1,000 for the place. Alas, he could not find ready money and fell behind with his instalments, which led to his sad reduction to unemployment on the half-pay list.

Messrs. Corri and Cockayne, attorneys of Lyon's Inn, also acted for Mary Anne. Colonel French was able to give her a proportion of patronage in the nomination of officers for his new levies, and she further arranged that she should get a certain sum out of the bounty for each new recruit.

She visited Margate and enjoyed the excellent air of that resort, feeling all the better for the rapid turnover of her

F

business. Prices were kept down too; an Ensigncy was obtain-
able at half-price—£200; one of her Lieutenancies would cost
no more than £400. She would gazette you Captain for £700
cash, and your Majority would mean but £900, a clear saving
of £1,700.

Yet, in spite of it all, her financial position remained as
unstable as that of every one else connected with the royal
brothers. Her own allowance was in arrears, paid in trickles,
although doubtless more than anticipated in the bills she ran
up. Creditors were pressing. None of them had any illusions
about the financial affairs of the Commander-in-Chief. Mary
Anne had to raise all she could; she borrowed from Mr.
Donovan, surgeon, of Charles Street, St. James's Square, who
wrote making frank and manly offers for appointments in which
his friends were interested.

Frederick got little benefit from the shameless unorthodoxy
of Mary Anne's ways. Place-giving and seeking is always
corrupt, but the straightforward sale of public appointments,
however unclouded by concealment, has a barefaced shame of
its own. And after all, there was no need for him to keep Mary
Anne. Three years of her, with all her charm and wit and mirth,
was a sufficient quota of bliss for one man. He was fond of her,
but the time had come to part.

Mr. Adam, his man of business, arranged the parting. The
terms were as had been agreed, a pension of £400 a year. But
it was to be payable subject to her good conduct. Presumably
Frederick did not expect her either to live on £400 a year or
to refrain from the employment of her charms, so he must have
referred to the obtaining of money on the pretext that she was
able to use his influence to secure favours. He gave her a couple
of hundred pounds on which to leave town, wrote her affec-

tionate notes—"My darling shall have the ticket for the box the moment I go home. God bless you"—but Mary Anne was once more alone in the world.

She had plenty of choice now, Lord Folkestone, Captain Gronow, Colonel Gwyllym Lloyd Wardle, supporter of the Duke of Kent and friend of Major Dodd, Kent's military secretary. They all knew the frail beauty with the dazzling eyes, "beaming with irresistible archness and captivating intelligence; her skin delicately fair without being dead white: a sufficient colour adorning her cheek. She was thirty-six and the Duke had left her."

They actually parted in May of 1806, and for a time, for reasons which can be interpreted one way and another, Mary Anne lived in obscurity. Frederick undoubtedly was nervous that she had compromised him, wanted her to keep out of London, and was relieved to pack her off to Devonshire. But unfortunately he was unable, or unwilling, to maintain the payments that alone would keep her down there. For even in Devon she had to live. After the parting, she says: "I submitted to a life of undeserved seclusion with more fortitude than falls to the generality of my sex under such circumstances. Pursued by my creditors—harassed and distressed by threats, which afforded my future life no other prospect but the walls of a prison—is it to be made a matter of surprise that any woman, so situated, with an infant family to support and protect, should be glad to *catch* at any *offer*."

For now the plot began.

Mary Anne was desirable enough in her own right and had the *réclame* proper to a fair Cyprian from the royal stables, but she had, for the duty-devoted Colonel Wardle, an even greater value.

For Edward, Duke of Kent, newly and ignominiously recalled

from Gibraltar, where he had grossly exceeded his duties by reducing drunkenness and misconduct and halving military mortality, had a bitter grudge against his Commander-in-Chief brother. Major Dodd, Kent's military secretary, had the duty of searching out and supplying to the press, for public consumption, any titbits of scandal he could find about Frederick, anything which would discredit him.

Edward's animosity grew. At first he was more furious than bitter. Through 1807, his jealousy increased. Mary Anne, back in London for sheer need's sake, glad to conceal herself from creditors by sheltering with a Mrs. Andrews at Hampstead, was not as yet involved.

She did not always lodge with Mrs. Andrews. The laws governing debt in those days made it a very inconvenient thing to be found by one's creditors, and it was useful to have an address that was reliable for friends to use and incorruptible so far as bribing foes might be concerned. Mary Anne was often with her mother, who lived at that time in Bloomsbury, at Bedford Place, Russell Square. The children were a constant anxiety. Life just then was very difficult.

Then, in the second year after their parting, Frederick began to touch her life again, to inspire it with hard cash and pleasant publicity. Mrs. Andrews came in from Hampstead with letters and messages.

She had another boarder, one Sir Richard Philips. Sir Richard was known to a gentleman whom Mary Anne doubtless remembered well, Colonel Wardle. Colonel Wardle was also, incidentally, an M.P., and exercised his Celtic charm not only on a wife and family, but also on a Miss Davis of Gloucester Street, a mistress "so *fair and young* that he did not suffer the air of heaven to blow on her."

Colonel Wardle, hearing from Sir Richard that Mary Anne was known at his lodgings and seeing in her the very person who would help him, had come to seek her. But one never knew. Mary Anne had had trouble from Frederick already, and there were the Devon creditors, to say nothing of others with uncompounded bills dating from the Gloucester Place days. So Mrs. Andrews had refused to give away the Russell Square address, but had taken letters and messages and brought them to Bloomsbury.

It was a difficult situation. Mary Anne had no desire to create more complications for herself, but she needed money badly. The three women discussed matters for a while, and finally sought legal advice from Mr. Stokes of Golden Square. Mr. Stokes thought that the affair was worth following further. The bad blood between the royal brothers was well known. It must be worth something. There was no harm in Mary Anne's seeing Wardle.

She saw him, and he made himself as pleasant as he possibly could, for she could be extremely useful to him. It is not surprising that she, on her side, thought that he could be more than helpful to her, particularly in the article of hard cash. She hinted delicately at the need. Dodd was produced, and Dodd came out into the open with assurances of generosity. Again Mr. Stokes was consulted, and Mary Anne returned to the kind gentlemen prepared to do everything she could for them, to unearth any possible evidence they could use against Frederick. But now, instantly, and for ever, she must have and be assured of money, plenty of money.

Dodd readily gave her this assurance. Frederick's paltry unpaid pension of £400 was nothing. She should have this plus a lump sum of £5,000. Further, her debts were to be entirely cleared, and she was to be presented with a house, a house of her own and furnished to her own taste. She took £100 off Dodd on account, and embarked on a nebulous and difficult game. For she had to be helpful, very willing indeed, and yet somehow more helpful and more willing when money flowed freely, and yet never so helpful and so willing that they got all they wanted and left her stranded once again.

No more Hampstead for her, anyway, neither baker Nichols nor the worthy Mrs. Andrews. No more Wiltshire or Devon either, if she could possibly avoid it. A cottage at Putney came into the picture, but she allowed herself to be persuaded by Wardle, perhaps on one of the days when she kept forgetting things and memory needed a spur, to take a house in Westbourne Place.

That was a practical step, but furniture was necessary. Both Dodd and Wardle would have supplied her freely with any money that the Duke of Kent gave them for the purpose, but he had no money to give. Mary Anne had been useful; she had introduced them to tradesmen who knew a great deal about the private life, financially speaking, of the Duke of York. Now, she began stalling. In the end, after an intricacy of plan and counter-plan and the signing of a £500 bill of sale, she secured some furniture.

In the summer of 1808 the three of them went away to the south coast on a pleasure party. They also went to Maidstone and visited the Martello Towers, new-built invasion defences. On Romney Marsh they investigated the end of the Royal Military Canal and talked to the engineers. For not only on the score of selling places were they seeking evidence against Frederick. If any fault could be found in his conduct of the Army's regular business, that also would be used. Discussion went on all through the Christmas season but in the end it was decided to stick to the corruption and place-selling line. That at least was open and easy, that could almost certainly be proved.

In all the fog of intrigue, it is not easy to see the exact motive guiding every one at every time, but it is safe to assume that at no time was Mary Anne actuated by anything but the purest self-interest. It was remarkably hard even for her always to see just which side of her bread bore the greatest likelihood of butter. There was the once adoring Frederick, who might even now return to his post as financial prop. Edward's friends were providing a dismal poor resource. She squeezed them hard, made the most of every opportunity, and turned to account all she could, but when, in January, Colonel Wardle rose in the House to ask a question about abuse in the matter of army appointments, promotions and exchanges, Mary Anne was by no means certain which side could be the better friend to her.

The Whigs, in tedious opposition, hoped for much from this attack. The Government took on the defence of the Duke of York.

Mary Anne's mother was away at Bath when the public enquiry began, and when, on February 1st, 1809, her daughter had to appear for examination at the Bar, she was unsupported. She moved down to Ellis's coffee-house and took lodgings there, with friends, for the period of her attendance. There would be much to do, many people to see, and she must be available.

First of all, she needed to create a good impression, and she chose her clothes with care. She selected a gown and coat of light blue silk. It was edged with white fur, and she carried a white fur muff, which is an efficient weapon in the hands of a vivid, small blonde, alone on a vast and dusty floor. She wore a white cap and veil, but decided not to let the veil down, to allow the full effect of charm and expression to be felt. Even so, when she made her first entrance, she was exceedingly pale.

Her business there was to give evidence which might compromise the Duke of York, and her status was his ex-mistress. But it was quite impossible to hector or bully her and, while she certainly gave evidence of her own traffickings, she took very shrewd care how far she went.

She stood up to all attempts at hectoring in a way that endeared her to the Members and the public and won their admiration. On her second entrance the vivid colour came to her face, but neither then nor later did she seem daunted or embarrassed.

She heard cited the case of Captain Tonyn of the 48th. He had been introduced to her, had agreed to pay her £500 on getting his majority, and the business was fairly and squarely arranged, the money being given straight to the stakeholders and then to that invaluable man, surgeon Donovan. The £500 had gone to buy some plate from a Mr. Birkett. It had been insufficient, and Frederick had paid the rest of the bill.

Now the whole point of the public enquiry was to prove that Frederick knew what had been going on. With the facts as they were, the Government could hardly deny that large and frequent payments had been made to Mary Anne for help in securing positions, but the Government was seeking to establish that Frederick had known nothing whatever about it from beginning to end, that she had, in fact, been taking the money and rendering no service therefor, or taking the money and perhaps persuading her lover to pull an occasional string, but in no case letting him benefit by the cash side of the transaction. He did not in fact even know, the Government maintained, that a cash side existed.

Behind the scenes argument raged. Edward was not paying. Where was the amply furnished house? Where the £5,000? What was to be done about her unpaid debts? Her evidence had been invaluable, had turned out to be almost the sole ground upon which their public action against Frederick could be taken, and look at this shabby treatment! Certainly there was considerable argument behind the scenes.

In the House, however, Wardle passed to the case of Colonel French's levy and its implications, including the Colonel's money-raising activities on Frederick's behalf. The determined Tories massed to his defence, found Mary Anne's evidence had a slightly uncertain quality that must have been very comforting to them. The more she quarrelled with Wardle, the more she confessed to her own most improper practices, but the vaguer grew the picture as a whole.

Mary Anne's butler was called as a witness, but his alcoholic habit made him most unsuitable.

Captain Sanden was the man most quickly implicated. Hundreds of notes were produced in evidence, frank statements of this or that transaction. Within a fortnight he was committed to Newgate, while his fascinating fellow-worker continued under examination.

Her lively wit gave her an enjoyable time on the whole. She played shamelessly upon the Members' sense of humour, took advantage of the good will which she had the art to create. On one occasion a note was slipped into her hand—"Three hundred guineas and supper with me to-night." That was the mood to which she tried to bring them.

Placidly she allowed her past to stray into the picture,

including the vague Mr. Dowler who had remained on her visiting list in Park Lane and even in Gloucester Place. Time and again she was caught out in obvious falsehoods. She would save herself with engaging blatancy, refusing once to repeat a remark made to her in the lobby by a previous witness. She protested to Mr. Windham, "I cannot tell you because it was indelicate."

The eight charges created eight times their real value in furore. Mary Anne won publicity, admiration for her coolness and respect for her lively answers. Now and then she produced a plum, as when she admitted that Frederick "told me that if I was clever I should never want for money." It was a juicy morsel. Her housekeeper, Martha Favery, appeared to testify to domestic stresses. Her devoted friend, the interesting Miss Taylor who made a living by keeping boarding school, was examined and as a result lost three-quarters of her livelihood. Of the twelve scholars at her establishment near Sloane Street, Chelsea, nine were withdrawn by parents and guardians.

Mr. Taylor, Bond Street shoemaker to the brothers, blossomed on her witty tongue into "the Morocco ambassador." At another time she involved Colonel MacMahon, henchman to the Prince of Wales.

She had adventures outside the House too. Returning late one night down York Street, Westminster, after a fortnight of examination, she came upon an outbreak of fire. She stopped her carriage to warn the householders. The blaze was in the cooperage of one Mr. Askell, next door to a brewery, which was for a time in very serious danger. Mary Anne enjoyed every moment of it, the energy of the Queen's Guards and the Tilt Yard Guards in subduing the outbreak, the rescue of

Mr. Askell in his waistcoat and small-clothes, the rush to and fro of excited and unsuitably clad citizens. She lent her chariot to ladies who had fled insufficiently clothed, until neighbours could receive them.

It was all very eventful, but not so eventful as the happenings that took place three days later. For on February 17th a large collection of papers was admitted as evidence.

These papers came from Nichols, the worthy baker of Hampstead, who had not found Mary Anne worth suing, in spite of her tendencies to blackmail.

On one occasion she had given his servants a mass of documents to burn, and this rubbish had come under his eye, and he had preserved them as being "too *curious* for the fire." Doubtless the idea was to have some grip over Mary Anne, to whom, now, these very papers proved a positive little gold mine. In fact, on this day was brought to the public eye the raw material on which she and her family prospered and lived happily ever after.

Quite apart from the business notes that constantly went to and fro between Mary Anne and Captain Sanden ("The present for my trouble for the Majority is seven hundred guineas," "Will you ask again about an Indian Lieutenancy? as the Duke assures me there are two for sale") there were letters from Frederick to her, a good many of them. It is hard to see who could have thought their preservation an act of injury to the lady. Addressed to "the lovely charmer of my soul," they were as good as an annuity in the hands of an astute agent.

Frederick was furious at the publicity given to his naïve epistles, which added considerably to the social gaiety of London. "My dear little angel, how can I sufficiently express

to my sweetest darling love, the delight, which your dear—
dear pretty letter gave me, or how do justice to the emotions
it excited! Millions—millions of thanks for it, my angel, and
be assured that my heart is wholly fixed on your affection. . . ."
In a purple passage, he longs for "Wednesday se'nnight that I
may return to my love's arms."

The Tories, and Sir Arthur Wellesley with them, put up an
adamantine defence, and it is true that Frederick was acquitted
by 278 votes to 196 and cleared from the imputation of knowing
what depths his charmer had plumbed. But it is hard to see
on what grounds this was done, when one of his letters read,
"How can I sufficiently express my thanks to my love for her
dear, dear letter, and the assurances it contained of love. Oh,
my angel, how you are beloved! Every day convinces me
more and more how much my happiness depends upon her
affection. . . . General Clavering, my love, is mistaken. There
are no new regiments to be raised; they are only second
battalions that are to be formed; so that his business cannot
be done, and tell him so."

Duly cleared Frederick was, although he thought it well to
resign from the Horse Guards. Frederica, his wife, had come
up to town to give him face before the barrage of ridicule.
All would be well in time, and two years later he was to be
reappointed, but for the moment London was aflood with
light-hearted and scurrilous comment. Some of it, of course,
was inspired in his defence, some pens leaped naturally to his
aid. "A Lady," probably Lady Olivia Serres, disapproved of
the proceedings, "especially when we reflect on the dangerous
tendency such procedure may have by rendering the industrious
and lower orders of people perverse and discontented with the
rulers they may have placed over them." She pleaded that

her interest was not the sale of commissions, which had gone
on for a long time, but the bitter treachery on the part of the
lovely serpent. It was true that "the generosity of his disposition should induce him to grant that favour to a beloved
female," but how wrong of her, how ungrateful and unworthy,
to use it as she did!

Satiricus, a robuster critic, summed the tale in verse, and
ended cheerfully:

"And now, shrew'd Mistress Mary Anne,
Having thus far my couplets ran
On thee, and thy notorious acts,
Since all I've said are public facts,
Thou can'st not say with whip of Carter,
Too hard I've lashed thee :—little *Tartar*:
For there's a something, fierce about thee,
That will not let me too much flout thee;
Since I am guided by this rule,
I love a *knave* far more than *fool*:
Not that I mean as such to stile thee,
Let *Justice first* as *base* revile thee,
When, should my Muse find naught to do,
I might once more this course renew,
Till which dear Cyprian Clarke, adieu."

Hard words break no bones, for she had the letters; thanks
to Mr. Nichols's wisdom and perspicacity.

Since Frederick had been acquitted of known connection
with her traffickings he should really bear her no particular
malice. He had left the Horse Guards, so Edward should
be fairly pleased. From one or the other, or perhaps from the
Prince of Wales, who might be interested in a *fracas* between
his brothers, surely some money must be forthcoming.

From Bedford Square she sent word to the Prince of Wales,

informing him of the existence of material in which he might be interested. Mary Anne Clarke was not mentioned. Her mother's name, Farquhar, was used. None of the royal brothers could entirely resist a scandal or an assignation, and so Colonel MacMahon was duly despatched to investigate. Later he rose in the house to explain the whole thing openly and frankly.

He told of meeting the lady, of a conversation of so "extraordinary a nature that I am confident this House would not for a moment entertain it, because the tendency and intention of it was to make bad blood between two illustrious brothers, whose affections could never be shaken by such representation; at least I am confident that the illustrious person I have the pride and glory to serve and love would be incapable. She then told me that she would show me letters to prove and to establish that there was a hatred on one part to the other; I declined seeing any letters."

All this gossip and the spate of pamphlets did not worry Mary Anne much. On the contrary, still in very low water financially, she decided that the material was too good to waste and made her own contribution to the literature of the subject. She produced *The Rival Princes*, of which the title is sufficiently explanatory, and it proved a success.

Frederick continued to leave her pension unpaid, being in any case furious at the public laughter she had raised. Wardle, "the pure, patriotic Colonel," produced neither the house nor the furniture, neither receipted bills nor lump sums, let alone an income. The Prince of Wales did not appear to be interested. Sir George Jackson, who saw her in March, in a box at the theatre, found her prettier than he expected, in a fine shawl and feather, but she was really seriously worried. There was her mother, and the much-loved son and the little daughters to be considered. A relative, Captain Thompson, had to have his debts paid to release him from a spunging-house. She tried to get a fund started for the children, and all through the early summer she was striving to get some of her moneys due from Kent.

But Wardle's purpose was served and Kent would certainly not fulfil the promises his lieutenants had made in a moment of need. Mary Anne was well able to fend for herself, and she had in actual practice made a point of getting everything from Wardle that she could. An upholsterer even took action against the Colonel for certain furnishing charges.

Her pen had helped her already. Now she decided that what was wanted was a little light on the justice of her claims. With the assistance of two others, she set out to destroy any vague remnants of Colonel Wardle's good reputation. She made a very thorough job of her pamphleteering and Wardle took action at once. He prosecuted the three of them, but once again a verdict of "Not Guilty" cleared the situation, and on December 10th she was acquitted.

What she wanted, she said plainly, was money on which to live. "I am of the opinion that there is not a person in England at all acquainted with the proceedings of the House of Commons . . . who is so credulous as to believe that Colonel Wardle has lately endeavoured to make the people of England credit as a divine revelation; namely that I incurred the exposure of myself, children and family, together with abuse, anxiety of mind, and fatigue of person . . . from a purely patriotic zeal to serve the public. If there should be a person in the country that indulge such an opinion of my patriotism, he must be the most insane and most weak man that ever lived." She was nothing if not a realist. Firmly she announces that "*if I had not been well satisfied of receiving the remuneration agreed upon* not all the Jacobinical parties in Europe should have introduced my letters and my person to the notice of Parliament."

There was, she decided, to be a sequel to *The Rival Princes*. Westbourne Place was a thing of the past, she was back with her mother in Bedford Row, and finances were very shaky. She would return to authorship and would now publish all Frederick's letters to her.

Sir Richard Philips, the fellow-lodger of Hampstead, had been in service once in connection with the sale of correspondence. Now she appealed to Mr. Adam, her former lover's man of business. If only the pension were promptly paid all this fuss and bother could stop at once. She would go on with her activities. "Yet, before I do anything publicly I will send to every one of H.R.H.'s family a copy of what I mean to publish. Had H.R.H. only been a little more punctual, this request had never been made."

Mr. Adam had apparently a useful Civil Service mind. Wrongs for which reparation could not under law be enforced were nothing to him. He got his salary, others could lack their pensions. It is possible that he was given no discretion in the matter.

She wrote again, "I have employed myself since in committing to paper every circumstance within my recollection during the intimacy of H.R.H. and myself. The fifty or sixty letters of H.R.H. will give weight and truth to the whole. On Tuesday I have promised to give these up, if I hear nothing further after this last notice; and when once given out of my own possession, it will be impossible to recall."

That was enough. Sir Herbert Taylor was commissioned to acquire the letters, and he offered terms that are quoted as £7,000 down and the old-established £400 per annum.

The book had been printed, and now every copy was burned, except for one which was deposited in Drummond's Bank.

One would have expected Mary Anne at last to be tranquil, but authorship was to be her undoing. Her next publication was a decidedly outspoken "Letter to the Rt. Hon. William Fitzgerald," to which that Privy Councillor took grave exception, and he brought her to court. "Pray, Madam," enquired Lord Ellenborough, with icy discourtesy, "under whose protection are you now?" She replied with rapid charm that she trusted she was under his, but the quip incensed where it should have soothed, and she was sent to gaol. Her many sympathisers thought it a vindictive sentence, although the actual term was short. The lot of female prisoners was revolting indeed.

Elizabeth Fry had not yet left Earlham for the task of redemption. Samuel Whitbread, in June of 1814, mentions to Creevey that "I have just received a petition from Mrs. Mary Anne Clarke, complaining of cruelty and partiality in her mode of confinement, and stating various instances where indulgences have been obtained for money." Mary Anne was apparently now upon the side of the angels, but it is perhaps permissible to hope that her charms did not always fail to work, and that an occasional gaoler was kind to her in small items of food and luxuries which she must so often have craved.

However, it was not for very long, and then she was out again, still undaunted. From now onward things were to be easier for her.

She put the past behind her and went to live in Brussels.

G

That was the place for English people with financial or other
worries, and it was also, just after the defeat of Napoleon, a
centre where one could certainly meet the passing world. She
took with her her money, her reputation and her daughters.
She had managed to educate the girls well, and abroad even
penniless young things could be given a good showing, and
they were, apparently, by now provided for. It is reported that
they had a pension each of £200, while a lump sum provided
for their brother.

Mary Anne made the journey successfully. Brussels was
not a permanency, however, and she advanced on Paris with
the conquering armies of the allies. Never again, she determined, would she go back to England, as once years before
she had vowed never to return to the squalid Gravel Pits of
Kensington.

The girls married, and married well. Mary Anne herself,
with her irresistible archness, her wit and captivating charm,
established herself as a blonde in her early forties, and began to
enjoy the fruits of a large acquaintance.

Captain Gronow reports that no old friend visiting Paris
failed to pay his respects. She became an institution. It was an
institution that took a certain amount of upkeep, but it was one
that they did not want to lose. Lord Londonderry was reported
a lover. Others came and went. Her flow of anecdote concerning the royal family became famous; Frederick had been
just a big baby, the Prince of Wales could be managed if you
knew how. Her stories grew apocryphal, but remained
popular. Undoubtedly it was a wise arrangement that she
should stay away from London, and she lived on to a ripe old
age in France, lively, sprightly and full of fun, retaining
pleasing traces of past beauty. It was admitted that her best

friend would serve as well as anyone else for the object of a joke, but Mary Anne was a law unto herself.

She lived on well into her seventies, and died at Boulogne on June 21st, 1852. The *Gentleman's Magazine* duly recorded her obituary, but Mary Anne Clarke died, as she had been born, not by any standards a Lady.

MRS. JORDAN

THREE SISTERS went out into the world to seek their fortune.

The Reverend Mr. Phillips, in his Welsh living, was probably no better off than the gentleman who was passing rich on fifty pounds a year, and his three daughters decided to go on the stage and seek careers for themselves. Two of them went to Dublin and appeared with success. There was apparently some degree of talent to back their ambition. One of them, Grace, perhaps had greater powers than she realised, if it was from her that her daughter inherited her gifts.

Her daughter was Dorothy—Dora Bland-Francis-Jordan-Ford-Jordan, name and name about, whose only real surname throughout her life was one she never seems to have used— that borne by the reverend gentleman in Wales. For Grace and Francis Bland, Dora's father, were never married. He had expectations and decided that he could not risk it. His family were prejudiced against the stage, which had already swallowed up his elder brother, and they would never consent to an actress daughter-in-law. Dorothy appears in the register of St. Martin's in the Fields, on November 11th, 1761. She was, to her cost, not their only child.

Grace and Francis Bland were obviously together for some years, and when his family did recall him, she was deserted indeed. He married a more eligible lady, but possibly he made

80

some provision for his children. He might have done more, but unfortunately he soon died, and his widow firmly declined to have anything to do with Grace or her offspring. Grace went to live in Dublin and her daughters, Hester and Dorothy, she put to training for the millinery business, while she made plans to return to the stage. But she was no longer young, and it was not easy to obtain a part, so in the end it was Hester who made a timid appearance at the Crow Street theatre. Hester had not the right temperament and she was so overcome by stage fright that she was unable to speak a single word. Tydei, from the theatre, went round next day to see her mother, and there he met Dorothy, who never remembered to garter her stockings properly and boasted that she could jump downstairs in fewer bounds than the boys.

It was Dorothy, then, who acted Miss Tomboy in *The Romp*. She laughed, boundlessly gleeful. The audience laughed at her, she laughed at herself, and they laughed again. Then she sang. During her life Dora Jordan made three theatrical reputations: in Dublin, in the English provinces, and in London. Each time she did it with *The Laugh*.

Dora was a success, a gay, Irish, penniless success. Unfortunately Crow Street theatre was growing steadily poorer. Dora might hand over her earnings as cheerfully as she liked, but they were not large enough to keep the entire family. Smock Alley, the theatre under Daly's management, was prospering. It was clear that Crow Street would not make anybody's fortune, but two new openings now presented themselves to Dora. She was offered an engagement at Smock Alley, and another sort of engagement, one that would end in matrimony, to Charles Powlett Doyne, cornet of horse. The first promised more laughing successes, but even a Smock

Alley success could not bring either wealth or social ease. Her cornet of horse, it was true, was penniless at the moment, but there were always those dim shadows known as expectations, and there was the chance of promotion. He might catch the eye of the right man with the right place in his gift. Anyway, Dora was used to poverty, and she was no longer a giddy girl in her teens; she had passed into her twenties, and what she wanted more than anything was a home, an establishment, and a family of her own.

It needed all her mother's protestations of helplessness, all her sorrowing wails for a more adequate income, backed by all their friends' prophecies of theatrical fame, to induce Dora to dismiss Charles and accept Daly.

Smock Alley brought her good parts, and good money for Dublin. However, this was always Daly's method when he wished to ingratiate himself with a new young actress. He set his heart on Dora, as he had on others before, and he tried his whole repertoire of tricks. When lavishness failed, he fell back on small parts and a pittance to induce her to look at him. When that failed too, he got her under contract, that her wings of escape might be clipped.

Charles Powlett Doyne seems to have vanished. He was not to give Dora that happy family of her own which she craved. But Daly succeeded where he had failed. He used methods rather different from those of the honourable cornet of horse. After getting Dora under contract, he persuaded her to accept loans, threatened her with imprisonment for debt, and still failed. Finally, he fell back on kidnapping and rape! Dora was to bear his child, now surely she was securely in his power?

She had conquered Dublin with her gallantry in breeches parts, with the golden laugh and her gay singing. Now she had to face a problem of a strictly feminine nature. Grace cannot have been much help. She appears to have been a woman of the type who drools a mournful "the Lord will provide!" and then makes such a science of martyred worry that her family regard themselves as forcibly cast for the rôle of Providence. Even now, it was apparently Dora who took the decisions.

She could not and she would not stand Daly. This was the last horror. Whatever might come of it, she was finished with him.

From the legal point of view, she very much feared his powers, for she was in his debt and he threatened imprisonment. She gathered up her dependants, mother, sisters and brother, and secretly fled with them to England. She really was penniless now, as well as pregnant.

Grace was at least helpful in that she guided them to Leeds. She already knew, and had acted with, Tate Wilkinson. He was known as The Wandering Patentee, from the number of provincial theatres whose patents, or licences, he held, and he surely would be willing to help the girl. Dora agreed to apply to him, but she refused to go alone. Grace must come too. Either they were so entirely without money that they could not afford to eat, or, more probably, Dora's misery and the whims of pregnancy had made her refuse food. When she met Wilkinson, she was too weak to give him any example of her powers until he had provided her with some refreshment.

Quite leadenly she rose to her feet. The mamma, pattern of theatrical mammas, who had been gushing her praises, stopped suddenly and hushed the brother. Wilkinson waited while Dora's mind wandered listlessly among the speeches of her various parts. Then, quite suddenly, she began, and as she spoke he saw her more clearly. She was not just a merry girl with a gift for making herself liked, blessed merely with sufficient personality for her natural gaiety to make itself felt across a theatre. She was an actress. Standing just back from the table with its dirty wineglasses and empty claret bottle, in the face of a hard-breathing family and a silent theatrical manager, with the unborn child of the detested Daly rounding within her, she played and won her battle.

Dora was engaged. She at once started to build up the second of her theatrical reputations, an even larger one than the first. Leeds applauded. They wanted more of her. She remembered the old Crow Street days, and *Melton Oysters*, the song she had sung so often after the piece was over. She would use it again.

Wilkinson was not anxious for her to sing as well as to play comedy, tragedy and farce. When he had asked her which she did, in the pre-claret stage of their first interview, she had answered "All!" Never, to quote her, was a middle-aged gentleman so surprised. He was surprised again when she insisted on singing, sang, and increased her reputation.

It was lucky that success came so soon, for she needed a few months of fortune to buoy her through the winter ahead. First, she was pregnant and unwell. Then, Daly had traced her and was threatening imprisonment for debt and breach of contract. Thirdly, her actress aunt was ill, and Dora felt an illness in the family more than one of her own.

It had been a bad time for her ever since she had sent Charles away and turned her face towards providing for Grace and the family. It was time something went right, and something did. Tate Wilkinson introduced her, the young success, to a dramatic critic of York, Cornelius Swan, who not only liked her, but saw most clearly her possibilities. He set himself to help, both by coaching and, when he discovered what was worrying her, by clearing every penny of the debt owing to the infamous Daly, and drawing that individual's fangs for good and all.

Dora was able to visit her aunt before she died, and for once was the richer for one of her kindnesses. She gained a wardrobe and some necessary linen. Either the aunt or Tate Wilkinson evolved the name of Jordan, as the matrimonial fortress into which she must retreat. Wilkinson says that he invented the name, since she "crossed the water." There is a theory that the aunt had at one time married a man named Jordan, had a baby called Dorothy, and lost the child. It was her dying wish that the name should live on in the cousin, in the career for which she may perhaps have intended her daughter. Yet another account says that Dora christened herself, on account of the tears she had shed, equal to that great river's flow.

Be that as it may, she laughed on as Mrs. Jordan, so successfully that Wilkinson in his turn got her under contract. He did it before her baby was born, so that offers from London might not tempt her away afterwards. "Gentleman" Smith, an actor friend in whose benefits she was to play in later years, had seen her and returned to Drury Lane with her praises.

Just at the moment, in spite of the contract, Dora was willing to leave the stage, or at least to make it her minor theme. She still hoped, above everything, for marriage, a home, babies. And she seldom missed an opportunity for making herself the slave of anyone sufficiently unworthy of her. Mr. George Inchbold was in her company. She felt for him something more than a passing whim. He scarcely seems to have been worthy of anyone, and at any rate he did not at the moment return her regard.

In November her daughter Frances was born. Dora acted as long as she could, for she needed the money, and then she stayed at home, waiting. Perhaps at the end even her courage was a little shaken, for she never forgot the needs of women in like condition. After her first confinement she was never without bundles of the necessary linen, which she lent out to the needy.

She went back to success. With success, she grew ambitious. There was London ahead of her. She was getting talked of now; she was important enough for people like Mrs. Siddons to predict carefully what a failure she would be in London, and this from the tragedy queen showed that she indeed promised to be a powerful rival, for Dora seldom touched tragedy. For the great middle period of her career she devoted herself to comedy almost entirely.

The provinces began to seem small beer, and she took less trouble. Here and there her casualness won an almost chilly reception, and she scarcely heeded. Drury Lane was beckoning.

Then, quite suddenly, came the definite offer. Among other things, she was to understudy Mrs. Siddons herself. Dora did not hesitate. She accepted, and for the rest of her time in the north her acting grew more and more careless. She had never the power of giving minute attention to artistic perfection as an art in itself. In her way, she was right. She had a natural vital genius, owing nothing to stage effect. When she did not want to act, when she was annoyed or vexed, then she could not act, whether or not she had to put in an appearance on the stage.

Drury Lane offered her four pounds a week. That was

where the real attraction lay. She had her mother, a dead weight on daughterly hands, her sisters and a brother. She took them with her to Henrietta Street, across the Strand from the houses which bordered on the unbanked Thames.

She opened in London with an old success, which was to be the staple rôle of her career. It was as Peggy, in *The Country Girl*, that she first appeared at Drury Lane. The play was a version made from Wycherley's *The Country Wife*, which was not considered "nice" for representation in the days of the Regency. It was revived a few years ago in London with the greatest success.

She earned just enough adverse criticism to make her a topic of continual interest. The world in general came to see her small, neat figure, so attractive in breeches parts, to listen to her sing, and to fall in love with "the Laugh."

Drury Lane put up her salary. Four pounds a week had tempted her; eight almost overpowered her; and then a rise to twelve made her realise that she had a market value. Mother and sisters could wax fat and possibly lazy. Little Frances could have the last word in eighteenth century baby equipment.

Dora was delighted, and she showed it, as she did resentment, in her acting. She responded to success in a bubble of glee. Possibly for the first time in modern stage history there began to be a stage-door crowd. The crowd came to see her arrive and depart, for rehearsals as well as for performances. Mrs. Siddons was the reigning star, but although she might be worshipped, the austere nature of her genius prevented her from becoming London's darling as Dora did.

By the next year she had more than an assured position. She also was rising to be a star. In May, she took a holiday, and—her instinct was towards family—she spent it in Edinburgh where her uncle was acting. This was her father's brother, the one who had pained his family by going on the stage. John Bland and his son, Dora and her brother, all acted, sometimes together, on Edinburgh boards. Her Scots success was repeated at Glasgow.

For anyone with a deep love for the security of home, there is no holiday quite so pleasant as the one which is to end in certain return to a certain job. The end of summer saw her back in Henrietta Street, and in the September of 1786 she created the part of Matilda in *Richard, Cœur de Lion*. With this, the great rivalry between Jordan and Siddons began in earnest, and Dora entered on a brilliant season.

She was fond of the public who applauded, and for that reason made them the more fond of her. She would not now slack off through lack of interest, but there would still be off-days, seasons of worry or distracted interest when her spirit struck no similar essence from the audience. She bore a humble and passionate generosity of soul, but she also had a single-track mind. When it was distracted from her work, then she could not act. She would say that she was ill; this was true enough in a way, but also untrue enough to annoy the people who had paid to see her play that night.

There was another good reason for occasional indisposition. From the first of her English performances on through her long career she was exceedingly often pregnant. Even now she again imagined herself to be on the brink of marriage.

In November of 1784 Daly's baby had been born. In 1787 she moved from Henrietta Street to share No. 5 Gower Street with Richard Ford.

In between these two dates there are a couple of shadowy admirers. Inchbold watched her success, remembered her

partiality, and came to her feet. He was firmly dismissed.
Then there is the rather faint outline of Mr. Bettesworth. He
takes firmer shape later on, in the legacy which came from him
to one of her daughters. As friend, suitor or lover, he seems to
have touched her life more kindly than most of the men she
knew.

Out of them all, there appear to be a few whom she herself
chose for the free gift of her love. One was that distant cornet
of horse. Then Inchbold. The third was Richard Ford. Her
meeting with him came about naturally enough. His father,
Dr. James Ford, had an interest in Drury Lane. Whereas the
father's interest was in the theatre itself, the son's was in its new
star. Dora loved him, accepted his proposal of marriage and,
with fond female generosity, allowed him to anticipate the
ceremony. He pleaded the same difficulty with his family which
had also deterred Francis Bland. It would be hard to slip an
actress, particularly one with a child already, into the social
circle. So she took his name in a private fashion, and they
moved to Gower Street.

The move was either just before or just after a tour of the
north. Drury Lane was jealousy-ridden, pleasant to leave for
a spell. The jealousy was all the more potent in that it had a
full-length cloak of love of art over its personal hates. The
Siddons faction, the stately and respectable devotees of high
drama, scorned and sneered at the noisy exhibitionism of
loose women, which was to them the current definition of
comedy.

A little girl was born in August, while Dora was up north,
perhaps a Ford, perhaps a Bettesworth. As her mother was
the only parent who paid much attention to her, it hardly
seems to matter. Now Dora had two small girls, she was

looking forward to marriage, and prepared to leave the stage without very much reluctance.

She had done very well, but there seemed to be a great many difficulties. Tom King, Drury Lane's manager, was firmly rooted in the successes of yesteryear. During the past season he had hardly given her any parts. The Kembles and their small-part following had supported his policy for their own reasons. Sheridan, also interested, scarcely ever gave more than half his attention to anything—he would have played atrocious golf! Richard's father was preparing to sell out, and that would deprive her of all her Drury Lane backing. Above all, she was going to be married at any moment.

But the careful Richard was too careful for that. Admittedly his behaviour was contemptible, but he still had one or two quite powerful motives. In the first place, marrying Dora would mean marrying her family, bloodsuckers to the backbone. Helplessly they clung round her and her bank balance. She was affectionate and generous; above all, she had the urge to be the centre of the group, a family group of dependence and interdependence. Richard would have found them inconvenient. He did not know, either, what his father planned to do when he sold out and retired. Possibly there would be satisfyingly large lump sums, potential legacies for those who had not lost the parental favour.

Dora, therefore, had to go back to work. Although she was already three months gone with her third child she acted all through the summer. For the first time, she played Harry Wildair, in *The Constant Couple*, a part in which she was not to be forgotten for a very long time. Breeches became her. There was a fashion then, inversion of the Elizabethan boy-heroines, for the better-known actresses to play men's parts.

Already the stage-door crowd had created itself in her honour; now she received her first marked attention from royalty.

George III paid a visit to Cheltenham and took its waters with almost fatal enthusiasm. Thither, therefore, flocked the camp followers of refinement. Dora had an engagement to appear at the local theatre. His Majesty postponed his visit to the play until she arrived.

That summer may have held a foreshadowing of the great event of her life, for it may have been then that she met Prince William. She would of course have seen him before in her audience, but this may have been their introduction as friends.

In October her third child was born, and still Richard Ford did not marry her.

Many people had assumed the marriage, or believed after consideration that it had taken place. Rather desperately, Dora saw those first irregular months, which could so easily have been forgiven and forgotten, lengthen and establish their precedent. Her position changed from fiancée to mistress, at any rate in the mind of Richard Ford.

If Dora was the Child of Nature, she was also the Victim of Human-Nature.

That title, the Child of Nature, was a legacy from the Inchbold connection. The admirer had been rejected, but his mother wrote a comedy (in which Dora did not act), under that name. It was a cap that fitted. Popular lips made it Dora's own and only title. Of her, Hazlitt wrote, "The child of nature, whose voice was a cordial to the heart . . . to hear whose laugh was to drink nectar . . . whose singing was like the twang of Cupid's bow . . . she was all exuberance and grace."

Now that the prospect of marriage was receding, the trouble

at the theatre began to prey on her usually sound nerves. She again became a little unreliable in her appearances. She had a good enough excuse, for another infant was expected, but the public would not always believe in her ill-health. Adoring and very vocal, they sometimes decided that her indispositions were diplomatic rather than medical.

Drury Lane was a very uneasy camp. Covent Garden, where Harris ruled with reasonable intelligence, was wise enough to profit and put out feelers. The feelers took the form of a definite offer, and Dora bore the offer for discussion to the busy Sheridan. He disengaged himself for long enough to smooth out her path for her at Drury Lane, and Covent Garden did not, after all, acquire a new star.

In the turmoil of this season, she turned to Edinburgh, to the merchant wealth and comfort and the Scots warmth of heart. After a short engagement at Richmond she went north. In Scotland the winter began well for her, with plenty of success while she still felt the sap of youth and future rising. The delayed marriage still grieved her, but it seemed to be her only cloud now that stage troubles had been cleared.

Then her mother died. She had been a constant drain on Dora's finances and had demanded endless love and attention, but Dora was heartbroken and inconsolable. She wrote a long elegy, in the classic poetic style, but even in the elegant periods of grief she was sincere. What indeed is home without a mother if the shadow cast by the mother has been the only abiding factor of home? Dora was many times a mother herself, but her own mother had always been the focal point of her life.

The return to London, with a new baby in her arms, was a grey pilgrimage. She had experienced difficulty, too, in getting her money from Jackson, the Edinburgh manager, and she

Dorothy Jordan, mistress of the Duke of Clarence (William IV)
Represented as Miss Tomboy in *The Romp*
From the portrait by George Romney

Adelaide of Saxe-Meiningen (Queen Adelaide)
Wife of William IV

needed it. There were still many relations calling on her for support or help.

But now, in 1790–91, she was about to become a person of consequence apart from the theatre.

She was still at Drury Lane, as popular as ever, but oppressed with a growing load of worries and loneliness. Daly had re-appeared. Ireland was the oyster he could not quite open, and he had come to London. His former young lead—had he forgotten the shaken despair of those sobs? the small physical strength which was all he could break?—his young lead was now London's comedy favourite. Her eldest daughter was his child.

He tried to see Dora, to induce her to act for him. He even tried to see his child. He failed. Dora was thirty now, no longer a defenceless slip, but a rather distracted, friendly, capable woman, with a grace of heart which would never let her condone his brutality and meanness. Daly had no chance.

Other men might meet her, speak to her, fall under her charm. Among them was Prince William, Duke of Clarence.

In 1791 he was just twenty-six—the King's third son and among the more innocuous of the royal princes. Now he fell in love with Dora with all the zeal of stupidity, and the force of a dull wit turning for nourishment to vitality.

He paid court without any attempt at concealment. It swelled her fame. She had been seven years in London now, and had been at the top of the tree for most of the time, but fame was still growing. Her tour of 1791 was marked by the cattiest of feelings and conduct on the part of colleagues and their mammas. It was a sign of poignant jealousy.

Richard Ford showed the same emotion. In his case, it took the form of incessant affectionate attention. She bore

H

him a dead child, the last of her babies by him. Already gossip and caricature were bestowing the honour elsewhere, but they were premature. Ford was constantly at her side, squiring her, demonstrating his overlordship, and she became more and more worried and unhappy. The one thing she desired was marriage and quiet settlement, but this was the only way by which he neglected to maintain his hold over her.

The Duke grew more and more ardent. Ford became more and more attentive, escorting her everywhere, complicating matters by introducing her as his wife. Friends who were not fully informed advised her to stick to her husband. But she had no husband to stick to. They told her that trouble comes to mistresses of royal princes. But it could lurk also for the mistress of a Mr. Ford.

Dora was the prototype of a bourgeoise matron, devoted mother of rather undisciplined children, certainly not the hard opportunist who would regard a royal duke as a worthwhile catch. She pondered over the problem from the point of view of her children. Under which protector would they be happiest? Her life was built round them, and round some shadowy ideal of reliable masculinity which she might call husband. If it had not been for that domestic dream, that shadow figure, there would have been a third path open, an independence in which she lived alone, earned the income, was father as well as mother.

Meanwhile the matter was under public debate and argued in the newspapers. Ford's motive was questioned. Was it genuine affection? Or dog-in-the-manger? The sound commercial instincts of the monopoly holder? Dora's supporters decided that he was a scoundrel, prepared to sell her and standing out for a high price, waiting for William to reach his ceiling offer. The opposition, partly Ford-inspired, cried fie on Dora for not, in reality, caring a rap for those precious children of hers. She was, they said, selling them for gold and glamour. On careful thought, the idea of any of those stout brothers ever possessing very much of either quality is surprising.

If William could offer any financial advantage, it would certainly count in his favour. Ford's decision not to marry her grew clear. There were the children, the brother and her sisters, all a drain on her resources. William was determined and seems to have pressed his points cleverly, for there were meetings all through the summer of 1791. June, July, August, Dora wavered, weakened, was persuaded. Even then she moved slowly. The change of lovers was arranged as carefully as a royal betrothal.

In the autumn she and William duly set their hands to an agreement as formal as a marriage contract.

She was to receive £1,000 a year and a pension. It was a security which would apparently last for life. In actual fact, the money frequently failed to materialise and was of the nature of an invisible asset. On Dora's side, she was to give over half her income and all her personal savings to her existing family. She had to do a great deal more than that for them before she had finished. The personal savings were a lump sum that she had in hand at the moment.

Then she got into the carriage and went off with William to Petersham. No. 5 Gower Street was a camp struck and abandoned. Richard Ford had lost her.

While she was honeymooning, the town was busy discussing the articles of her new association. They were still inclined to be critical. Dora "belonged to her public," as later lovelies have so affectingly said, and she had in the event to write them an explanatory letter, explaining the provision she had made for her children. It was broadcast through the press, and enlivened the tables and coffee-houses where her admirers gathered.

During her London years thus far, she had lived right in the heart of town, close to the theatre. Now she made a complete change. She took a house for the children on Ham Common, and one for herself in Brompton. The rearrangement of life fretted her, as earlier uncertainties had done. She could not appear. Her public had fresh ground for complaint in an illness which they could not credit. Her first appearance after the new establishment was before a hostile audience.

But the new life soon settled into something satisfactory, she could feel the earth underfoot, see the future. She had never been so gay or so full of vitality, and that audience melted like any other. She charmed and controlled them, and finally spoke severely to them for their own good. Royalty was present. It was a big evening. When it was all over, her public credit floated free again, in mid stream. She continued to act.

But if Dora was pardoned, it was at William's expense. If she were exonerated from the charge of selling her young, he was accused of living on his wife's earnings. Living on the earnings has never been thought a manly peccadillo. Caricaturists saw the sudden splendour of the situation and he was depicted drawing her pay for her. They found further scope in drawing a parallel between the positions of Dorothy Jordan and Maria Fitzherbert.

The Prince of Wales was feeling unsettled. His father's temporary mental recovery had removed for the moment his hope of becoming Regent. He and Maria had worked hard for a free-handed Regency, she in the hope that he would do something

—it is rather hard to see what—about regularising their union. Now that moment had gone. He was angling instead for some kindly gesture from his country in the shape of payment of his debts, and undoubtedly the pill which he would have to swallow with this sugar would be a royal and Protestant bride. He could believe that it might not be as unpleasant as it sounded. In October of 1791 his brother, the Duke of York, had married Princess Frederica. Frederick of York had been as wild a night-hawk as any of their cronies. He was now, apparently, as happy as the innocent lark. Had marriage, then, more compensations than one judged?

Maria could guess that the Prince was making a decision, and she bitterly resented caricaturists who approximated her position to that held by Dora. The fact that there was an even wider gap between her position and that held by the Duchess of York might tend to establish her, in the public eye and then in the eye of her lover, as an obstacle removable on pension. Kind as she was, she could not help showing her hostility to Dora at this time, and the caricaturists capitalised it.

All this affected Dora a good deal less than it did Maria. It did not complicate her position, and as for the publicity, she had lived her life under the lights. All through 1792 she acted like a bird, gayer and happier, more heartfree than ever before. This was almost all she had wished, if not marriage, at least an establishment. William improved enormously at her side, in manners and habits. She brightened him up, smoothed his corners, and secured from him the wondering beginnings of a real affection.

The gallery of theatrical portraits of Dorothy Jordan begins to date from this period, portraits painted by Gainsborough, Romney, Morland, Hoppner and others, each of them trying to capture something of that sparkle of natural glee which Hazlitt strove to describe.

Her children throve. She was not at the moment expecting another of them. Financially she was more comfortable than she had ever been. Through the next year she acted less. When she chose to appear, she could get her own price, but most of her performances were in "benefits," in which she seldom refused to help.

Early in January of 1794 a small daughter was born, the first of a large family which she and William were to have. For them, as for their mother, a name had to be found. They became the FitzClarences. The father and mother were happy. At Petersham, Dora entertained royalty in the shape of William's brothers. At Drury Lane, she was treated almost like royalty herself. Her lying-in on this occasion must have seemed almost exotic in its luxury when compared with the birth of Fanny.

Fanny's father, Daly, bobbed up yet again. He was slipping hopelessly. Once more he tried to induce Dora to act for him. She refused utterly. Again she declined to see him, speak to him, or to let him see the girl. Dora's inability to forgive him would seem to offer convincing proof of his infamy.

With the following spring the sequence of small girls was over, and she bore her first son. There was all suitable rejoicing, but undoubtedly the honeymoon was over. William showed a regrettable tendency to behave as though he were married, and started wandering from the fold. Dora brought him back, but this year financial anxiety returned to her life. She had to take more engagements, in fact she had a miscarriage through over-work in the year 1796. The £1,000 a year did not assume tangible form. Much of her work was still done at benefit and charity performances, but she was glad now to earn money too.

Then, just when it seemed that the foundations she had built were again to be swept away, William was given an appointment which opened the long, settled phase of their life together. The office of Ranger of Bushey Park fell vacant; William was appointed and they moved down together from the tempting perils of town to the quiet of Bushey House. Here she made her home, the one loved home of a changing life.

Regularly she added to her collection of FitzClarences, a brood to which she was devotedly attached, although she never lost day-by-day touch with earlier families, boarded out in suitable surroundings.

She had got William away from the bright lights, and she continued to turn him into her idea of a kindly family man. His dignity suffered—not that he had much of it to suffer—creaming her face, counting her earnings, arranging her tours; and he made himself rather ridiculous—but he was slightly ridiculous already—officiating as censor and dramatic critic. But it was an entirely blameless way of keeping him out of mischief and under her eye. A domestic lute can have a surprising number of rifts in it without losing its value as a musical instrument.

Their life was cheerful, open-hearted and above-board, exactly as Dora liked to live. She might in some moods have reflected that it would have been more pleasant still to enjoy life among the FitzClarences without the need to work. But as the £1,000 retained its mythical quality, her earnings were needed to swell the common purse.

Life continued to be gay. She was popular wherever she

went; she was received in houses she could not have expected to enter, and hardly anyone felt compelled to decline to meet her. People came to her parties, where the babies were duly paraded. If any of the family's royal brides could have produced the babies, even without earning a handsome living as well, they would have been worth their weight in crown jewels.

All through the next years she worked very hard indeed. In the summer of 1797 she played at Richmond, which she was to make a habit of doing, and at Thanet. Next year's baby, again a girl, was born after the second Richmond engagement.

Then she took a long rest, earned and deserved. She had been buxom at thirty, she was almost plump now, penniless, popular, gay and affectionate, the same with a royal duke or a daily help. A letter to a governess shows her in high relief. "Why will you, my dear girl, make yourself uneasy about me. Believe me, I am very well; however, I think a little bark may strengthen me. I am sincerely sorry that you are going to leave us, but won't blame your friends for their anxiety to see you again. Let me request you will not stay long away; believe me, you have not, among the people who love—and who must love—you, one who more truly values your friendship than I do. My poor little girls will miss your society greatly. You give me great pleasure in saying that you think Mrs. Betty may answer; God grant she may. And now, my dear girl, the money I owe you is among the least of the kindnesses I have received from you, and it is the only one of the many I can make return for. Let me know how much it is, and I will so far gratify your good heart as to let you have it as I can spare it. The dear little ones are all well. God bless you, and may you be as happy as you deserve and as I shall now wish you. Your affectionate friend, Dora Jordan." There was a postscript: the Duke desired to be remembered, and remembered affectionately.

For months on end she was at homely, untidy Bushey. She had occasional trouble with William over her generosity to her family, more because he was always short of money than for any other reason. She was earning well, her tours continued. William never forgot that he had been in the Navy, "The Sailor Prince," and when these theatre voyages began again, they were suitably renamed the Cruises. When she was away she wrote to him daily, a scribble or a screed as occasion allowed.

After the birth of a child—there were ten FitzClarences in all—she rested until the spring of 1799. She was thirty-eight now, her personal life had taken its shape, not hereafter to be changed, but to abide by its consequences as all lives must. She was the Child of Nature, idol of English comedy, she was the owner of "the Laugh." As she had perforce to go on acting, she not unnaturally developed views on the theatre. And she had the benefit of unlimited theatrical advice from her Sweet William, as that fragrant dianthus considered himself something of a stage expert. She took now what was a perilous plunge, professionally. She challenged the Siddons on the respectable heights of tragedy. Not since the days of long ago, since Tate Wilkinson's time, had she done so, and she had an amazing success. It was a sweet moment for her professional vanity. It may be noted that she played under her usual handicap, there was another baby coming.

The stage had given her a good literary education. You cannot spend much of your time conning and speaking other people's good English without acquiring some of your own, and of natural fine feeling she had plenty. Her elegy on her mother was not only uninspired, it was neither insincere nor unpolished. She tried her hand at playwriting. *The Spoiled Child* is partly hers. And in spoiling children she had acquired considerable practice. People are ready to believe, and it is a pleasant belief to hold, that she also wrote and composed *The Bluebells of Scotland*. Certainly she sang it with tremendous effect.

It was a very good season, that which began the new century. She acted before the King. She was in the theatre, although not on the stage, on the occasion when an enthusiast rose up and fired on His Majesty. He took it with Hanoverian courage. Dora also was unshaken, except in the first crashing moment, and helped to calm the audience, while behind the scenes the fairy godfather of Drury Lane wrote his famous extra verse to the national anthem.

Life had its rhythm, Drury Lane, Richmond, the Cruises, home again to Bushey.

Margate was, one day, to see her last stage performance. In 1802, however, that impatient resort tried to forestall the event and she was nearly burned to death. A lamp set fire to her clothes. The garments flared up, the lady was not of a slenderly mobile build, but fortunately the fire was extinguished and she lived on uninjured.

Meanwhile Daly's memento, young Fanny, was growing up. She was nineteen, it was time that she was "out." Poor Dora! Even if she had been able regularly to make over £500 a year to her first family, without working, it would still have been insufficient for all she wanted to give them. As it was, she made the best arrangements she could, counting the pennies as she went along.

She took a house in Golden Square and established the girl

there in 1803. Soon, surely, the sort of good man would appear whom womankind is prenatally destined to make happy. She would realise in her daughter, if not in herself, her golden glow of domesticity. However, she was happy at home, successful in her career, and unaffected by William's latest theatrical craze, the exploitation of Master Betty.

This lad, the infant prodigy of his day, almost eclipsed the Siddons during his heyday. Dora had proved herself a fine tragedy actress, but she belonged essentially to comedy, using the same parts year after year. They were her media, the scaffolding on which she displayed the gaiety her public loved. Master Betty's reign had no terrors for her, meant no neglect or falling off in esteem or income. 1805 was one of her really triumphant years. She was stout by this time, many times a mother, strong still in her early vitality, although now nearly forty years old.

Then, just twenty years after she had first captured London as Peggy in *The Country Girl*, and just when she was beginning to weary a little of Peggy and all her other tomboy parts, she thought she saw a pleasant chance of retirement. Trafalgar brought William a considerable sum in prize-money—the advantage of being a naval officer—and the Bettesworth legacy came to one of Fanny's young sisters. This daughter, too, was set up in a house of her own, at Richmond. The household seemed to be better off, the maze of debts cleared a little.

Dora decided to retire. William was agreeable. She saw visions of a sunlit autumn after a successful career.

The pity of it was that in her valiant edifice of makeshift home life she had not quite succeeded in getting her partner into his right category. She had certainly improved him as a human being, and she tried now to see in him a middle-aged woman's middle-aged spouse. But he was also a royal duke and, for such, a young man. His career lay ahead. Dora's was nearly over, William had not even started.

However, she retired. His birthday in 1806 was celebrated with fine magnificence. The brothers came to dine. The Prince Regent led in Dora, who was certainly an entertaining dinner-partner. The band played, the latest FitzClarence was carried in by the proud nurse. It was a scene of domestic splendour which the crowds watched from the town. Certain sections of the press suddenly went on record as shocked beyond measure, although not beyond expression, by this display of illicit love life.

Dora may often have forgotten that it was illicit, but she could not now forget that it was rapidly growing bankrupt. The brief essay in solvency was over, debts piled up again. In the spring of 1807 she had to come from her retirement and return to the stage, weary in body and now rather fat. Her age, and the drastic slimming methods she adopted, damaged her health. For ten days she had to stop work. The era of youthful and ill-founded *malaises* was over, there was no question now of her not being strictly an invalid when she said that she was "ill." Rather the reverse, in fact. She was over-anxious not to appear aged and infirm. In October she was ill again, twice tried to get back to work, twice was beaten, and retired to bed at Bushey.

The end of her happiness was in sight. The family was beginning to break up. William, an affectionate father, put their eldest son into the Navy. Fanny married a gentleman named Thomas Alsop. Another daughter also married, choosing, or being chosen by, a Frederick March. Both are described as "clerks." William had to provide the girls' *dots*, against money that their mother had lent to him, but there was a certain amount of bad feeling about it. The truth was that Dora was tired and ill. The end of feeling happy is sometimes also the end of being happy.

However, she made the first of a series of visits to Bath and had a success. Either that, or the returning cool of the year revived her, and in the autumn she was better, well enough to go back to full work at the end of the year.

1809 was troubled. There was the scandal about the sale of Army commissions, involving the Duke of York and Mary Anne Clarke in arc-light publicity. Frederick had to pay in cash for his mistress's commercial instinct, and his brother's mistress had to suffer too. Just as a comparison had once injured Maria Fitzherbert, now Dora was the one whose position was undermined. The spirited Mary Anne, courtesan by profession, made their joint rôle rather notorious, and she and Dora, a world apart, were yet more akin to each other than any of the other ladies.

Then, it was a season of London conflagrations, and among them was the tragic burning of Drury Lane. Drury Lane was Dora's unchanging home. She might want to retire, but while she was forced to act, there had always been Drury Lane to welcome her. Now substitute platforms were arranged and William organised an extensive cruise. Bath gave her a series of ovations, and the inhabitants complacently decided that they had been privileged to see Dorothy Jordan at her best.

That was one brighter moment; another was the return of George FitzClarence on leave between the battles of Corunna and Talavera. It was at this time that Dora paid her first visit to Dublin after an absence of more than twenty years. She took with her Lucy, now the eldest unmarried daughter. A paltry supporting cast ruined her stage appearance, but nothing could detract from her successful reception; in Dublin she was already a legend. It was a gay interlude, cloudy with recollections.

She returned to find that William was unwell, but she could not even stay to nurse him. She had to be off again, to the everlasting jolt of a laboured trot, and the bumping of hard wheels on bad roads, to tour the north-west. To her joy she was home in time for a great family gathering at Christmas, a party including her sons on leave from the Services. It was just what William liked, she said.

With the New Year Lucy became engaged. She was married in April to Colonel Hawker of the 14th Dragoons, a widower with a grown daughter.

All through that year Dora continued trying to build where no sound foundation lay. Her finances and William's were hopelessly intertwined. His passion and her stifled dreams had settled down to his affection and her devotion. But she was an actress within a year of fifty, and he was a royal duke of forty-five. William's future was approaching more rapidly now.

There was an interlude. While she was playing at Glasgow, he fell ill. Back she came, driving night and day, leaving her carriage neither to eat nor sleep. William's sentimental heart was surely touched, for he subsidised some months of home life, until the stamina of his purse was hopelessly undermined.

His mother's attitude had changed too. She was no longer so ready to regard Dora as an insurance against wilder courses, in fact she was beginning to think of her as an incubus. He was beckoned from St. James's, where they were beginning to speak of marriage. But Dora could beckon too, and with gold pieces when she was at work. For that reason, if for no other, she ploughed on. 1811 opened rather heavily before her.

The worst was beginning to happen. William's thoughts were turning to marriage. It was not at the moment the prospect of an officially arranged match, with a suitably increased allowance from the country. St. James's had not progressed as far as that yet. This was his own idea. He had had many years' alliance with a skilled worker, and his simple but not unshrewd mind had realised that, high as is the wage of skill and merit, much more is forthcoming from a well-endowed capitalist, however undeserving. He seems to have reflected aloud, for once at Bushey, Dora was so cross that she threw a tea-cosy at him.

Still in William's mind the capitalist dream took shape. Miss Tilney Long's bank balance was drawing admirers from far and wide: William, an affectionate soul, took his elder daughter with him when he went to make himself agreeable. It showed that he had certain solid qualities, but apparently they were insufficient to attract the heiress.

Dora played on, inimitable still, within her the prescience of disaster that comes to all builders on sand. She was at Cheltenham when it happened. On the night of her last performance a note came to her from William, and he asked her to meet him. She was to go to their Maidenhead house, and there they would arrange the terms of their separation.

She went back on to the stage to finish the piece. But when that famous laugh should have carolled round the theatre an uncontrollable burst of tears came instead. The actor playing opposite her altered his line with brilliant presence of mind—"Why, they have made you *crying* drunk!"

Did she, one wonders, remember Cheltenham so long ago, when the King postponed his visit to the theatre until she came down? Was it indeed at Cheltenham that she had first spoken to Prince William? If so, how strange and cruel the circle of destiny.

She went from the stage to her travelling coach, in costume and make-up, to change and cream her face as they trundled along. Even now, Dora would not face defeat. After all, this was no marriage arranged at Court, this scheme of William's. It was entirely of his own devising, perhaps as impossible as marriage with herself would have been. It was, also, no rush of importunate adoration, as when he had last wanted to see her to "arrange terms."

William, however, was not the only one who thought that the time had come to make an end. His brother Ernest, Duke of Cumberland, took a hand in the game, met Dora, recounted the Tilney Long episode in detail, and made trouble between the two of them.

There had, after all, been provision for a pension in her original contract. It was a job, like any other; it had ended, like any other. By the end of 1811 the FitzClarence ménage broke up.

William was certainly not ungenerous. He not only readily promised, but he often tried quite hard to perform.

As usual, Dora thought passionately for her children, and insisted on having the care of the four youngest daughters. They were to have their own income of £1,500 a year, and £600 for their house and carriage. Both the girls and the money were, William stipulated, to revert to him if Dora went on the stage again, for this was to be retirement. It is a strange touch of solicitous paternity. For herself, Dora was to have

£1,500 a year too, and £800 to divide between her first four daughters.

It was not a gigantic income, she could have earned more even then, but it was generous and enough for retirement and comfort. General Hawker, her son-in-law, was named as her agent, and Thomas Barton would act for the Duke. Thomas Barton was a shrewd and hard-headed fellow, a man of business who, unfortunately, did not regard human affairs as human. He was managing an estate, by name Dorothy Jordan, and in the management of it he proposed to be as carefully economical as possible.

With the four children, and their governess, Miss Sketchley, Dora retired into private life. There, quiet at last, and lonely, but perhaps not really unhappy, she could watch William. As yet neither his family nor his country felt any very strong urge to go to the expense of marrying him off, and he hawked himself slowly round the more eligible heiresses in a sort of oblivion. He made no attempt to prevent Dora from seeing any of their children. The new year came, and it seemed that Dora was at last to have a year of complete peace.

But in the autumn Daly's love-token, as ill-omened in Dora's life as long ago her father had been, brought the beginning of final ruin. Fanny was weak and silly. Her husband turned out to be weak and vicious. His finances crashed, and he fled abroad.

Fanny rushed to mother for help! Mother gave all she had and mortgaged her future to pay his debts. Money she had to have, Fanny wailed for it. There was only one thing to do, go back to work again. That meant that she must give up Fanny's four small sisters, the girls whom she and Miss Sketchley tended between them.

I

With a heavy heart she did so. They went back to their father, to come in the end under the kindly care of Adelaide, for William's future was approaching fast.

Dora got engagements. That was never a difficulty from the time of Tate onwards, but the mainspring had gone, she was ageing quickly. Life was breaking up, like any ship on any rock. Nevertheless she kept on, with occasional illness. One of these breakdowns was caused in 1814 by worry over the two young sons, now involved in a court martial to clear a superior's name. They had to leave their regiments and were posted to India.

Fanny was still worrying her. Miss Sketchley remained devoted, but Fanny grew discontented. Perhaps now and then Dora spoke hardly of William, lamented on occasion the long unrest of her life and the insecurity in which she now stood. It must be remembered, of course, that if William was a bad payer, Dora was a bad manager. However it was, Fanny finally decided that she was the injured party and wrote threatening letters to William. At the time she was staying with the March family, her sister and brother-in-law, and when Thomas Barton came down to deal with the matter, he at least succeeded in frightening March.

Fanny, however, appeared to think that her letter-writing had achieved results and could well be continued. To Barton, she assumed the proportions of a vampire menace. To Dora, away on tour, she was a nagging persistence, the source of an endless flow of begging letters. It was enough to make her ill, and so it did. To quiet the demands she sent March notes of hand, left blank as to amount, and drove ceaselessly on at her work. In the spring of 1815 two of her sons sailed for India, and by May of that year she was ill once more. In August she recovered sufficiently to return to the stage and she appeared at Margate. She was still at Margate when the final crash came. March had filled in her blank notes of hand for unexpectedly large amounts. Thomas Barton massed her debts so that they loomed colossal. At all costs he was determined to frighten this family, and William was, apparently, never informed. Dora was cowed at last, terrified, and, as she had done so many years ago in Dublin, she broke down and fled. Miss Sketchley, still devoted, went with her, and together they crossed to France.

There were no more expedients. She could not help herself, and no one else had ever helped her. Two of the FitzClarences were in Paris, and, love-drawn to the last, she managed to move near them, to Saint-Cloud and then to Versailles.

On July 5th she died, after waiting all day for a letter to come, a letter from home, a letter which might bring a little hope.

Strangers buried her. At the last there had to be a public advertisement, for the final fifty shillings of the cost. And at the bank, had anyone cared to ask, there was a credit due to her.

So died Dorothy Jordan, "the child of Nature, to hear whose laugh was to drink nectar," and of all that galaxy of lovers— Duke William, Inchbold, Richard Ford, Bettesworth, Daly and Charles Powlett Doyne, cornet of horse—there was not one to mourn her or to stand beside her grave.

QUEEN ADELAIDE

ON JULY 13th, 1818, Amelia Adelaide Louise Theresa Caroline, Princess of Saxe-Coburg Meiningen, fell heir to the former partner of Dorothy Jordan.

William, Duke of Clarence, third son of the late King George III, was now fifty-two years old. The Princess was twenty-five, not quite a girl, but certainly not fifty-two.

One of the best known of her portraits shows her as a lovely fragile-looking woman, but curiously enough she is invariably reported as quite plain—rather small, with pale flaxen hair and eyebrows, a ginger-bread complexion and weak eyes, according to Lady Brownlow, her lady-in-waiting. Greville coldly summarises her as very ugly, with a horrid complexion but good manners. They were not the good manners of long training, amid much society, in the niceties of social etiquette, for she had been brought up simply enough. Adelaide's manners came from the simple amiability and kindness of a very charming woman—her mother. Greville may have spoken of *manners*. To less inhuman observers, it was manner, and an attractive one. Lady Brownlow agrees that she had a very pleasant expression, and Lady Granville that she moved very gracefully, and entered or left a room " *à ravir.*"

Like the majority of people she had no particular talents. She had sound domestic accomplishments, could run a palace with comfort and economy, could draw well enough to get a good likeness, and was devoted to needlework, particularly to Berlin-wool tapestry. She even took it with her to Ascot—an epitome of her whole life.

She was born on August 13th, 1792, the first child of a ten-year marriage, born heir to her father and welcomed by his people, the first princess to arrive at the castle of Meiningen for nearly a century. She was baptised on the very next Sunday, August 19th, with much song and feast-making and the ringing of bells.

When she was five her father provided her with a tutor and started his own supervision of her education. At the same time, he founded in the town a school for girls. Meiningen was in the full glory of the Liberal eighteenth century and education was valued there. Up at the castle, tutor followed tutor, always under Duke George's eye, and further children followed Adelaide into the world. But, when she was eleven, the Duke died, and although her mother endeavoured to carry on his policy with his family, she was very soon to do so under a grave disadvantage. The next few years were to mark Adelaide for ever, to scar her life with a complex of fear.

Napoleon was marching.

He and his opponents crossed and recrossed, marched and counter-marched through the small State. The people of Meiningen were powerless. They could do nothing. What could one do? They helped the wounded, a hospital was even founded, and they stared at the columns of the Revolution in hourly fear. At long last came the Russians, as deliverers, and the joyful word of Allied entry into Paris. Adelaide was by then a woman grown, a Princess who behaved by choice like a lady of the manor.

And then, in her middle twenties, came the proposal for her hand on behalf of the Duke of Clarence.

The 1818 brides owed their positions entirely to the death of the Princess Charlotte, and when Adelaide made her calm reflections and planned her gentle, unswerving course through the intricacies of her married life, she accepted and remembered this. She did not demand, she did not exact. She resigned herself so pleasantly that she ended by having a devoted husband and loyal subjects; she may even have enjoyed considerable happiness.

Her mother brought her to London, to Grillon's Hotel, but, by way of a beginning, there was no one to meet or welcome her, until George FitzClarence was sent to present greetings. At any rate, she could unpack in peace and could choose what to wear from the 10,000 Fl. worth of trousseau with which the little duchy had equipped her. She chose, she tried on for the last time, she rested, and she and her mother took dinner. Then, after dinner, the Regent arrived. He could charm when he pleased, and the Duchess was quite delighted. The evening was complete when, with a rattle and clatter of hooves, the Duke of Clarence drew up outside.

Adelaide could acquire—she knew it herself—a sudden spiritual loveliness when she was deeply moved. Was she moved then? Did Duke William see a small, plain girl with a bad skin, or a lovely uplifted woman? At any rate he behaved most amiably, excused himself for being out of town, and the bridegroom and his elder brother stayed late, talking, one supposes, mostly to mother. Did Adelaide produce some needlework then, or did she sit quietly, with her little, deft fingers curved in her lap, and cling to the thought of her sister Ida and of Altenstein, her home?

She had been officially married, William appearing by proxy, before she left Meiningen, but she had the customary second wedding in England. She shared it with the Duchess of Kent, the lady who was to succeed where she would fail. It was very quiet, performed at Kew, in front of the old Queen Caroline. Afterwards the whole family dined and then drove to a cottage in the gardens to drink tea. It was a very cheerful party. The other bride was a sensible young widow, with healthy pink cheeks and some determination of manner. After it all, William drove his wife and mother-in-law to St. James's Palace, where his apartments were somewhat inconvenient, situated in the stable court.

Charlotte loved Kew as Adelaide was to love Bushey and later, during her reign, Windsor, and at Kew, Charlotte was dying. In spite of this, the Clarences were to go over to Hanover almost at once, where another of the newly-wed brothers, the Duke of Cambridge, was Viceroy. It was not long before Adelaide came down again to the scene of her wedding, to say good-bye to her mother-in-law.

Charlotte died, as she did everything, with a good deal of firmness and dignity. It was her affair; she knew what she was about; and she disliked people to make enquiries or to say the long farewell to her. Adelaide said her good-bye formally and, with the others, left the bedroom. Then she broke away gently from Court regimentation and performed one of those little acts of independent domesticity that were to make every one about her so comfortable. She crept back down the corridors whose winter cold had sapped Miss Burney's strength, and timidly opened the door a little. She might never see her husband's mother again, and her husband's mother was, of course, almost her own mother.

She peeped in, just to see her. Charlotte was not asleep, she called out. Perhaps she was tired, but she had never made much of weariness and she had seldom failed to appreciate a good intention. Adelaide came right into the room. She went back to the bedside, and for a while they talked again, quietly, leaving everything understood and unspoken as they touched on casual topics.

At Hanover, Adelaide and the Duchess of Cambridge made friends. Both were German princesses and of much the same age. Nine months after her marriage Adelaide punctually produced an infant. (The Duchess of Cambridge, a month less prompt to the call of duty, produced one too, in the same forty-eight hours.) Unfortunately, Charlotte Augusta Louisa, born on March 29th, died in a few hours, and Adelaide was taken to her mother's villa near Meiningen to recover and to take the waters at Liebenstein. William was with her there.

She liked Liebenstein. Fifteen years later she went back there to pick up her strength once again and to get rid of a cough. This time they liked it so well that they put off their return from month to month and made an autumn journey in conditions so bad that Adelaide fell ill at Dunkirk. Even then she had a bad crossing to face, which she endured bravely, but which certainly did not help matters. Once back in England, she grew worse again, and lay very ill indeed at Walmer Castle for six weeks.

After such an autumn that winter can have been by no means pleasant. The St. James's Palace apartments were in a very bad state, not at all fit for an invalid, or even a convalescent. However, in the spring William took Adelaide down to Bushey, which had been newly done up for her reception.

William's reasoning is easy to follow. He liked Bushey and

had been uncommonly happy there; he liked Adelaide and wanted her to be uncommonly happy; therefore he took her to Bushey.

She found it full of keepsakes from Dorothy Jordan's day, in the shape of all the FitzClarences. They seemed to be innumerable and she was a married Princess of only some twenty-six summers. But she opened her heart and adopted them all, children, hoydens and young bloods. She adopted the Duke too, and the house. One and all throve again under her care; she was a woman of domestic tastes and capabilities.

William was now a royal prince, royally married, with a very good hope of becoming father of the next heir presumptive. He was also a simple man, almost a simple gentleman, though stout, middle-aged and excitable. His first love, Dora, had been a gay and confident person, some years older than he was, who had been able to do the managing. Now he had someone to protect, a young bride reasonably ignorant of the gayer world and with conventional feminine tastes. As is usual in such cases, he fell quietly and happily under her influence, and she improved him still further in manners and character.

Adelaide was excellent at entertaining, both public and private. She made friends with all her sisters-in-law, including the allegedly scandalous Frederica of Cumberland, and she received anyone whom William cared to ask to the house.

Her own preferences still lay in the direction of Germany, and she made good and fast friends of the wives of the envoys of Hanover and Prussia, Countess Münster and Baroness von Bülow. Baroness von Bülow had children, and Adelaide, who was expecting another herself, adored children. In Meiningen, her interest had lain in founding and visiting schools. "I enjoy seeing happy children," she wrote to the Baroness, when she

sent her her own theatre pass to use for herself and the family.
"I assure you, I had rather know you were enjoying those
amusements than go myself, so I trust you will allow me to
continue sending you my theatre pass from time to time, and
I hope you understand the private greeting which never fails to
accompany it."

In 1820, when the Princess Victoria was a fat little baby girl,
"*le Roi George en jupons !* " Adelaide bore her second daughter,
who managed to survive her first perilous weeks of life. For
three months Victoria was deposed, and the Princess Elisabeth
Georgina Adelaide took her place, but only for three months.
Then she too died, and Adelaide had Chantrey make a little
marble effigy of her babe, which she kept always in her room.

She never had another, but perhaps her love for little children
deepened. When Victoria was two, she wrote to her: "My
dear little heart, I hope you are well, and don't forget Aunt
Adelaide, who loves you so fondly," and in May of 1822 she
wrote to her again for her third birthday. Uncle William and
Aunt Adelaide sent kisses to every one, including the big doll.
"They also hope," she ends up, "that dear little Victoria will
not forget them, and know them again when Uncle and Aunt
return."

She was off on a round tour of Continental relations. It must
have been an enjoyable one, for it began with her sister Ida,
Duchess of Saxe-Weimar, at Antwerp and at Ghent. She went
on to her sister-in-law, the Landgravine of Hesse-Homburg, at
Coblentz and Frankfort, and thence to her brother Bernard at
Meiningen, to visit Altenstein once more and go round her
schools. Finally she and William went to his sister, the Queen
of Württemberg, who shared Adelaide's taste, which was then
not uncommon, for sketching. She took her guests for a barge

trip up the Neckar, and together they made their pencil sketches and washed in the blues and greens, exchanged their little recipes for catching the ripple on the water, or the shadow where trees overhung the bank, or the sweep of sunlight across the vineyards.

She must have enjoyed herself thoroughly, for in 1825 she was back in Meiningen with her two younger stepdaughters. Dora Jordan's wide-eyed hoyden brood probably found life there rather dull, and if they did, most likely they showed it. Adelaide was no hand at checking or repressing. She saw what was good in them and doubtless she sighed over the rest, but she established no control over the lesser details of their manners. Perhaps she thought that very strict training was a matter of *noblesse oblige*, and that while it was correct for princesses to be drilled and schooled, it was not at all pleasant; she may have been glad that she was not forced to be so strict with her only quasi-royal charges.

To combine the certainty of steamboats with the cleanliness and silence of sail, the royal yacht used to be towed by a steamer when it crossed the Channel. On their return this time, William and Adelaide met with such bad weather that the cable parted. Adelaide remained quiet and unflustered. The crew, under a commander probably delighted to show their mettle against the floating tea-kettle ahead, brought them safely in to Yarmouth.

Next year, Adelaide and William saw the field of Waterloo. They were making a tour of the Rhine and Netherlands, and with William's nascent admiration for the Duke of Wellington, Waterloo could not be missed. She was to hear him frequently on the subject of Waterloo for the next eleven years, in spite of the fact that William was a sailor at heart and should have preferred Trafalgar. But people are unreliable in their favourite victories. Timidly respectable maiden ladies cherish a fanatical preference for Badajos, so why should not William love his Waterloo? It was fine, straightforward fighting to words of command, just as he could appreciate. No fire could have daunted a Hanoverian.

Adelaide listened. Perhaps she brought her needlework, or perhaps he encouraged her to reproduce the "*circ de bois, de coteaux, de vallons*" in mild water-colour.

Then, in 1827, William found employment for the first time since he was recalled ashore. He became Lord High Admiral, with no duties and spacious apartments for the entertainment of royalty and elegance. He made innumerable duties, stood up for his sea officers, and filled the spacious apartments with them, their wives and families at enormous free-for-all entertainments, which Adelaide found very uncomfortable.

She made no sign of unwillingness and received everyone whom he produced, but unfortunately he did so much work that he very rapidly became a thorn in the flesh of the authorities. He neglected the "Lord High," and took to the "Admiral" with all the thwarted passion of a seaman who has been too long rusting on the beach. All of his simple faith came to him, he used to say, during his first storm at sea, and he was bound for ever to serve the welfare of men who had shared his experiences.

He asked questions and he tried to get through all the work he could find to do. Naturally he had to retire.

He retired not only fuming but positively sizzling, and Adelaide turned her attention to him rather anxiously, in the quiet of Bushey. The threat of his father's fate always hung over his head. He, of all the brothers, showed the most signs of that excitability which was the first symptom of their hereditary insanity.

They were still quietly at Bushey when, in 1830, George IV died and William became King. The messenger brought the news to them there and Adelaide wept. She gave him, as a souvenir, the prayer book which she held in her hand. As was to be expected, she looked upon the accession more as a sacred calling to high duties than as a matter of personal aggrandisement.

In those first days it seemed as though the peace of home life were gone for ever. She passed them in a babel of officials, pressing crowds, and the pawns of William's insatiable hospitality. One could do nothing for a day or two, but in a few weeks she had reduced her royal household to something like order, written the necessary letters and caused sentries to be posted where they could enforce a certain amount of privacy. She always disliked her private life being treated as a peepshow, actually or in print.

William's excitability was the immediate embarrassment. It flared up now from another cause than thwarted energies and baffled intention. The whisper ran round in buzzing circles, his father's long years of madness were recalled. Quickly and very quietly Adelaide came forward. Where William went, henceforth she went too, for she knew that at her touch or look he would always calm himself down a trifle. The unfounded rumour buzzed a few weeks longer, and died down. The King was not mad at all, but he was furiously energetic and genuinely interested in his job.

Just as at Bushey, their private circle was pervaded by FitzClarences. Perhaps from habit formed in dealing with this family, Adelaide would tolerate almost the same degree of boisterousness from irrepressible young ladies-in-waiting, rather than reprove them. For herself, she had no intention of making her private life very different. She still did needlework every night, in quantities which it makes one's fingers ache to contemplate. She liked whist, although it seems unlikely that she was ever a very good card player. And she liked music; her band really was a good one. She still continued her riding and walking, which were her outdoor amusements, and at times rode so far that she returned with only her gentlemen, the other ladies having fallen by the wayside. She was careful to see that permission to turn back at any point should be understood, and that, on long walks, carriages should be waiting at strategic points for those without route-marching tendencies.

Of the royal palaces, Windsor pleased her most. It was in the same countryside as Bushey and amid the same neighbours. She quickly made her flower garden and added to it a model dairy and "Adelaide Cottage," a *Petit Trianon* after her own taste. Her care took in the labourers on the estate and, of course, all their children. Her ideas on housing were rather in advance of those of her day. At least at Windsor and in Norfolk there were landowners who did their complete duty, although the Coke outlook on agricultural practice was decidedly the better informed. However, she attended carefully to all that lay within her power. She introduced some form of etiquette into the King's "crush parties" by keeping herself and the quasi-princesses at a table apart, though she still, as always, received anyone whom William might care to present.

She had reduced the pattern of the last twelve years to something like regularity, and where she could she carried the comfort of her routine with her when she became Queen. But all the same, as was inevitable, the next six years held more problems than any she had faced before. She found that she could not, as before, withdraw tranquilly into her own life. She had duties, obligations and responsibilities which she performed well, and which she tried always to keep far from politics and publicity.

The great burden of her queenship was the Reform Bill.

On the face of it, Duke George's daughter should have been as pro-Reform as her husband. It had been her father's gesture to bury his mother in the ordinary churchyard of the town, as "worthy to lie among her subjects." He had been the friend of Schiller. In matters of housing and schooling she was something of a reformer herself. But between the philosophy and liberalism of the eighteenth century and her accession had come the French Revolution which to most of Europe meant the horrors of war in all its actual presence, and sudden Napoleonic piracies of established thrones. The wars of the Republic, the Hundred Days, Waterloo, and the slow, impoverished gasps of crushed States and Nationalities, had destroyed in her any liking for reform. In her mind it stood for revolution, foraging armies, the tumbrils, *déportation verticale*, and the guillotine.

She was the kindest of gentle, unassuming women; she wore English silks and asked other ladies to do the same, in order to benefit the English industry. She would lend at least commonsense help to any practical scheme of benevolence, but she set her face entirely against the granting by law of the treatment she was so ready to concede by grace.

There were other excuses for her. The London mob at this time was more out of hand than it has ever been in the whole of London's arrogant and self-centred history. From the Lord George Gordon riots down to the Chartist era, it now and

again held the streets in something like terrorism; it released
prisoners, fired houses and generally behaved as mobs may be
relied upon to behave. The English were rough in those days,
far rougher than the German peasantry and burghers among
whom Adelaide had been brought up. The riots, which failed
to do much more than inconvenience English-born ladies, terrified the Queen, although she concealed her fears heroically.

These were her opinions, and those of the Charlotte-trained
princesses, and she made no attempt to conceal them. But she
also made no attempt to press them on the King. Her idea of
her rôle was that she was entitled to think for herself like any
other human being—behold the eighteenth century peeping
through the succeeding barbarism!—but that it was not the
function of a queen consort to meddle in politics, or even to
speak one word that might concern that side of the crown's
duties and privileges. This attitude was consistently misunder-
stood by the people at large. They knew her opinions. With
the violence of partisanship proper to the nation which invented party-politics, they assumed that she was forcing her
views upon her husband, in season and out. The injustice of
the situation naturally added to her distrust of the people. The
one played on the other, and the Queen looked up from her
needlework to find her subjects scowling at her.

She could keep out of politics. She could not quench public
suspicion because she could not prevent her name being used,
at any rate while Brougham, of the acid mind and biting
tongue, was writing articles for, and inspiring the politics of,
The Times. Grey, unsuspected adorer of Dorothea de Lieven,
had been called upon by William to form a Whig pro-Reform
government, and this in spite of the royal admiration and
affection for that magnificent Tory, the Duke of Wellington.

Grey himself had the wit to learn and understand Adelaide's attitude, but Brougham was Lord Chancellor.

All through 1831, London raged over the Reform question, and England raged round London. Faction ran so furiously high that it divided families and friends. Adelaide's Chamberlain was, naturally, an opponent of the Bill. How else could she have endured normal day-to-day conversation which, in any age, must to a certain extent be topical? Lord Howe, broadly speaking, agreed with her. William liked him, knew that Adelaide found him trustworthy and helpful, and saw no reason to dismiss him from a purely Court position because of his political convictions.

But the gadflies of Brougham's spite stabbed with their poisoned stings, sharp as so many pins. *The Times* "took sides," and its attacks on the Queen, its innuendoes, its malicious paragraphs, grew more and more marked.

The rioting continued. Adelaide was mobbed on her way home from a concert. To her terrified mind it was Revolution, the frightful result of promised emancipation. William, by now a most devoted William, was furious and refused to attend a Lord Mayor's banquet.

Both sides were curbed. Howe was tactfully asked to restrain his expressions of opinion. To Grey it was hinted that he might get his team under control. Then came final proof of *The Times's* source of inspiration, for Grey spoke to Brougham, and on the next day it published a report of the rebuke.

In the end Howe had to go, although the Queen made a point of asking him as her guest to the next occasion on which his successor had to attend her. It was hinted that there was more than met the eye in her partiality for him, but even the

K

generation of Gilray and Rowlandson had to drop that morsel of gossip. However, the fact of its ever having been mentioned did nothing to make her regard the English world with greater trust.

At the time of the coronation she had further worries. Quite naturally she had assumed that she would be granted at least the same sum as had been given to former royal ladies on their accession. Hurrying ahead with preparation, she had actually spent slightly more, in advance, on what she needed, including jewels. She had reckoned without the defunct George IV. Owing to the late King's extravagances, Earl Grey suddenly announced that he dared not ask Parliament for the Queen's grant. Again William was furious and stepped promptly into the breach by assuming her liabilities.

Parliament was won. It was agreeably ready to take the credit for William's generosity and voted her a dower of £100,000 a year, and Bushey and Marlborough House.

Adelaide certainly agreed with William about the suitability of a very quiet and economical coronation, the "half a crownation" of city catchword. Whenever possible she avoided involving him in too much cause for excitement. Also, to her, it was more a divine sanction, a dedication ceremony, than a display of pomp. Seven years later when Victoria's way led her in her turn through the acclamations to the Abbey altar, Adelaide wrote to her niece, "The guns are just announcing your approach to the Abbey . . . and my prayers are offered up to Heaven for your happiness, and the prosperity and glory of your reign." She waited then at Marlborough House, listening with her pen in her hand.

At her own coronation, as the result of William's generosity, she was able honestly to wear "a gold gauze over a white satin petticoat, with a diamond stomacher, a purple velvet train lined with white satin having a rich border of gold and ermine." Dr. Doran describes the magnificence for us. She disliked wearing feathers, but perhaps on this occasion their splendour contributed to her feeling of solemnity.

Lady Brownlow, her lady-in-waiting, was charged with the duty of wiping Adelaide's forehead after the anointing, and of securing the crown when it had been ceremoniously perched on her hair. Like her mistress, Lady Brownlow seems to have been a very feminine woman with nice neat little ideas, all her little arrangements planned and just so. The cotton-wool and the cambric for the wiping she had in a little white and gold bag hanging from her girdle, but the four long, diamond-headed pins for securing the crown she had prudently run into her dress. "So," she points out, with the dislike for making herself conspicuous which is so proper to really nice women, "so, I had all ready and there was no bustle." Yet, poor lady, she never felt so nervous in her life, and her own coronet was but perilously poised when Adelaide's crown was lowered and she had to produce the four diamond-headed pins.

Adelaide relied on that great inner strength of hers, and went through the ceremony with grace and charm. But she held her first Drawing Room with her knees bandaged, to lessen the fatigue of bending them so often. For she was getting on for forty, and neither so slender nor so supple as the years had once seen her.

From that Drawing Room there was one absentee. The Princess Victoria was not there, pleading her delicate health. It was a sorrow to Adelaide; she loved the little niece who was now heir presumptive, although she had almost grown to dislike her sister-in-law, the Duchess of Kent.

The Duchess was openly hostile to William. It was she who kept Victoria away, prevented her from meeting her aunt and uncle, although she was the heir to the throne. In this way she kept the young princess from contact with the rowdy Fitz-Clarence family, and furthermore, semi-seclusion restricted possible matchmaking to the purely theoretical.

The Reform Bill came to its crisis. The Wellington boot turned its forcible toe abruptly in the other direction, and the Bill became law. If Adelaide could still be regarded as a schemer, it must be as a foiled and bitter one.

It would be unjust to imply that she took no part in William's official activities. She did. When they came to the throne, he found that the path of duty led to glory through some forty thousand arrears of signatures, the legacy of his elder brother. He settled down to them every evening after dinner. Adelaide stood by, to blot and to remove signed papers. When his gout forced him to stop for a moment or two, she still stood by, silent—for he liked his sympathy like that—until he felt able to continue.

She did not change when she became Queen. She behaved as decorously in the royal chapel as any other gentlewoman in church. She kept her family friends, her old acquaintances. She gently cleaned the Court of the elements which she could not consider respectable. Although she never deserted the FitzClarences, she declined to countenance either the old Duchess of St. Albans or Lady Ferrars, both of whom were supposed to be ex-mistresses of her husband. She was kindly but she was firm.

The Duke of Wellington, of course, was the iron idol in the shrine of William's devotion. Adelaide, who had reconciled Sussex with Cumberland, as well as opening the family doors to the Duchess of Cumberland, now set about reconciling Cumberland with Wellington. They were both high Tories of an uncompromising nature, and Tories do not as a general rule get on remarkably well with each other, but she succeeded in time. She prevailed upon the Wicked Uncle to allow Frederica and their blind boy, Prince George of Cumberland, to call upon the Duke.

She loved the child for his own sake. She was fond of all children. Baroness von Bülow said that it made her quite sad to watch Adelaide with them. "First she let them run about wherever they liked, and then she took us into her bedroom and showed us all sorts of pretty things, and the King came just as she was holding Linchen up in her arms." If she was to have none of her own to replace the baby daughters of long ago, she very soon had a beloved foster-child. Ida's daughter, Louise of Saxe-Weimar, was delicate. In 1831 her mother brought her over and left her with her aunt, and Adelaide loved and tended her like a daughter. It was good to have the child there, to have a young thing to fuss and plan over. She took her down to Brighton for the sea-bathing, but it was at the height of the Reform Bill unrest and, even with a sick child in her care, she had the unpleasant experience of being mobbed.

It was at Brighton that she met Maria Fitzherbert. Maria had at last shown William the proof of her marriage, to which she had been so loyally and so silently true. William wept, took her to the Pavilion and put her servants into his own liveries.

Then, in 1833, the Queen's little niece died. William treated her tenderly, as though she had again lost a daughter of her own, and Adelaide mourned sadly. But the other children whom she loved could not complain that she turned away from them. If Victoria were cut off from her, it was not Adelaide's fault. Louise had been like an adopted daughter, and now she all but adopted the younger brother, Edward of Saxe-Weimar. There seemed to be more boys about her now. The Duchess of Cumberland often brought her son to Windsor, among all the magnificence that he could never see. The Duke of Cambridge was still Viceroy of Hanover, and his son, Prince George of Cambridge, was growing up. His aunt received him too. He came to her under his tutor's charge, to continue his education.

She was even offered the guardianship of the young exiled Queen of Portugal, but it seemed wiser to her to decline the honour quickly. She pleaded the incompatible difference in religion.

Windsor, near to her old home Bushey, remained her favourite residence. They moved to Brighton in the winter, but she did not altogether care for it. As she wrote to the Baroness von Bülow, the change took her away from her "bright, cheerful rooms, full of the busts and pictures I specially value, and above all, the graves so sacred to me. To be near them does me good." They were the graves of her niece and her younger daughter.

Seeking to distract her, William had arranged illuminations for her birthday in the year when she lost Louise. But the fog had come down and blotted them out. Next year, he arranged a fête in her honour. He did it thoroughly. Whether or not she was entertained, she must have been touched. He was very devoted, and that alone was much more than she could have expected when she started out from Altenstein so many years before.

One of her gifts was the ability to find ways out of small

difficulties, not only when they arose as crumpled rose petals
in William's path, but also in other directions. There was a
day when the Countess Münster and the Baroness von Bülow
found themselves in a predicament because she had invited
them to a dinner "without trains," and they found at the last
moment that they must first attend a Court ceremony at which
these trailing glories were essential. The Baroness turned to
Adelaide, and quickly she sent back her advice. She herself was
having a light, detachable train made for the first event. The
Baroness passed on the solution, and the dress problem of the
three ladies was settled. It was another of her little arrangements.

In the spring of 1834 she was coughing. From week to week
it went on, and William began to look at her anxiously. It was
one of those nagging coughs which fix their shaking grip on to
middle-aged ladies who are very run down, rather worried,
and need a change. But William felt it was no good suggesting
a change to Adelaide. For one thing, she would never consent
to go anywhere without him. And for him to go away at that
moment was impossible. Earl Grey, worn out and ill at ease
in the new world of his building, was retiring, and the Government needed further patching and bolstering.

Without saying a word he made all arrangements for her to
go away, intending to spring it on her as a *fait accompli*. He
chose Liebenstein and her old home as most likely to do her
good, and told her only when all was ready. Adelaide was
touched and she agreed to go, but it was with a little nervous-
ness. She never left William if she could help it, because she
was never quite sure that the little irritable excitability would
not return. It was important that she, who could best calm
him, should always be on hand. However, she agreed to go.
But before she left the country there came another of those

periods, disturbing to the inner political circle, heart-rending to Adelaide, when he grew overwrought. Adelaide thought quickly, and as usual produced a little plan which soothed every one and met the need.

It was charming of William to arrange this holiday; she would enjoy it and of course it would cure the cough. But as he could not come with her, might she not wait just a few weeks? Then her own brother could come and fetch her, and what could be better than that?

It was arranged. She watched over William tenderly, and before Duke Bernard arrived he had happily quieted down again. She departed with public acclamations that moved her to tears, coming after so long and nerve-racking a series of misunderstandings. Two steamers towed the royal yacht this time, so that no more parted cables might endanger her passage. At Rotterdam, Ida came down to meet her brother and sister, and they went on together, through Holland and into quiet Germany.

In July she came to her beloved Altenstein. She showed Lady Brownlow her old home, and the bedroom that she had shared with Ida until they married. Greville tells us that it was a hole "which an English housemaid would think it a hardship to sleep in." In the winter its bare floor must have been extremely chilly to the feet of the two Princesses, and when they undressed at night, they must have been glad—and Adelaide remembered it—to slip quickly into the two small beds with the white dimity curtains. And now she and Ida were matrons, and Bernard, the baby brother, was the reigning Duke.

This time, as before, she delighted in Meiningen. She gave a donation to the school, and founded another where there was need of one. In England she was a Tory and a Die-hard Queen.

Here she went back to the days when she had been a Liberal princess.

On the return journey she visited her sister-in-law, Elizabeth, but this time she took care not to leave her sea journey until too late. She was back in England just before the end of August.

As she had been god-speeded, so she was welcomed back with a great reception, and clearly it pleased her. She stood on deck, apparently restored to health and certainly cheerful.

But if she rejoiced at the burial of the old suspicions and prejudices, then it was premature rejoicing.

In November, Spencer's death translated Althorp to the House of Lords. Grey had retired to recover his good humour at Howick. Melbourne inherited the Whig party, and an uneasy estate it was. He regarded Brougham with the distrust with which most of the world regarded that eminent statesman, and he suggested dissolution.

The alternative was the Duke of Wellington. William and he might be poles apart politically, but William had an endless admiration for the Duke as a man, so he turned to him now. On the instant, Brougham took up his poisoned pen, and next day *The Times* announced roundly that Spencer's death had given the Queen her chance. She had seen it as an opportunity to get the Whigs turned out and the Duke invited to form a Tory government. The paper was compelled at once to withdraw the statement. William took the matter up with energy. He came up to London and demanded the resignation of the ministers.

It distressed Adelaide very much to find the old bitterness cropping up again. Perhaps this was partly responsible for her failure to pick up strength again. However, whether or not she realised it, the bitterness was now only Brougham's, not the nation's. The hero who "could if he wanted to!" when Coke asked him if he could swim, was much the same to every one. But the bitterness against Adelaide was particularly unjust, because she had never entered his political arena, had never even attempted to do so. On the contrary she had kept out of it.

She grew no stronger, rather the reverse. Time was no longer on her side. In 1837 she was too weak to be able to attend Court ceremonials, and yet once again, for the last time, she had to leave William and set off alone. She hurried over to see her dying mother. William stayed behind; he was waiting by the deathbed of his eldest daughter, the Lady de Lisle. When Adelaide returned she found him in the deep mourning which he continued into his own last illness. She watched over him then, nursing him as she had Louise, until the end.

He lived past Waterloo day, as he wished, and on June 20th he died in her arms.

All that Adelaide was, every quality she possessed, her gentleness, her strength, her kindness, her piety, her devotion and her sheer affection for people, come out in the letter she managed to write that same day, a reply to Victoria's letter of sympathy. "I have the great comfort to dwell upon the recollection of the perfect resignation, piety and patience with which the dear King bore his trial and sufferings, and the truly Christian-like manner of his death. . . . My heart is overwhelmed and my head aches very much. Accept the assurance of my most affectionate devotion, and allow me to consider myself always as your Majesty's most affectionate Friend, Aunt and Subject."

Then she broke down. She recovered, it is true, but from then on she remained an invalid, and many of her old acquaintances heard from her no more.

She went back to Bushey, to her first English country home, with permission to take with her from Windsor anything she might like. She chose a silver cup, which William had admired, and out of which she had given him what he could take as the end grew near. She took, too, a portrait of Dora Jordan, now dead for more than twenty years, with her children all about her and William's bust amongst them.

Before she moved she wrote again, gently and kindly, to the young Queen. Next year she thanked her for announcing that she would continue the FitzClarence pensions; so it came about that the Victoria who lived on into the then immensely distant turn of the century, helped in her girlhood the children of Dora Jordan, who had travelled out of Dublin so long ago.

Maria Fitzherbert had died at Brighton the year before. Adelaide went to St. Leonards for a while, and that winter she went to Malta. She wrote again to her niece from there, asking for funds to establish the English Church there, which is her own foundation.

She was in England for Victoria's coronation, and later for her wedding. When the ceremony was over, and etiquette required her to come forward and make her congratulations, it was Victoria, the fat toddler to whose doll she had sent kisses, who moved quickly and came to claim not formal well-wishing but an embrace.

From then on, Adelaide travelled in search of a kindly climate and some distraction, for her life had been emptied when William went. She rented various residences, although she always had Bushey and Marlborough House. She went to Madeira, where there is a road of her building, and of course she went to Germany, to see Ida again, and Bernard.

One of her brothers-in-law, the Duke of Sussex, died a year

or so later, in 1843, and she went to see his widow, the small and plump "Ciss," created Duchess of Inverness by Queen Victoria.

Four years later she was in Madeira with Ida. They could sit quietly there, in the warmth, far from the world in which they lived, and talk of the old remembered things, of their mother, and Louise, and Altenstein. She lived to be brought back to England; in fact she lingered on until 1849, and died at last at Bentley Priory in Middlesex.

At her own request, she was borne to her grave by sailors, a last little tribute to William, from which it is pleasant to think that she became as fond of him as he undoubtedly did of her. She was not sixty years old, and yet she seems to have worn herself out. By the time she died, she was very tired.

To her belongs the distinction, although she did not produce an heir to the throne, of being the only one of our Ladies who became Queen. She was not one of our more outstanding Queens, but she was certainly one of the nicest.

On the whole, women with a taste for Berlin wool-work knew how to make themselves valued, at least in their own homes.

MADAME DE ST. LAURENT

ALPHONSINE THÉRÈSE BERNARDINE JULIE DE Montgenet was one of a family whose fortunes during the French revolutionary period cast many of its members into strange places. Geneva, always a refuge city for men and a cradle-town of ideas, still harboured one of the young de Montgenets two years after Waterloo.

In 1789, George III's fourth son, Edward, was in Geneva. France was, of course, impossible. Spain had been isolated for some time. The alternative to Hanover and its related German Courts was a trip to Switzerland or Italy. Edward, future Duke of Kent and father of Queen Victoria, was sent there, and Baron von Wangenheim accompanied him, as military tutor. His rule, however, was of such Prussian severity that his charge fled from him, and back to home and father.

Edward, the radical disciplinarian, almost a sadist on the parade ground, practically a democrat in politics, had a chastening upbringing. It moulded him into a man rather different from his brothers. He and Ernest of Cumberland stand out amongst them as characters who were able to take something from the tyranny of Kew and form it into an original material.

Now, however, his father refused to see him. For over a fortnight Edward and his brothers tried to make George III change his mind, and failed. As with most large families, there

137

were strong ties between the brothers. When one was in trouble, the rest rallied, but now all their rallying failed.

Edward was not sent back to Geneva. (Was it because of one of the Mesdemoiselles de Montgenet, a girl of his own age, gay and graceful, lighthearted and charming? Here, alone among the ladies, is one who links us with the civilisation of France.) He was sent immediately to Gibraltar, but he was not left for long even there, and the next step was Canada, where he was sent in command. He was in his early twenties then, a rigorous young officer with a taste for justice and mercy blended in a mixture not altogether to our present-day taste.

Just after the War of Independence, Canada was in a changing state. The colonists there had rightful grievances. Many of them were new to the land, and some of the newcomers from the United States preferred to keep their allegiance. There were the rough old settlers; there were new adventurers, and there was a very large body of French-speaking citizens, until recently the subjects of France. They ranged from sturdy backwoodsmen to French families of cultured and long-formed tradition, such as the de Salaberry family, whose name is part of the history of Canada.

Here, then, Edward landed in 1791 and went to his residence, the Castle at Quebec. On the Saturday after his arrival, he received—officers and men of note came in the morning, their ladies in the afternoon. It was not a big world, although educated, liberal and intelligent, and in some ways far ahead of the populated German principalities where some of his brothers learned to think. The de Salaberry family, with their army tradition, were amongst his first friends. This was the beginning of the great friendship that was to continue for so many years.

The beautiful Mademoiselle Alphonsine Thérèse Bernardine

Julie was in Canada too; she had joined Edward on the far side of the Atlantic. From now onwards we know her as Madame de St. Laurent, Baronne de Fortisson, as "the French lady," Julie of the wide St. Laurence.

Edward's first official residence, which had been built by the last French governor for his fascinating young beloved, was in St. Louis Street. Now it was suitably rechristened Kent House, and its routine moved with the exactitude that Edward liked. In the last twenty-five years, the type of official sent to the British colony had greatly improved, and Edward could find friends among officers, residents and settlers, who were likely to be reasonably critical of his actions. They do not appear to have disapproved when he set up a country residence at Haldimand House, at the Falls of Montmorency, and Julie was installed there at his side. She was a young woman of piety as well as affection, and it is unlikely that she consented to companion Edward during the quarter-century that lay ahead, except on terms of which she could approve.

There, then, they set up housekeeping. Edward drove in daily to his work, at the Castle of St. Louis, leaving punctually each morning and returning when the duties of the day were over.

The de Salaberry connection continued warm and affectionate. Edward was writing, in March of 1792, to Louis de Salaberry, at home at Beauport, that "the moment you inform me the roads are passable, I will not lose an instant in repairing to Beauport with Madame St. Laurent." Three months later, Julie was writing rapturously to Madame de Salaberry about the birth of her son to whom she, Julie, was to be godmother. Her letter gives a sudden, bright picture of gaiety and spontaneity, affection and sunshine. Julie was never exceptionally strong, but she seems to have shone in the eyes of those about her.

"Hurrah! Hurrah! Hurrah!" she wrote, like a true British officer's wife, "a thousand rounds in honour of the charming *Souris* and the newborn. In truth my head is full of joy and my hand trembles so much that I can scarcely hold my pen. And it is another boy! How I wish I was one of those powerful fairies who were able to bestow their gifts in such profusion; how the dear child should be endowed.

"Unfortunately all this is but an illusion, but never mind, something has said to me that the pretty little fellow has been born under a happy star; kiss him for me, my dear friend, and tell him this prediction of his godmother.

"O! no! I was never so happy in my life. I have this moment sent the news to our dear Prince. It is needless to await his reply to assure you how delighted he will be. I know his sentiments too well to have any fear in expressing them. Mrs. Stourton will excuse me and I will go to Beauport to-day about seven o'clock; to-morrow I will go again, and every day. Ah! I wish it could be this very instant of my life. I reserve it to myself to congratulate M. de Salaberry in person on the happy event; and in the meantime I embrace the whole household without distinction of age or sex."

Not only was Edward's lighthearted adored Julie godmother, but he himself stood for the boy who bore his name and whom they were to love so much and to lose so tragically.

And then Edward was transferred once more. All his life he suffered from transfers which almost always cost him the loss of a complete kit; and for very little, if any, of this expense, was he ever indemnified. Away back in the Geneva days, when his allowance of £1,000 had been increased to £6,000, the

Baron von Wangenheim gave him only a guinea and a half a week for spending money. Small wonder that even then he started incurring debts. He was given but a day's notice of his first posting to Gibraltar, and storm and wreck followed the vessels that bore his linen and top-boots. He could allow only a bare £400 a year to Julie, even after they had been together for some years.

His new appointment was to the West Indies. She waited behind for him, in Quebec, until he returned to Canada and could send for her to join him at Halifax.

He spent the summer of 1794 preparing for her arrival, building a house at the head of Bedford Basin, the inner harbour of Halifax.

The Lodge was a two-storey house, in wood, gay with paint and gilt. Long, winding avenues were cut out of the forest, for it stood about six miles from the town. It was easy driving distance, but the site itself stood in high and desolate country, with long, lovely views and falling streams. One of these was diverted to form artificial falls, elaborate gardens were laid out, an arbour of lattice-work supported a flowering vine.

There they could entertain in the summer. There was a bandstand near the house, topped with a great golden ball. In a clearing, stood an ornamental Chinese temple, decorated with jingling bells. Long after they had gone, and the Lodge fallen into decay, the fences down, the avenues overgrown by forest underwood, the blistered wood ravished of its fresh colours and the metal eaten and consumed with rust, there would still survive a bell on the forlorn little temple, to tinkle alone in the breeze that murmured in the trees.

But they were not gone yet, they were but just arrived.

Julie travelled down alone from Quebec, catching a nasty

L

cold on the way. She was never strong in the chest, and every winter colds and lung complaints were a burden to her. However, she was enchanted to be with her dear Prince again, and they quickly took the lead in Halifax society. If it was a little boisterous, they were determined to civilise it.

To begin with, although they entertained a great deal, they set their faces against drunkenness and gambling. Cards were allowed, a permissible distraction, even Julie played now and then, but they were purely for pastime. They would accept no invitations for Sunday card parties.

By November, Edward was writing to the de Salaberry family that Julie was in good health. His own excursion to the West Indies apparently had done no harm, and Halifax was decidedly the better for their presence. In the previous September, Quebec had paid him a compliment in opening the Quebec Sunday School, under the special patronage of H.R.H. It was to be a centre for free tuition, and there were special references to classes in English, made simple for those recently come under English dominion. It must be remembered that young countries and new colonies have great difficulty with their second and third generations, who do not arrive already educated in the culture of older lands, and who are born too early for their young motherland to have much to offer them. A colonist might be able, intelligent, a power in the land, and yet barely literate by European standards. The Quebec Sunday School would not have the same type of scholar as the Sunday schools of England, striving to civilise the brutalised child of the industrial era. Pupils would be older, more eager, less handicapped, keener to learn, healthier.

In Halifax, Julie passed a pleasant autumn and winter. It was milder there than in Quebec, and they had hopes that she might preserve a fair measure of good health into the spring.

The New Year came and went, and in 1795 they had once more to be parted, when Edward was for a while absent again on active service.

It did not break the life they had built between them. Julie was always bustling and busy with the domestic side of their affairs, running with French efficiency the sort of orderly establishment that Edward liked. She was in his complete confidence and acted often as his secretary, although towards the end of the spring this was for the time being out of the question. She gashed her hand and could not write. It was Edward who sent letters north to their Quebec friends, giving punctilious news of her. In July, he wrote that she "will soon have news on a subject interesting to ourselves and our friends. . . ."

Time passed pleasantly for them. Julie enjoyed games of skill—chess, backgammon, cards. She liked music and dancing, and home life with Edward. He, adoring and formal, grew ever more rigid in what he conceived as suitable, ever more exigeant in matters of service and ceremony. And yet, because he was not primarily self-seeking, or at least admitted other motives, he was never disliked as much as some of the brothers. When, in the autumn of 1798, he had a very bad fall from his horse and lay seriously ill, Julie was not the only person who was genuinely anxious.

She took over the duties of the sickroom and sent for the doctor. Time passed, but Edward did not recover as he should. The doctor advised England, the waters at Bath, modern medical care in place of backwoods physic. It would, he decided, be as well if His Royal Highness returned to England for attention.

Julie was a little nervous, but she could have the delight of being closer to her own people, to her sister, Comtesse de Jeansan, her brothers, the rising generation. This was not quite enough to quiet apprehension, for she did not know England except as the home of the most ruthless royal father of recent English history. She had had contact with some of Edward's family by correspondence, but the first meeting is always a little unnerving.

However, she set about preparations for the trip. It was the beginning of the North Atlantic winter, and they sailed in time to reach England before Christmas. Winds were good and the trip fast; they did not take quite three weeks, but it was a cold voyage, with rough seas. Both of them were overcome, and, by the time they landed, poor Julie felt very little stronger than crippled Edward.

They went to Kensington Palace, and Julie was duly installed in Knightsbridge, in every comfort. She was well received by the Royal Family. All the brothers liked "Edward's French lady," and Maria Fitzherbert, the illicit if legal wife of the heir to the throne, became her very good friend. Like Julie, she was a Roman Catholic, was gay and charming, good-looking and good-humoured. She had been educated in Paris, and could talk merrily with Julie, who had not taken easily to the English language.

Edward bought a house from Maria, a place at Ealing. He needed an English home, for his trip had other hopes than merely a cure for his fall. He felt that he needed to press his claims for help and promotion, and for this a headquarters on the spot would be advisable. He could plead and pester with the necessary courteous formality and far more efficiency.

Castle Hill Villa, at Ealing, made a very convenient country home. There was Julie's town house in Knightsbridge and his own apartments in Kensington Palace. She had stayed with him there at first, living in the very room in which, many years later, his daughter Victoria was to be born.

Edward's bones healed and Julie's health picked up quickly in the English spring. By April she was perfectly well, and Edward restored. They went to Bath for the cure and took the waters.

There was one trouble that remained constantly with them. Edward had by now lost a half-dozen different outfits and never could he persuade anyone to reimburse him. The cost weighed on him as an almost hopeless burden; in fact, he never managed to clear himself. The last of his debts were paid by Victoria after she came to the throne. His exaggerated sense of his own importance demanded a princely manner of living far beyond his means. His honesty was ever at variance with his vanity and his financial affairs were hopelessly insolvent.

However, he got his dukedom, became Edward, Duke of Kent, and he got his grant, which eased matters a little. He was appointed Commander-in-Chief, British North America, and in July he and Julie set sail across the Atlantic once again. By September they were back in Halifax, and Julie was glad to see old friends, open her rooms, unpack new fashions, and prepare for the winter season of entertaining. They were certainly still financially embarrassed, but that was nothing new. Edward was a little restive at this continual banishment from London, but prepared to do his duty.

Now it was poor Julie who had a bad fall and slightly injured her head, and the winter, which was to have been so cheerful, was threatened. However, she recovered quickly, and Edward surrounded her with care and precautions. In the spring of the

following year he was able to write to de Salaberry that
"Madame de St. Laurent has wholly recovered from her fall;
she has passed the winter without any sickness, a thing which
we feared as the climate of North America is by no means
favourable; but for the last few days she has been a little in-
disposed. As to the future, I flatter myself that after a little
she will be quite well again."

Edward was anxious for promotion to more agreeable posts.
He kept an eye on the horizon and was struck by the political
implications of the Irish Union. Why should he not become
Commander-in-Chief, if that was to be his rôle, in some more
centrally situated spot than British North America? Why not
Ireland? In any case, little could be done from Canada in the
way of taking soundings and holding discussions. He decided
to go home again to urge the matter on the spot.

On the plea of illness, he packed up, and embarked again for
England in August of 1800. The Lodge was abandoned now,
to fall into decay, for this was to be Julie's farewell to the
Americas. From now onwards she would live and move
amongst the other Ladies.

They landed in September and went straight to Weymouth.
It was a favourite watering-place and seaside health resort of the
period. Although they had made a good voyage, Julie had
caught a cold on landing, and it lasted well into November.

Edward went to see his father. He found, however, that he
could not persuade that stubborn and self-opinionated gentleman to make the appointment. If George III nourished the
idea that Ireland had done little to deserve one of his sons, he
will not perhaps be wholly condemned.

Meanwhile, after leaving Weymouth, Julie had to set in order
her English homes, Castle Hill Villa and the town house. Kent

House, in Knightsbridge, was to be their winter establishment, and all through the autumn Julie laboured at her settling-in. Her cold weighed on her. Edward had rheumatism (whether of a medical or diplomatic nature is not stated, but certainly he was well suited by being detained in London). It was a trying time for them both.

Julie at least was approved by Edward's mother as an admirable influence. Queen Charlotte did her best to be amiable, admitted her to the royal circle and invited her to some very dull evenings. Julie, gay of heart and loving, could have found little that was sympathetic in the grim circle of unhappy princesses and their dragon mamma.

Edward was trying to become a public character now. His Radical views—politically he was one of the "Reddish" brothers —attracted a certain amount of attention; he was interested in public and philanthropic works, and was generous of the gift of his patronage.

By Christmas, they were well installed and organised, but he was writing that they were neither of them in good health again, and "Madame and I consequently abstain from any amusements whatever." There was certainly part climate and part politics in this, for they were both people who could enjoy themselves cheerfully at theatre or opera.

While Julie began to entertain again with the returning spring and summer, he continued to hope for an appointment. Ireland was not for him. It was not, in fact, until March of 1802 that he got anything at all, and then he was offered the Governor-Generalship of Gibraltar.

He lost no time in making for his headquarters, sailing before the end of April and arriving early in May, but he retained the appointment for a bare twelvemonth. What Halifax could survive was too strong a dose for the Rock. He and Julie could purify Colonial society if they liked, but to improve the notoriously lax discipline of the Gibraltar garrison, and that in the most necessary article of curtailing its drunkenness, was the road to disgrace. It was hard that they should have had to suffer, for Edward's reforms, notably the closing of many of the wine-shops, resulted in halving the soldier mortality. It was also accomplished largely out of his own pocket, as part of his income came from the wine-shop licences.

But that was not the only way in which he earned unpopularity. His discipline was even more rigid now than when it had surprised Quebec a decade earlier. His brother Frederick, the Duke of York, was Commander-in-Chief, and he found young Edward's uncompromising zeal extremely awkward. In 1803, the younger brother was recalled, with a grievance that would last him for a considerable time, to languish in unemployment that grew yearly more bitter.

It was perhaps entirely due to his recall from Gibraltar that the scandal of Mary Anne Clarke ever shook the august walls of the War Office.

At any rate, the unfortunate Julie suffered for being the wife of a disappointed man, and it may have been at this time that she learned to dislike London and its dank gloom, even if her good-natured heart could not let her entirely condemn it.

Edward had not only lost all brotherly accord with Frederick, Duke of York, but he was now busily quarrelling with the Prince of Wales; he was additionally embittered by a rising tide of debts, although these did not yet interfere with the course of his life. Julie's allowance had risen from £400 to £1,000, as naturally befitted her position, and Kent House was provided with elaborate furnishings and efficient staff.

And now Julie was preparing to receive the three sons of their greatest friends at Castle Hill. For in the spring of 1805 she had a genuine cause for happiness. The three young de Salaberry boys, their godson and his two brothers, came over to stay with them in England.

Edward and Julie were ever constant in affection for the de Salaberry family, but the name soon began to have an over-familiar ring in the ears of those in high places. Edward was constantly asking a place, a favour, or help in some direction for a de Salaberry. He and Julie were loyal friends.

The boys were as charming as could be wished. Julie wrote to Canada at length reiterating assurances of the care she would take of them, praising their manners and deportment, behaviour and charm. In April she wrote to their father as joyously as of old, dating her letter from Edward's apartments at Kensington Palace. "Nothing could be more delightful than your letter but its author," she assures him. "I have read it with extreme pleasure, what you say of Maurice enchants without surprising me. During his infancy I was always struck with something chivalrous about him, and you will recollect my passing my fingers through his fair, sunny hair, and comparing him to the famous Maurice, Count Saxe. I do not think less of my *little chevalier* now that he is at least as tall as you are. . . ."

Her nostalgia peeps out as she ends, "dear and ever dear de Salaberry. I have only a minute left to dress and go out. It is go and come from morning to night. Oh! London, I will not call you a *hole*—the greatest and most beautiful city in the world—but every place has its drawback." And his sincere friend signs herself, as always, primly, "J. de St. Laurent," Julie of the wide St. Lawrence.

They welcomed the boys with delight, and one of the boys'

letters home to the distant parents assured them that "Madame is really a sweet woman, and is as handsome as ever."

The great pleasure of the next two years was the constant presence of her godson, Edward Alphonse. He came to them at Castle Hill Lodge, and, being younger than his brothers, became a child of the establishment. She wrote to Canada of him and his perfections. She and Edward showed him London, took him to the play and the opera, sent him to school, rejoiced in his return for the Christmas holidays. His complaint was the commonplace of happily spoiled childhood; he was embraced too much.

Not only did she love them but the youngsters had also found the core of affection that enlivened Edward's correct heart. They came to him, as it were, on the Julie side, and surprised a good fund of sensitive love in him. The same lighter spirit and more tender manner appears when he conducts his correspondence in French, and again one feels that Julie's lover is a different man from the martinet Duke on the barrack square.

She was happy that winter, charming to look at, prettily dressed, driving the boy round in a curricle, playing with him draughts, chess, dominoes, backgammon, and taking care not invariably to win her games.

The Clarke scandal matured and Edward continued to embroil himself with his elder brothers. Julie shared in his difficulties but contrived to remain cheerful and serene in her own surroundings and atmosphere. From Castle Hill, where they spent as much time as possible, Kensington and Knightsbridge she continued to send across the Atlantic letters that were mainly devoted to accounts of the boys. "I could write a great deal longer on this interesting subject, but have not time at present, having a large dinner-party to-day. . . ." She and

Edward had sent over gifts, and she was "delighted that my dear *Souris* has decided to try the wig (for my little finger tells me she has done so). I hope she will wear it for my sake. It is a headdress which she will find very comfortable when she has become accustomed to it. Everybody wears it. . . .

"The room paper is for Beaufort, that home dear to my heart, and which I delight to call to mind."

Her godson, in his own letters, gives a vivid picture of her life at the time. "H.R.H. and Madame de St. Laurent are at present at Knightsbridge," he says on one occasion, "which is some distance from here (Kensington Palace). It is a superb mansion, beautifully furnished; I have dined there several times. I dined there on Christmas Day with the Duke of Orleans and his brothers. I have been at the opera with H.R. Highness and Madame, when I saw the Duke of Cambridge, to whom I was presented as the godson of H.R. Highness and Madame. . . . H.R. Highness has given orders that we shall always have music at dinner. . . . The Duke and Madame have been very kind to me, and their kindness if possible is greater every day." He adds a pleasantly boyish postscript, "Madame de St. Laurent has given me six guineas since I came to England, a jolly sum for me." For the de Salaberry fortunes were not great. The three sons had been impressed strongly with the need for avoiding extravagances or appeals home, or debts likely to be a hindrance to others as well as themselves.

Julie certainly suffered under Edward's debts. Even her pin-money went towards clearing the more pressing of them. Edward was reputed to be generous and charitable, the friend of liberal thought and humane action, but fate remained irritatingly unproductive of the income necessary to support these characteristics. Then there was Kent House to be kept up as well as the Kensington Palace apartments. In addition, there was Castle Hill *Lodge*, as it was called on promotion, in its forty-acre park, run with magnificent, functional efficiency.

Edward could organise, and at Ealing he achieved a very high degree of organisation indeed. He was a man of great punctuality and, like the Duke of Wellington, had an irresistible urge to answer any letter he might receive. His personal habits were strict. A manservant remained awake all night to light his fire in the early morning. At six, another servant brought him a cup of coffee. Another yet removed the tray. Innumerable were the bells which summoned specialist after specialist from his highly trained staff.

The Kensington apartments were rich in musical clocks, which did not greatly facilitate conversation, rendering it liable to regular and prolonged interruption.

The mounting debts did not proceed from lack of method, for he audited the household accounts daily. His punctilious manners, softening engagingly towards Julie and the lads, made him reasonably popular, even if he continued on bad terms with his brothers. He hoped, when Frederick was forced to resign after the Clarke investigation, to get the appointment himself, but this did not happen. He remained unemployed.

The two elder de Salaberry boys were taken from them now, as they were posted to India. Edward, as well as Julie, wrote to their father. He also, rather touchingly considering his own load of debt, paid a tailor's bill for them. It was done unasked, unless Julie discovered the trouble and suggested some relief. He seemed in his dealings with the youngsters to understand the needs and sympathies of youth.

(There are echoes here of Emily Crawford's strange trio, the Cameron Kent family—John George Frederick William,

Jemima Charlotte Augusta and Edwina Caroline Elizabeth—passing as godchildren to the Duke of Kent and alleged to bear a closer relationship. Did the girls not speak perfect French, from their Canadian residence? And, except for the first names, they seem to have been christened exclusively from the fund of convenient labels used by the royal family.)

Edward de Salaberry went on to Marlow, an educational establishment for cadets, while his brothers were on the high seas. Julie's correspondence was now to be triangular, with the boys out in India and the parents in Quebec. Gifts went to and fro between them. She wrote to Canada in 1807, thanking *Souris* and the family for gifts of their own making, embroidery and fine needlework, and a flag. They were on her table as she wrote, from Castle Lodge, and Edward was staying there.

That establishment was only one of the burdens which overweighted their income. It was of all their houses the one run most perfectly according to Edward's desire. She lived her gay, charming and rather motherly life there, in a splendid routine which Mr. Justice Hardinge fittingly describes. He had just paid a visit to Castle Lodge.

"I was received in due form by a porter in livery, full trimmed and powdered. He opened his iron gates for me, bowed as if I had been the King, and rang the alarum bell as if I had been a hostile invader." That was done to give due warning, so that the second stage of the welcoming drill might begin. The drive was flanked by coloured lights. At the garden gate, the head gardener, duly in his best clothes, was ready to appear. He too bowed and sounded yet another tocsin. Six tall footmen, a guard of three a side, stood to usher him in, to be received by a French house steward of considerable age and dignity and with the appearance of a Cabinet Minister.

Elegant, chaste and princely was the exterior. The interior added to these qualities the true, awe-inspiring palace hush, that silence of infinite control, perhaps in this case broken only by Julie's quick, lively voice. Passages and staircases were lit by lamps of different colours. All the state apartments were open and lighted. Dinner was a gourmet's dream, "an epicure would have travelled barefoot three miles in deep snow to have been in time for it."

All liveries had always to appear as new, and it was necessary to keep a hairdresser for the servants who wore them. Not that there was waste. Money judiciously laid out could preserve in use a curricle that Edward had owned for twenty years, at home and overseas. "I never was spilt from it but once," he was proud to say. "It was in Canada, near the Falls of Niagara, over a concealed stump in a wood just cleared."

It was no wonder that his income had to be largely devoted, and then deliberately assigned, to the payment of his debts.

Their happiness, at least, continued to flow evenly. Mary Ann Clarke, in *The Rival Princes*, refers to Mr. Glennie's praise of Edward for his "affection for his old French lady, whom, he lamented, he could not marry." This was "a proof of his steady disposition and domestic good qualities, added to which he regularly went to church." Edward's agents had approached Mary Ann to provide evidence for their attack on Frederick. It was his agents, too, who had proved financially disappointing to the lady, which was hardly to be wondered at in view of the state of his own finances.

The de Salaberry boys continued to be Julie's happy interest. One of them fell deeply in love, contemplated the possibility of a romantic match with a pretty cousin on no better support than his pay. He wrote to Julie for advice, and she consulted

Edward. He dealt kindly with the boy, although he managed to persuade him against such desperate courses, while she wrote to Canada, telling the full story of the adoring couple, of Edward's sound commonsense advice, and of the young man's consent to abandon a design which could bring so little advantage to the lady of his heart.

The winter of 1808–09 was a particularly trying one for Julie. Even the pleasure of godson Edward, who spent his holidays with them as usual, could not cheer her much. Edward, writing at the end of January to Maria Fitzherbert, had to say "I know you will be sorry to hear that Madame de St. Laurent has been confined to her room for six months with one of those violent coughs and rheumatic colds so that the house is quite an Hospital."

It was a deprivation to her. No one more enjoyed driving out, garden parties, flowers and sunshine. She was fond of the theatre too. In October, young Captain de Salaberry had been summoned by Edward to escort her to Richmond. They had planned to see Mrs. Jordan's performance and Edward had found himself detained by business.

Then, in the very next year, it seemed as though fate abruptly decided that there had been enough of peace and happiness for Julie de St. Laurent. Trouble began to find its way to her.

The three beloved boys were all to be lost. Maurice died in India, loved and mourned. Edward, the most precious, fell one April day at the costly taking of Badajos, killed on the field. That was in 1812. The very next year Julie was to weep again for the death of the third brother. So short a time before all three had been with them. Now there was loneliness at Castle Lodge and desolation in Quebec; heartbroken, heartbreaking letters passed to and fro.

In the spring of 1814, Julie was really ill, confined to her room and unable even to come down to dine at six-thirty, as was her custom. Edward worried over her and did all he could. There is a note of gentleness in his letter to de Salaberry. "I am sure you will be pleased to learn that what our life was when we were beside you," he writes, "*that* it has continued during the twenty years that have passed since we left Canada, and I love to think that twenty years hence it may be the same."

On the Continent events moved to their tremendous climax. The Hundred Days came and went, Waterloo broke the spell, and the looming menace of Napoleon's France was suddenly over. Not so the dark cloud of Edward's debts. Money troubles were worse than ever, and in 1815 he appealed to the Regent, his brother. It was in vain. There was to be no recompense for those lost outfits, and no relief in present straits. Edward felt that he was already economising to such an extent that he should almost be ashamed of his betrayal of the dignity due to his position. But it was an untenable position. If he could get no help, and he was given no appointment, then he must leave England.

There was no question of going back to Canada.

The Continent was open now. Englishmen who had to economise and who wished to preserve some comfort and appearance on the tattered remnants of an income, were finding Belgium a cheap resort. Edward rented Vice-Admiral Donnolly's mansion in Brussels, the property of the Count de Maldegham. At least it was the largest residence in the place. He took it for a year, paying £300, and at once had it altered and decorated, and had a garden laid out for Julie. This at any rate was economy without actual squalor.

At the end of the summer they left England. Edward took Julie over to Calais; she had left Castle Hill for the last time.

At Calais they separated. Edward was to make a little tour, and Julie went straight to her sister, the Comtesse de Jeansan, in Paris. It was a delightful treat for her. Her brother, M. de Montgenet, the *Ingénieur en Chef*, was there. In mid-October, Edward joined the family group, amiably ready to escort the two sisters to their private box at the theatre, by day enjoying sightseeing with Julie's nephew. Julie lingered in Paris until November, to see her youngest brother who was there from Geneva. Only then she tore herself away and followed Edward to the new house at Brussels.

Before Christmas they were very comfortably settled. Two or three times a week they would go to the play, and on other nights friends were invited to dine and to make up Edward's whist table.

Maria Fitzherbert had a letter from him describing the new way of life with more than reconciliation. "My house, though old, thanks to painting, papering, whitewashing, carpeting and putting up a number of stoves, is very tolerably comfortable, totally *isolé* from any other, not overlooked. . . ." He commended the flower garden, the shrubbery, the fruit trees.

Julie was happy and comfortable, with reminiscences of her first family reunion for over a quarter of a century. It would be pleasant if they could now remain without worries, her family within reach, while Edward's debts were cleared.

Three-quarters of his income was left in the hands of trustees to satisfy his creditors. Castle Hill, Kent House and Kensington Palace had to be forgotten, and they were never to return into

M

Julie's life. Meanwhile, exact and careful regularity continued to govern their hours. Meals followed each other with appropriate ceremony. It was pleasant to be among French-speaking people, and far less expensive than keeping up the position of a Royal Duke in England.

Then in November of the following year the position changed overnight. Princess Charlotte died, and the hunt began for the—almost—missing heir. Worse than no alternative, dark Ernest of Cumberland already had a son.

Unfortunately, it is from the sharp pen of Creevey that we first learn how Edward took the news. Creevey was in Brussels in the December and Edward sent for him, hoping that he had the ear of the Whig party. Small hope from the Tories for a Radical of his complexion!

Creevey noted down Edward's words. ". . . Should the Duke of Clarence not marry, the next prince in succession is myself." Edward seemed to assume that marriage would automatically bring sons to his brother William. He went on with simplicity, "God only knows the sacrifice it will be to make, whenever I shall think it my duty to become a married man. It is now seven and twenty years that Madame de St. Laurent and I have lived together; we are of the same age, and have been in all climates and in all difficulties together; and you may well imagine, Mr. Creevey, the pang it will occasion me to part with her. I put it to your own feelings," he said, rather pitifully, "in the event of any separation between you and Mrs. Creevey. . . ."

Julie knew well what now confronted her. She had learned it with tragic abruptness.

"As for Madame St. Laurent herself," Creevey reports Edward as saying, "I protest I don't know what is to become of her if a marriage is to be forced upon me; her feelings are already so agitated upon the subject. You saw, no doubt, that unfortunate paragraph in the *Morning Chronicle*. . . ." It had appeared just after the death of his niece, Charlotte, and referred to the possibility of his marriage. "Upon receiving the paper containing that article at the same time with my private letters, I did as is my constant practice, I threw the newspaper across the table to Madame St. Laurent, and began to open and read my letters. I had not done so but a very short time, when my attention was called to an extraordinary noise and a strong convulsive movement in Madame St. Laurent's throat. For a short time I entertained serious apprehensions for her safety, and when, upon her recovery, I enquired into the occasion of this attack, she pointed to the article. . . ."

The harm had been done. Julie could only grieve and suffer now in Admiral Donnolly's house in Brussels with its newly made gardens, the gardens which Edward had laid out to please her. Christmas came and went, and *Nouvelle Année*, but where was the hope of the following spring? Beauport and home were far away; indeed, what home could she ever have but at Edward's side? Maurice lay dead in India, the cherished godson Edward in far Spain. At her side her lover plotted uneasily.

He was trying to spare her, and that may well have made her pain the worse to bear.

"From that day to this I am compelled to be in the practice of daily dissimulation with Madame St. Laurent to keep this subject from her thoughts." Luckily Edward knew the editors of the two local English papers, and they agreed to spare Julie's feelings by keeping their pages clear of any reference to his approaching marriage. For it was now as positive as that.

If the Duke of Clarence had not completed arrangements to marry before Easter, then Edward would find some pretext to go to England in the spring and discuss matters.

Julie must, of course, be "provided for," and his ungainly, if orthodox, demands have a certain pathos. "I shall hope and expect to see justice done by the nation and the ministers to Madame St. Laurent. She is of very good family and has never been an actress, and I am the first and only person who ever lived with her. Her disinterestedness too has been equal to her fidelity." He recounted gravely to Creevey the tale of her allowance, the small income she had received at first, its later augmentations, her willingness to sacrifice it in the cause of their common finances. "If Madame St. Laurent is to return to live amongst her friends, it must be in such a state of independence as to command their respect." Solemnly he haggled for servants, a carriage, and Julie, as the summer of 1818 bloomed in her garden, cared less and less for these things.

Without Edward, they meant nothing to her. He might be a figure of fun in the eyes of English statesmen, a pompous martinet, or just a plain nuisance, only important now in his character of potential father to an heir. But to her he was the beloved, the husband, the partner, the tall young officer with dark hair and long legs who had loved her when she too was young.

Without him, she wanted nothing. It seemed clear that she was to be without him.

If she had cared to go back to England, there was her old friend, Maria Fitzherbert, but she preferred to remain in France. And in France too were many who would help her. Louis Philippe was on the throne now and he took up her interests.

Her final decision was to enter a convent, and it was accepted. Her own small income would, she said, be enough. At any rate she wanted no more from Edward, even if he insisted upon her accepting gifts.

In 1818 the long story ended. Julie de St. Laurent, Madame la Baronne de Fortisson, renounced the world for ever. By next year, de Tottenberg was writing to de Salaberry in Canada, "Madame de St. Laurent has retired to a convent." Edward was already married to a suitable, and buxom, German princess.

Her friends did all they could for her, particularly Maria, living quietly now at Brighton with her two adopted daughters. They thought of her in her seclusion, and very soon had news for her that they would have preferred not to send. For, not two years later, in 1820, Edward died, away down in Devonshire, killed by a neglected cold. How often could Julie recall their care of each other in similar circumstances. This time she had not been there; another woman had care of him and she had let him die.

Now indeed there was very grave danger of Julie's just dues being forgotten, and Louis Philippe wrote to Maria, "You have been so good to my lamented friend, the Duke of Kent, and also to Madame de Montgenet that I must send you duplicates of all the letters that are now going to London in her behalf. . . . I am sure if you can give her a lift, you will do it." For Maria had cleared up Julie's affairs at Edward's marriage, and now, at his death, she did her best for the grieving woman in France.

Quietly, in her convent, Julie lived on into old age, never appearing again in the world she had known.

When Maria Fitzherbert herself was a very old lady, it

seemed wise to her to deal with the enormous private correspondence that she had accumulated, letters to and from every
member of the Royal Family. All the Kent correspondence
relating to Julie and her affairs passed into the hands of the
young Victoria.

THE DUCHESS OF CUMBERLAND

THREE TIMES in successive generations were there marriages between the English royal family and the ducal house of Mecklenburg-Strelitz, that Baltic province edged on three sides by Prussia, on the fourth by the sea. Each marriage turned out well, but between the first two brides, Queen Charlotte, wife of George III, and Frederica, Duchess of Cumberland, bleak hatred reigned.

They were to become aunt and niece and they were mother-in-law and daughter-in-law!

Frederica Caroline Sophia, born in 1778, was the youngest of four gay, handsome, witty, intelligent, musical and charming sisters. Their mother was a Princess of Hesse-Darmstadt. She presented Charles, hereditary Duke of Mecklenburg-Strelitz, with four daughters in succession—Charlotte, Theresa, Louisa and Frederica. Then, in August of 1779, little Prince George was born.

Duke Charles was neither the reigning Duke nor a wealthy man. He had taken service with the Hanoverian forces and was stationed in Hanover, holding the post of Commandant and living at the old Fort in the town. Hanover and England were sister nations, under the same crown, and the Queen of England was Duke Charles's sister. He had visited London when he had taken her over for her marriage.

If Duke Charles's children could hope for little material

wealth, they were rich in unexceptionable connections and, greater treasure still, in a warm family love that bound them together. Little George, the baby over whom Frederica chuckled, was later to be her hot-headed champion, rashly fighting her battles with the Queen, their aunt.

In 1782 the family in the old Fort tempted Providence too far. The mother died at the birth of another child, which died with her. The Fort became a haunted spot for the Duke, and even for the elder girls, Charlotte and Theresa, who were as devoted to each other as were Frederica and Louisa. It was decided to move to Herrnhausen, stately palace of the kings of Hanover. Many years hence Frederica was to come back to Herrnhausen, to reign there as Queen of Hanover.

Life went on well for them, as it does for the gay at heart. In 1784, Duke Charles married again, choosing his sister-in-law, but in the following year she too died, at the birth of her son, Charles.

There were now only three little daughters at home, for Charlotte had married, from the schoolroom, the Duke of Hildburghausen, and had disappeared into the Thuringian forest with her former governess as Mistress of the Household.

It seemed to the twice-bereaved father that the best thing to do was to hand the children over to the care of their grandmother, the Landgravine of Hesse-Darmstadt, and so, under Louisa's wing, and with two baby brothers to look up to her in their turn, Frederica went south, to the pleasant lands where she was to grow up. Her time there was short, but it left her with that buoyant charm which is the legacy of a happy childhood.

The grandmother believed in happiness for children, in tender hearts cultivated by cottage visiting, in thrift taught by scanty pocket-money, in much music and laughter. She took care to educate the girls socially too, and they were certainly all that is eligible. Frederica and her two sisters were taken to visit their aunt, the Duchess of Zweibruecken, to Starbourg, Rotterdam and The Hague. Twice they were taken to Frankfort, for the coronations of the Emperors Leopold II and Charles II. They were taken to the country, to Braunshardt, near Darmstadt, and to their grandmother's own property at Broich, near Dusseldorf.

At home, their education was not over-bookish, although they were all intelligent. They were bilingual in French and German, and spoke too the soft Rhineland dialect. French was still the Court and society language of the German principalities.

Severe Mademoiselle Agier, the French-Swiss governess who took them to Darmstadt, was deposed in favour of the gentler Mademoiselle Gelieur (several versions are given of her name), who did not leave them until the very day when Louisa and Frederica set out together upon their wedding journey.

Theresa made that journey first. In 1789, she married the Prince of Tours and Taxis, and the two younger sisters probably went a couple of times to Frankfort in connection with her betrothal and bridal, as well as to the two coronations in 1790 and 1792. Both were already light of foot and flashingly lovely. Frederica had that half swooning vivacity which must thrust itself forward and onward into life. She had courage too, and of all the Ladies, she was to need it most, for the wars and upheavals that shook Europe as the French rose in revolution and then in aggression, touched her more than any of the others.

Darmstadt was not thought safe enough, it was too near the French border. Both girls were packed off to sister Charlotte, at Hildburghausen, a vital, sunshiny place set in the pine forests, with air perfumed of Paradise, and where there was music and dancing to their hearts' content—and within the limits of human endurance Louisa and Frederica could not have too much of dancing.

They were growing up quickly now and becoming ever lovelier. Ambitious yet vulnerable, they were afraid of separation. Marriage was their life, their career, and it would be well to succeed in it, but each dreaded the approaching day when they would lose the other to an unknown husband.

Ernest, Duke of Cumberland, the dark horse of the English royal brothers, constantly involved in scandals which omitted no reasonable or unreasonable vice, was in Germany at this time. He was in the field, serving under the dashing and chivalrous Marshal Walmoden. The following year, Ernest was to be gazetted Field-Marshal in the armies of both England and Hanover, but now it was 1793 and Custrine had entered Mainz. Frankfort was for the time being in the vile hands of the French.

The German forces of liberation were led by King Frederick William II of Prussia, and he had with him his two sons, the Crown Prince, that amiable and respectable young man, and the younger Prince Louis. The King's brother was there too, Prince Louis Ferdinand, bold, dissolute, charming, rash, much that he should not be, much that was enviable.

The whole set-up was tempting, for were not the two brothers the most eligible matches in Germany? The field was rich, too rich for a loving grandmother to resist. There had been vague discussions already, and rumours of the two young lovelies. Now the Landgravine came to hurry the girls back from Hildburghausen to Darmstadt, *via* newly liberated Frankfort. They must stay the night there; accommodation was found at the White Swan Inn. They were merely "breaking their journey," but, the King of Prussia being in the town, it was of course necessary to pay one's respects. There were delays and, after a visit to the theatre where the King saw the two princesses for the first time, an invitation to a supper-party which could not be declined. Frau Olenschlaeger entertained the two girls at breakfast next day, and they went knowing that the Crown Prince would be there to meet them. Something had been decided then, and both sides must seem happy, must create, at least for the moment, the haze of romance.

The Crown Prince could have his choice. Between the sixteen-year-old Frederica and her just-elder sister there was nothing to choose. One was third daughter, the other fourth. He kissed their hands, stood up, Mars selecting his sacrifice, and decided upon Louisa. It was all the same to his brother, Prince Louis, who it had been decided should marry the other. Prince Louis's affections were engaged elsewhere and he was entirely indifferent as to which bride fell to his share. It was suitable, too, that the elder sister should marry the heir to the throne, the younger live at her Court.

Frederick William II was not a model husband, but he knew how such things should be managed. He wrote to Berlin, in the warmth of March, that he had "been occupied with a constant succession of fêtes, especially designed to honour the presence amongst us of . . . Princess George William of Darmstadt and her two delightful grandchildren. . . . The latter are as beautiful as angels. I saw them for the first time in the theatre. . . . I was so overcome with admiration that I hardly knew what I was doing or saying when their grandmother presented them to me. I only wished my sons could see them and fall in love with them. Next day, however, the young people were introduced at a ball. The princes were simply fascinated. I did my best to let them see as much as possible of our fair visitors, that they might get to know them. As far as I can judge, the two angels are as good as they are beautiful. When we found that the princes were very much in love, we just settled the matter out of hand. The princesses gave their consent and the betrothal will take place in due course, probably at Mannheim. My eldest son will marry the elder princess, his brother the younger."

It was as simple as that. They were not to be separated.

All the girls were now settled, and well settled. Charlotte wrote to Theresa, "Just think how well everything has turned out! How delightful for the two to be together as long as they both live. It is what they always desired. . . . Papa," she adds, "is looking at everything through rose-coloured spectacles."

For Duke Charles it was indeed pride and joy and consolation, but no one seems to have recorded what it was like for the youngest of the party. Louisa began, in her grave, sweet way, to fall in love with the Crown Prince, and he returned her affection. Frederica, the child of sixteen, however, was to be handed over to a dissolute young man who was deeply in love with another woman. He would take her to one of the gayest and most licentious Courts in Europe, and, once there, would hardly care what happened so long as she yielded him a boy baby or two before they forgot each other's faces completely. But to Frederica it was an excellent marriage, the best possible bargain in the time she lived, and the happiest possible arrangement to be with Louisa.

There was no delay, and the twin betrothals took place in all gaiety at Darmstadt in April. The princesses saw a good deal of the young bridegrooms, who were in camp at Mainz, and of their dashing uncle, Prince Louis Ferdinand.

The world began to look at them now, penniless young princesses gathering their bridal finery, the future Crown Princess of Prussia and her sister-sister-in-law. Princess Anton Radziwill, shrewd and alert, decided that Frederica was not such a beauty as Louisa, "but she had an attractive figure, was exceedingly amiable and anxious to please, so that she was often preferred to the noble beauty of her sister."

Goethe was in the camp, and from the recesses of a tent watched the two girls pass as they came to visit their princes. Two celestial beings, he described them, unforgettable amid the tumult of war.

Wedding preparations began at once; the unchanging formalities were duly numbered in Berlin. The two girls set out on December 15th from Darmstadt, with the bells pealing, playing "Jesu, meine Zuversicht" (memories of that other Louisa!). A greeting to Charlotte at Hildburghausen, and then on to Weimar, to Leipzig and thence to Potsdam, where they arrived on the 21st, to meet the formal welcome of the citizens.

Both brothers were there to receive them, and Frederica, the little sister, the unloved bride, found herself somewhat over-shadowed. Louisa, the future Queen, shone in all her glory; Frederica, the future Princess Louis, slipped a little into the background. Two days later, at the state entrance into Berlin, Louisa's loveliness, her artless embrace of the welcoming child with flowers, drawing the usual rebuke on the score of the formalities, won everybody to her. Countess Voss, mistress of the young Crown Princess's household, and until the end her and her husband's friend, rode opposite them.

On Christmas Eve, Frederica sparkled with sudden gaiety in the full pantomime of Louisa's wedding. The public was admitted to the palace, there was a torch dance and ceremonial supper, there was even a touch of kindliness in that people were asked to give to the poor the sums they might have planned to spend on illuminations.

Instantly, not waiting for her own wedding two days after Christmas, Frederica helped her sister to claim the freedom they were both to establish. At Louisa's wedding they danced the waltz. The waltz was banned at the Prussian Court, and the Queen turned her back. She forbade the princesses ever to imitate these sisters-in-law. The King was fascinated by such grace, such verve. Men stood on chairs to watch and to argue which of the two excelled.

They were now to have their fill of dancing.

Frederica and Louis were to live next to Louisa and Frederick, and as Louis exercised the bare minimum of his rights, and as Frederica was as gay as a bird and could use quite an amount of flattery, and was sixteen years old, she seemed suddenly to surge forward into the lead. Her sister became perhaps more than a little dependent on her.

The two couples were incessantly together. The girls calmly took a greater share of liberty than anyone expected, went driving unchaperoned, accepted and gave invitations, and, as the Countess Voss says, "almost danced themselves to death."

They saw much, too, of Louis Ferdinand, the King's brother, who desired an *affaire* with Louisa now that she was safely married. She innocently allowed attentions, discovered their meaning, withdrew, and left him to press Frederica into service as a go-between. It was not long before she took the title rôle.

There was some considerable scandal. Already both sisters were pregnant. Frederica was to bear her first son, the handsome Frederick William Louis, in October of 1794, the year in which Ernest of Cumberland was gazetted Field-Marshal. Prince Louis Ferdinand, the admirer, was gallant, dashing, devoted for the moment, and on the spot, which is always an asset. Prince Louis, the husband, was indifferent; Frederica's affections were not of importance to him. Countess Voss, warming from Court lady to doting admirer of Louisa, now regarded Frederica as a bad influence in the family. Frederica was indifferent to both opinions. With a prince of Prussia in her womb, she danced into the dawn and woke at lunch-time with the famous complexion undimmed.

It went on through 1795. By the end of the year she was carrying her second child, Frederica Wilhelmina Louisa, to be born in September. She spent part of the summer at Sans Souci with Louisa, who was perforce left alone for a while. As always, the sisters were completely satisfying to each other, laughing and gay, demanding music and flowers, and doubtless giving not a thought to the indifferent Prince Louis, whether he was sailing on the Oder or lying in the arms of his love.

When his daughter was three months old, and on the day after his wedding anniversary, Louis died in a fever. Frederica, in her nineteenth year, was left a widow with two small babies, a reputation for gaiety, an endless appetite for parties, and an exquisite wardrobe.

It was a season of deaths and illnesses. Before her father-in-law himself died, he went to take the baths at Pyrmont. Frederica accompanied him. She had always to rise to the occasion and must never be defeated. She must lay comment low by giving it fuller measure still on which to catch its breath. The King took his mistress with him too, the Lichtenau, and sent later for the Queen, the Crown Prince and Louisa. He forced them all to be present at an evening party given by the mistress. Frederica laid aside her mourning for the first time and glittered once more.

She helped Louisa, so soon to be the young and lovely Queen of Prussia, to set the fashions, wearing with her the fascinating trifle of ribbon or gauze below the chin, to disguise the fact that the almost perfect elder sister was a little thick in the neck.

Frederica's future had now to be considered. Why regret the marriage that had served its turn? Louisa could not face the thought of a parting, but perhaps it did occur to Frederica that the rôle of widowed sister-in-law at her sister's Court might become a little savourless. At any rate, she raised no objection when, after due discussion, she was officially betrothed to Adolphus, Duke of Cambridge, perhaps of all the English royal brothers the worthiest and the most likeable.

The old King of Prussia was dead now. Louisa was Queen. Frederica was in high sparkle once more. The young King, an adoring husband, insisted that his wife brighten her wardrobe and no longer allow Frederica to set the pace. It was not a question of clothes entirely; that glowing complexion had to be matched, and the dutiful Louisa took to rouge and lipsalve.

And meanwhile was happening what must always happen when vitality and high spirits run riot. Within a few months of her husband's death, Frederica began to amuse herself again. Soon the Countess Voss was commenting on the visits of "the everlasting Prince of Solms." This was a handsome ruffian, under thirty, Captain of the Bodyguard. His full name was Prince Frederick William of Solms-Braunfels.

Adolphus, Duke of Cambridge, who was not there and was, in any case, unromantic, stood no chance at all. In 1798, Frederica went through a secret and irregular form of marriage with Solms-Braunfels, and jilted Cambridge. She had, apparently, no mind to be a duchess just yet. George III had already given his consent to the match, and Frederica found herself in a fine pickle when the Solms-Braunfels marriage was known.

Louisa was heartbroken at her sister's lack of confidence in her. The young King was furious. It was necessary to be firm. The couple were publicly remarried, Solms-Braunfels was found a post in Ansbach, and they were sent off there together. Frederica was forced to renounce all the trappings of royalty, for this was no alliance suited to a widowed Princess of Prussia— neither the man nor the manner was acceptable. She had to forfeit her title of Royal Princess, her coat of arms, her princely household. And she was to lose the babies. Louisa, weeping between her adored husband and her cherished sister, modified the terms a little. The tiny Frederica could go with her mother for the moment. Later, she must be returned to the Prussian Court for her education. Miserable and uncertain of herself, longing for Frederica to remain, wretched at her departure, still more wretched at her secretiveness, Louisa made her farewells and Frederica went out into the wilderness. The young Queen wrote to the Countess Voss away on a short visit to the country, "Now that I am separated from her, it seems to me that the memory of her here, where I have not been since her departure, is more strongly vivid, and that I must find her everywhere." She ends piteously, "The reasons that separate us, cut me to the heart."

To be candid, Frederica had made a fool of herself. The next few years were the worst of her life. They were hideously complicated by the French wars, the Napoleonic invasions of Germany, the fleeing from castle to castle, the winters on the icy Baltic, the beleaguered life of war. And very soon it was

N

obvious that the marriage was a failure. The swashbuckling Captain of the Bodyguard was a brutal and inconsiderate husband. Their first child, Prince Frederick (taste in names was strangely circumscribed!), was born in December of 1801, and Frederica's second and last daughter, in the summer of 1804. The baby was christened Louisa, for by that time the sisters were reconciled.

Louisa had gone with her young husband on a long tour of Poland, part of her domain, and aroused there the wildest enthusiasm for the Prussian royal house. On her return she was allowed to visit Charlotte, at Hildburghausen, for a family reunion. Frederica was there, and the only loveless years came to an end, the estrangement was over. They were not to live together again for a while yet, but the old foundation of love and laughter and trust was rebuilt.

It had need of good rebuilding to withstand the years that were to come, when Napoleon swept into Germany, conquering and devastating that smiling countryside. Anxiety and worry made Louisa ill through the long winter of 1805, and the new year was disastrous for her beloved Prussia. Auerstaft was fought, Jena next, and the young King escaped only by fleeing to Weimar. He and Louisa had to plunge on northward together, to Kustrin, and on, in 1807, to Königsberg.

Frederica had taken a house there, and in the bleak winds of March she bore her third son, Prince Alexander. The noble young Czar had at that moment all the adoration of Louisa, and consequently of Frederica. Not that there was much time for girlish hero-worship. At the first threat to Berlin, Louisa's young family had been sent to Frederica's former castle at Schwedt. Now Frederica herself, with her month-old baby needing care, had to nurse her sister through a three-weeks' illness. The wounded crowded into Königsberg after the battle of Eylau, and for these also she did all she could. Defeat and disaster followed each other; there is no record that they found Frederica unable to bide their company.

Louis Ferdinand had been killed in battle, dying gallantly and recklessly to meet the need. His body was found on the field stripped and with thirteen wounds. Ernest, Duke of Cumberland, had been sent out to Stralsund with Lord Cathcart and twenty thousand men to support Prussia, England's current ally, but he arrived too late. Tilsit had shown how far the Czar, too, would support his friends. Prussia had fallen exceedingly low.

The first phase was over now and there was the peace of national defeat. No need for Frederica to recall the day when she had packed off Louisa, in an open carriage in the snow, with Countess Voss ahead to search for sanctuary and quarters at Memel. No need for Frederica to remember how she and Princess Louisa Radziwill had remained in besieged Königsberg, defended with fiery ingenuity by Ruechel, "the Don Quixote of the Prussian Army." There had been compensations. At the end of that long and terrible winter, when the Baltic was blue again and the spring flowers out, Louisa had come back, a little better in health, but never to be strong again, and together they had weathered the fall of Danzig. They were very close then, sharing the house of Countess Schlieben, sleeping in the same room, never apart. There was merriment under the siege guns, she could remember that. They invited guests for teas, musical evenings and water parties as the year warmed, and lived in a mixed allied society, English, Russian and German.

Defeated Prussia had to accept her terms. It was learning the hard way, and Louisa mourned tragically. Frederica nursed her through the birth of her tenth child, Prince Albert. Brother

George, whom both sisters loved dearly, and who loved them with tenderness and passion, came north to them.

When the time came for the re-entry into Berlin, Frederica went back there with Louisa. Her banishment was over. Never again would there be any question but that she was the King's sister-in-law, the beloved sister of his lovely Louisa. Frederica was waiting at the Palace Unter den Linden when Louisa's carriage came rolling again down the road they had both travelled as brides, on that brilliant winter day long ago. Now another Frederica, her daughter, sat where she had sat before; while Countess Voss still rode opposite.

But the end of the war did not mean peace, either for defeated Prussia or for Frederica. She went home to her father at Mecklenburg for a long, quiet visit, rejoicing in the little Court, in George's company, in her grandmother's society, and recovering again that certainty of the light of heart that life is basically an *affaire du cœur*.

In 1810, Louisa too returned to Strelitz, her first visit to her father's home since she became Queen. Frederica had remained there, relaxing in agreeable company. She wrote gleefully to Louisa, who would come almost alone. Frederica would lend her the faithful Quint as a servant. The family would have a few days at Strelitz and then Louisa's husband would join them, and they would go into the country for a day or so more. Louisa wrote merrily . . . "Old Marten is undoubtedly going round with his leather apron and measuring rod through the whole castle, rides breathless to Hohenzieritz and comes back saying, 'I have found room for every one!'" She pictures Frederica's incessant, "Aber, Georg!" and his quick, "Just hear, Frederica!" If only, she adds a little wistfully, she could afford to take Frederica and their grandmother to Carlsbad! But although they were not so entirely destitute as during the war years, the Queen could not yet afford jaunts to watering places. This simple visit home must suffice.

George took Frederica down to the duchy's border, where they met Louisa at Fürstenburg. Their father came too, to bless the young Queen who had survived such great misfortunes, and they bore her home between them. That evening they were gay again.

A few days later Louisa lay dead, Frederica's hand in hers. Frederica had nursed her through her last pathetic illness, as she had tended her before. She was there when Louisa was bled, had stroked her hands through the long and hurtful hours. It was hard to believe that Louisa of Prussia had gone.

For a while the loss dimmed everything. Frederica emerged from it, sheltered still by George, by her father, by the affections she had woven, and she found life empty. Neither of her husbands had counted for much, temporary loves for still less. Her real heart had been Louisa's, and now her sister was dead. She could turn to books, to music, to current affairs—for she was a woman of wide interests—and she could turn to people, but for people her judgment was for the time being blurred. It was little comfort that dead Louisa's son was growing up strikingly handsome, and that young Frederica was fourteen, past the dangers of childhood and almost ready to embark on the career that was to make her reigning Duchess of Anhalt-Dessau.

War returned too, but this time the war of the receding tide, the road to victory over the young Republic. Ernest was in Germany again in 1813, successfully defending Berlin, that city of trials, in August against Oudinot, in September against Ney. He was at Strelitz, staying there with the Duke, and he thus met and came to know the daughter, Frederica.

Ernest found the Princess of Solms-Braunfels so attractive that he would not even yield her as a dinner partner to Bernadotte. Sir Charles Stewart had to devise a procedure which sent Frederica to the dinner table hand in hand with her grandmother, with Ernest and the Swedish Regent hand in hand behind them, so resolute was the Duke upon the matter. Already he intended to marry her. Nearly a year before the marriage actually took place he told his brother, Frederick, of his intention. Ernest had found his love. Solms-Braunfels had faded into the distance.

Napoleon was defeated, Elba received him; in Vienna, Congress danced. Ernest hurried to Hanover, stole the thunder of deliverer's welcome, and governed it until Adolphus, Duke of Cambridge, came out at Christmas as Viceroy. 1814 came in.

The Prince of Solms-Braunfels divorced his wife. It was he who produced cause and set the marriage aside. In April he died. In July Frederica bore a son, Prince Frederick William Louis George Alfred Alexander. As the tiny newcomer appeared at Strelitz, his eldest brother was cheered in England, a handsome young officer of the Prussian Army who had arrived in the train of his King and uncle. The Czar was there, and Blücher, victors who were to be cut short in their triumphs with the Hundred Days, whose victory had to be resealed at Waterloo.

A month after the baby was born Frederica was in Berlin once more, sitting at the King's left hand at the splendid thanksgiving dinner. The ceremonies, the triumphal entry of the widower king with girls strewing flowers, the open-air service, the opera after dinner, the music she knew and loved— at every hour Berlin was full of memories of Louisa. The Countess Voss was there too, old now and a little tremulous.

It was the end of an epoch both for Europe and for Frederica. Napoleon's army was broken at Waterloo, Wellington and Blücher were finally victorious. In the same twelvemonth came the announcement of Frederica's engagement to Ernest, Duke of Cumberland.

The news of it reached England in August and Queen Charlotte wrote in delight to her brother, Frederica's father. "I can scarcely find words sufficiently strong to express all the joy I felt on receiving your letter. . . . God grant that the brilliant perspective which both have formed may be realised, in which the age of both authorises the most flattering hopes, and in which the character you trace of your daughter gives me the greatest confidence."

In the traditional rôle of gentle, welcoming old mother, she wrote of her quiet life, of the welcome guest that Frederica would always be, of how she and her daughters would try to entertain her. She wrote also a long letter to Ernest, serious and happy, commending the little interval there was to be before Frederica's remarriage after her former husband's death. She wrote of *"the desire I feel that she should come to this country without incurring the criticism of those who are not the best inclined to the Royal Family."* It would be wise, too, to make known publicly the arrangements planned for the four young Solms-Braunfels children, to whom Frederica was so attached. Otherwise England, rather too accustomed to royal princes in need of funds, might grow restive. She assured him: *"this advice I offer only as a proof for your own ease of mind in Future and not in the least as harbouring any suspicion against the Princess or the Family wanting towards them, for I am sure that your heart will always Incline you to forward their happiness and Education when you have the means of doing it, nay, it would be absolutely wrong to withhold it.* . . . *I wish both of you,"* she writes, *"to set out in the world free from all uneasiness in a country where She is not known and where I could wish not any unpleasant opinion should be harboured against her when she arrives."*

The little warnings she sent were gentle. England was not Germany. Frederica should not receive male visitors in the morning, save such army men as the Duke might present to her. She should beware of unsuitable female friends.

Plans moved towards the wedding, which was to be a family affair at Strelitz.

Then came the abrupt *volte-face.* Queen Charlotte began to get more news of her niece, to understand that she was the Princess Frederica who had long ago jilted the blameless Adolphus, the virtuous Viceroy, now at Hanover. She learned too that Solms-Braunfels had divorced Frederica, for misconduct, before his death. She had thought the alliance was broken for state reasons. There had been almost no personal news from the Continent for so long that piecing the bits together, learning what had become of every one during the dark war years, was a slow and difficult process. Now she began to make out Frederica's story, and she turned upon Ernest a torrent of disapproval.

It did not deter him in the least, and certainly it did not frighten Frederica. The disapproval of an aunt, Queen in a country she had never visited, would hardly seem important to her.

Ernest went to Strelitz, and there, on a summer evening, they were married in the town church. Sir George Jackson, present as a witness, describes the glittering guests, all *en grande tenue,* a crowd of German princes and princesses making a

brilliant show to celebrate a post-war wedding. The bridegroom was waiting, looking very well too. The officiating
minister waited. Finally, the old Duke led in his daughter.

Frederica was brilliant. Now in her middle thirties, she still
had her grace of figure, her lovely complexion, and Jackson
records, "she was very well dressed and looked very handsome."
Marrying at long last a man she loved, she shone through it all,
through the ceremonial congratulations, through the splendid
supper. Little Mecklenburg-Strelitz stretched itself to the
utmost to give her the wedding of her heart's desire.

Only the witness was a little dubious, slightly mocking,
doubtful if the pair would be well received in England.

On the face of it, there was cause for a little mockery. The
marriage between this handsome, spirited, not-so-young
brunette and the lean and dangerous brother had all the hall-
marks of the most cynically arranged alliance. She had her
history. He had been suspected of every vice, and was yet to
live through more scandals than could be imagined. And yet
it was the most triumphant love-match of them all.

Both were genuine, entirely careless of opinion, dauntless,
intelligent, resolute in difficulty, clear in thought. The wicked
duke, devoted High-Churchman, high Tory, patron of Kew, and
the woman who had danced herself ill as a pregnant child, had
lived through sieges and two disastrous marriages, had ridden
in triumph and been banished in disgrace; these two were now
in love and with each other. They had a quarter-century before
them and yet, in a sense, Frederica's history ends here, on a
summer evening as she came up the aisle of the church in
Neu-Strelitz with her hand on her father's arm to be given
in marriage to Ernest of Cumberland.

Everything Ernest did occasioned comment and hardly ever

did he pay the least attention to it. Now he left his bride and
went alone to England, which was unkindly remarked. He
wanted to soothe down his mother's anger and stop her indignant comments on Frederica's morals. He went at once to
the Regent, before whom he and Frederica were to be remarried in the usual style. He consulted the Duke of York. He
went to Windsor. He went to the Prime Minister, Lord
Liverpool. Princess Charlotte, his niece, was asked to help.

Nothing would make the Queen change her mind. Neither
she nor her daughters would receive or even acknowledge the
new Duchess. Frederica could and should stay in Germany.
She might be received there, she never would be here.

Ernest had no more intention of giving in than had his bride.
He went to the Commons for the customary increase of
allowance on marriage. They refused it, by a majority of one.
Peter Pindar wrote satirically:

> "O fell *majority of one*!
> By which my hopes are all undone!—
> 'Tis cruel usage on my life,
> Deny me cash, abuse my wife!"

He puts the plea briefly into the Duke's mouth:

> "Can't they be still and say their prayers,
> And meddle not with my affairs?
> Let them *sing hymns*, with pious qualms,
> And leave me to enjoy my Salms."

Salms for a Royal Duke indeed! Frederica had faced much, but
she had yet to meet the British on their own ground. However,
one who had survived the displeasure of a King of Prussia and
the warfare of a Napoleon, could face most things. Her husband
sent for her, and her beloved and hot-headed brother, George,
brought her over. The Regent gave his public consent, saw

them remarried, but hedged as usual and made no mention of it either in the *Gazette* or in the speech from the Throne.

Brother George made considerable trouble, for he dashed into battle against his aunt and was worsted like any other nephew. The Queen wrote furiously of the insult against which age, sex and position should have sheltered her. Neither the King of Prussia nor the Duke of Mecklenburg-Strelitz could have known of the liberties taken in their name. She refused to meet or to recognise Frederica, finally and for ever.

It was exceedingly awkward. The King of Prussia was making an incident out of it, and the Duchess of York, formerly a Prussian princess herself, was drawn into it. Ultimately, both Frederica and Ernest left England and returned to Germany, to Berlin, and a life that both knew and could understand. Neither was English, for all that Louisa had called her sister "my English Frederica," neither had hands for English people and customs. They had been badly treated and would go back where they could settle with some contentment.

In 1817, Frederica bore Ernest a daughter, a stillborn princess, and in the same year her eldest son, Prince Frederick, married Princess Louisa, daughter of the reigning Duke of Anhalt-Bernbourg.

Then came the death of the Princess Charlotte, at Claremont, and Ernest and Frederica went quickly over to England. It now seemed exceedingly probable that Ernest would succeed to the thrones of England and Hanover, or that his children might do so, for he was the only married brother. The cast-about for brides had begun, and Adolphus, whom Frederica had jilted when they were all young, married Augusta of Hesse-Cassel. She was brought over for the most benign welcome from her mother-in-law.

This was hard and Frederica resented it. The old Queen was glad to know that she did. But it did not destroy the family friendliness between the two duchesses, who were already connected, Frederica's brother George having married Augusta's sister, Marie. This friendship infuriated the Queen to such an extent that on one occasion, when Frederica and Augusta met at Kew, "accidentally" by secret appointment, to talk for a while of their homes and friends and relations, her wrath was almost fatal to herself.

The Cumberlands returned to the Continent again, and in 1819 Frederica's last child was born, little Prince George of Cumberland. It was time she ceased adding to her own family, for in the following year she was to become a grandmother.

Ten years in all she and Ernest spent happily living on the Continent, mostly at Berlin, but travelling a considerable amount and paying many visits. Spa was fashionable, and on one occasion when they were there Wellington was at the resort too, and the Emperor Alexander, the Prince and Princess of Orange, and members of the Prussian royal house. Mademoiselle Mars, a little past her best, was appearing at the theatre.

Prince George of Cumberland throve, a strikingly good-looking child. The elder daughter, Frederica, bore a daughter in her turn, with the original name of Princess Agnes. Then, in 1826, there was a second grandson, brother to the first.

Frederica's second family grew up now. The boys went into the Prussian army, as convention decreed. Princess Louisa was married, in 1827, to Prince Albert de Schwartzbourg-Roudolstadt. All was well in Germany, but in England matters seemed to be changing fast. First, the old Queen died, and then the Duke of Kent, who left one small daughter, Victoria.

Poor mad King George III died at last, and Frederick, Duke of York, sober in his old age. The Prince Regent was now King George IV, a monarch whose health in 1828 was not particularly sound. The Duke of Clarence, who apparently would succeed him, seemed likely to remain without heir.

There was virtually only the infant Victoria—and the rearing of babies was chancy in those days—between Ernest and the throne. He lived quietly abroad, and it looked almost as if fate would reward him by dropping plums into his lap. Death alone—his own—could rob him of the throne of Hanover, from which Salic law debarred the little princess. Death alone —Victoria's—could easily give him the throne of England too.

He hurried over to England without Frederica, and from Germany she learned what steps he was taking to make himself felt. The situation needed watching. William, who had yet to reign, might go off his head, as his father had done. There had been rumours that Ernest himself was dead in Berlin. In fact he stayed several months at Windsor, in constant friction with most of the world, and eventually returned to Berlin very much alive.

In 1825, the extra £6,000 which had been refused on marriage was granted to him, ostensibly to educate Prince George. Now Ernest planned a full-scale return to England, a transference of his headquarters. It was fully time. Only one thing had to be arranged—that which had proved impossible ten years ago— the adequate reception of Frederica.

He argued with his elder sister with greater ease than he had with their mother. At last Frederica, alone once more in Berlin, received her summons, and in August, 1829, took Prince George with her to England. Ernest met them at Calais and took her to Windsor. All the Royal Family and

most of the Cabinet had been gathered there to receive her.
Dorothea de Lieven waited on her and reported her "an
excellent person."

Settling at last, and perhaps for ever, in the foreignness of
England, Frederica seemed to have found a good deal of contentment. All the Solms-Braunfels children were settled now.
Prince George was growing up tall and handsome, with a
naughty delight in making the sentries at Kew turn out for him
over and over again. George IV treated her with consideration.
Wellington urged the Duchess of Kent to write a civil welcome.
Adelaide, Duchess of Clarence, liked her as she liked them all,
and loved little George dearly.

Gossip and scandal still raged around Ernest and even touched
Frederica, but there is no proof that either husband or wife was
very much disturbed by these things.

Then George IV died, and William IV came to the throne.
Little Victoria still flourished under the total, if sheltering,
blanket of mother-love, so that it did not look to Frederica
now as if she would be Queen of England. But if Ernest lived,
and there seemed no reason why he should not, she would
undoubtedly be Queen of Hanover. They stayed on at Kew,
where Ernest took the deepest interest in the Church, and young
George grew on into his teens, tall and good-looking, with
charming, very German, manners.

The Reform Bill, to which Ernest was by nature and nurture
bitterly opposed, broke on them like the budding centre of a
new Revolution. Frederica and Adelaide were close together
now, affectionate with each other. Adelaide loved the tall
child who might yet sit on her husband's throne, or even
become Victoria's husband and reign with her. She persuaded
Ernest to let Frederica and the boy call on the Iron Duke at

Apsley House, when those two notable Tories were estranged. Adelaide was always a peacemaker.

Frederica did not share the Duchess of Kent's desire for seclusion from the family. She lived in and amongst them. The boy was often with his aunt and uncle. On one occasion, coming back in the carriage from the theatre with the King, they were pelted by the hooting crowd, and a stone fell in the young Prince's lap. It seemed then to his mother and aunt that revolution was upon them and anything might happen.

Then in 1832 the saddest of catastrophes befell Frederica— her greatest grief since Louisa's death more than twenty years previously. Playing at Kew, Prince George had an accident, and as a result of it, was to lose his sight.

Frederica would not accept it, she was a fighter still. He must go to Hastings, so healthy and warm. He would recover. She injected her own faith into Ernest. Resolutely she went on with daily matters, writing to Lord Eldon with flowers for his birthday "from Kew, which I beg of you to accept, and the cups which accompany this note, and which I beg you will not trouble yourself to answer, as you have better things to do and a night of great business in prospect. . . . Yours very sincerely, Frederica."

Yet her heart was sore, and she was grateful to the family when they all rallied round her; even the Duchess of Kent made formal enquiry. Frederica's heart went out to them. She even earned a rebuke from Ernest for one of their own aides. She had sent his man to the Duchess of Kent with a message about George's health and he was hospitably detained overnight, to be told fiercely by the Duke of Cumberland on his return that his duty lay in looking after Prince George, not in nursery-governessing Victoria. Victoria was not one of those people whom Ernest would have officiously striven to keep alive.

Slowly the sight in their son's eyes faded. He went on growing, tall and slim, charming, kindly, grateful and courteous for every service, uncomplaining and unharassed. But he was undoubtedly growing blind. Frederica resolved that the boy should be taken to see Baron Graefe, the German eye specialist. He had operated on Ernest with great success and there was no need to assume that he would fail with the boy. She decided to take him to Germany.

Lady Bedingfeld has left a record of the farewell party in her Diary: "Thursday, September 19th, 1833. I attended the King and Queen to a farewell dinner at Kew, to the Duke and Duchess of Cumberland. . . . When we arrived at the King's Palace at Kew, the Duchess of Cumberland holding the Arm of her Beautiful blind Boy, came out to meet the Queen . . . in a minute the King left the room with the Duke, and the Queen and Duchess began talking in a low voice in German. Poor Prince George was probably the subject of their conversation, so I kept the other side of the room and entered into conversation with him. (He and Prince George of Cambridge went out together.) . . ." She goes on to describe the dinner; ". . . The Dessert was placed on the table from the beginning, in the German fashion. . . . The King gave the health of the Duke and Duchess, with a few very affecting words on the Subject of the cause that takes them out of the Country! A dead Silence of some minutes followed, the Duchess was much overcome. At last the Duke arose, and in tone of voice that proved he *felt*, returned thanks. . . ."

The expedition was made, but it was unsuccessful. George returned blind and so he would remain until the end of his days.

Frederica of Mecklenburg-Strelitz, (1778-1841)
Duchess of Cumberland

The Secret Marriage of Prince Augustus Frederick (Duke of Sussex) with Lady Augusta Murray, Rome, 1793

From a contemporary drawing

Never again would he look out of the windows of his home at
Kew and enjoy the wilderness of summer green and see the
birds whose singing could still delight him.

His cousin, the Princess Victoria, lived on and reached her
majority, a secluded Princess, whom few people ever saw.
Only then did William die. Frederica indeed became Queen,
not of England, but Hanover. Ernest hurried over at once to
hustle Adolphus, the Viceroy, back to England and to sweep
away as much as possible of the work he had watched his
brother do.

And now Frederica, after many years, went back to Hanover,
to the Herrnhausen palace, with Monbrilliant to enjoy as a
summer residence. She went back to reign where her mother
had died.

It was the last epoch of her life, and the shortest. It was also
happy, for she was a popular Queen and she herself was glad to
be in Germany again and able to visit Berlin once more. She
was there in 1837 with King Ernest, their son, the Crown
Prince, and his elder brother, Charles Solms.

Then, towards the end of 1840, Frederica's great vitality
began to fail. She was not old, but life had been strenuous and
she was tired. 1841 came, and even the spring brought no
improvement. She was in bed for three months, the only long
illness of her life, and Ernest was constantly at her side. Prince
George stayed with her, and the other children came too. The
younger Frederica, Duchess of Anhalt-Dessau, was there with
Ernest and George when Frederica died.

After her death her rooms were left as they had been, the
candles lighted at night on the brilliant dressing-table, the
dressers and pages kept in attendance. And every night Ernest
went in alone to pray at her bedside.

o

In a letter to Viscount Strangford he writes her epitaph: " . . . your kind and sympathetic letter in this—for me—unbearably heartbreaking business, one which has completely annihilated me and destroyed all my worldly happiness, accustomed as I was for near thirty years to talk over with her, and consult her often and often when in the greatest difficulties. I always found the advice she gave me and the opinion she formed the justest, the truest; for of all Women I have known, believe me she had the soundest judgment and the clearest perception, void of all the pettiness one so often meets, having at heart but one wish, and one object, my Honour and Character; besides she possessed such a sweet and amiable character, that she knew how to soothe me and tranquillize my mind when irritated and disgusted at all the ingratitude and hostility I met. Her loss to me is irreparable, and I can say life is now become to me a burden. . . .

"Few men in any situation, certainly in my Rank of Life, were ever so blessed with one of the best, most amiable, and accomplished wives as I was. For believe me, her mind was the most accomplished, and having been witness to all the calamities that took place here on the Continent, was perfectly *au fait* with all that had taken place; this had formed her mind and given a solidity to her thoughts. Perhaps there never were in any family four sisters more distinguished for their Intelligence than the four Duchesses of Mecklenburgh, acquainted as they were with all the great statesmen of those days. They had thus acquired more the habits of political insight than many men. Excuse my dwelling so much on this subject, but my heart is so completely broken, my soul and mind so engrossed with my dreadful loss, that I am unable to do my own duties which my position here demands of me. . . ."

LADY AUGUSTA MURRAY

THE LADY AUGUSTA MURRAY was the daughter of an Empire builder. The Earl of Dunmore was one of those upstanding personalities which are an inexhaustible source of national self-congratulation. He helped to confer the boon of sovereignty on the American States, by the simple procedure of irritating the colonists until they decided to sever their home ties.

He and his wife could claim every advantage of lineal descent, drawing blood from royal houses of England, France, Scotland and Holland, and numbering William of Orange and the French Charles VII amongst their ancestors, as well as the illustrious Italian family of d'Este.

At about the time of the birth of his daughter, Augusta, the Earl became Governor of the City of New York (it was before the War of Independence). The city's Recorder, Thomas Jones, welcomed him on behalf of the Common Council, and Lord Dunmore replied suitably that, "With your assistance I am not under the least doubt of seeing the most perfect order and tranquillity reign throughout this City." He had entered the Foot Guards as a young man, and it is extremely likely that he had, in fact, no doubts at all on any reasonable subject. Six years later, a pen was lifted on that same side of the Atlantic, to trace out the strong, effectual words that begin with the *noble apologia* . . . "When in the course of human affairs . . . "

Meanwhile, Lord Dunmore had proceeded to Virginia, where he exasperated the colonists.

His Empire building suffered a brief pause during the War of Independence, but in 1787 he was back in the saddle as Governor of the Bahamas. Nassau, however, was made of tougher stuff than New York. He continued to be high-handed, but in the ancient Bahama House of Assembly he found men whose indomitable will to belong to the British Empire could survive almost any rough handling.

Augusta, the fourth daughter, was brought up by her mother, another high-handed individual, in the manner befitting her rank. She was reputed to be beautiful, witty and intelligent. She had a strong sense of duty, fixed and unalterable principles, was generous, devoted, widely travelled and cultivated.

The Countess of Dunmore, not invariably at her husband's side during his arduous duties, and reputed during her younger years to be not incapable of relaxation and consolation, liked to travel on the Continent. Rome, so secure from the troubled whirlpool of republican France, was a natural enough place to choose, in December of 1792.

There was always a large British colony in Italy, and events had increased it. The last of the Stuarts brought their followers. With the closure of France and the troubled state of Germany, Rome became the Mecca of the cultured travellers. Young Prince Augustus Frederick, son of the King of England, was in Rome too with a suitable escort of Hanoverian gentlemen. Augustus had been brought up as a Hanoverian Prince, and it seemed highly improbable that he would ever settle in England. Like his brother Adolphus, he was neither so headstrong nor so intelligent as his elder brothers. He had considerably more moral sense than some of them, and all the sentimental urgency of his race.

It was in Rome that he met Augusta Murray, seeing her first, by report, as she came out of the Church of Saint Giacomo. Her shoe-string was untied, and he knelt to fasten it.

The English colony was sociable. The young Prince, in his twentieth year, was welcomed. It was easy to make further acquaintance with the charming young woman, a few years his elder and much his mental superior. He was not bad-looking, in the heavy Guelph style. He was musical, liked to be considered cultivated and at the same time a good fellow. Unlike his brothers, he had remarkably little understanding, through lack of first-hand experience, of the disciplinary powers of his father. He had not yet come up against George III.

Soon notes and letters were passing between the pair in Rome. She was apostrophised as "Goosy" and "Gussy." Her own diary, at the end of March, recorded rather confusedly, "O Lord, Creator of all things, I am not worthy of the mercies you lavish upon me, but yet I dare not trust them." The naïve suggestion that total lack of merit is the title to infinite bounty may merely be a slight grammatical or sentimental lapse. Report says that the Prince had contrived to give her a copy of *The Tempest*, wherein, fondly underlined by the royal adorer, she could read, "O, if a virgin, and your affections not gone forth, I'll make you Queen of Naples."

Whether or not Lady Dunmore realised that Augustus was making proposals of marriage to her daughter, and without any form of authority from his parents or her own, she must have seen his devotion. So must the not overbright Hanoverian gentlemen accompanying the Prince, but they would not be likely to take so serious a view of the situation. With German ideas on the subject of royal marriages, they probably did not even consider a marriage possible.

Possibly it was the sheer romance of the situation that made the couple keep their affairs to themselves. Possibly, on the other hand, it is a tribute to the unreasonableness of George III that even a son who knew him so little should not trouble to approach him in the matter. His consent would never be given. It was nothing that Augusta was unexceptionable personally, as well-descended and well-educated as the pick of the fräuleinish German princesses who were deemed so eligible. English noblemen had never held sovereign powers over their estates, and they were therefore incapable of siring suitable brides for Hanoverian princes.

Quite apart from royal anger, the lovers had to face a difficult problem. For without the royal consent, a marriage between them would not be legal. Furthermore, Augustus was not yet of age. Had he been Prince of Wales he would at eighteen have been considered fit to guide the destinies of Empire, with the sole assistance of a royal conscience and the government then in power. But no prince or princess was able to marry without the consent of the reigning sovereign—who might be a younger first cousin—until the age of twenty-five. Even then, if consent were refused, it would be a long and battle-scarred campaign before the marriage could be achieved.

Augustus and Augusta, therefore, desired the impossible. In her diary she commented sadly on the proposed exchange of vows in place of a regular ceremony. "What are oaths unsanctioned there (at the altar)? They bind the honourable, but they do not satisfy the world." Virginity, for her, could expire in no less hallowed surroundings than the bridal bed. Those were her principles, and she was surely right in maintaining them.

They decided on a wedding religious enough to be satisfying, if its fragile authenticity had still to be guarded from hard, cold legal scrutiny. She searched for an American pastor, or, failing that, an Armenian patriarch. Both were Christian dignitaries, but surely so dissociated from the King's justice that they could hardly be said to move in the same world.

Finally, Augustus had the idea of approaching Mr. Gunn, an English clergyman in Rome. He would state the case at its strongest, appeal as a man desiring above everything to preserve the status of the woman he loved and to testify to his intentions. In other words, to enter into lawful matrimony. He told it all to Augusta. She wrote back, full of hope too, but still strong in her unshakable resolve to abide by her principles. "Then, my treasure, you say you will talk of honour to him. There is no honour in the case; if there is," she added with some fire, "I will not marry you. I love you, and I have reason to hope and believe you love me; but honour in the sense you take it is out of the question. I cannot bear to owe my happiness to anything but affection: and all promises, though sacred in our eyes and those of heaven, shall not oblige you to do anything towards me that can in the least prejudice your future interests. As for honour, with the meaning Mr. Gunn will annex to it, I am ashamed to fancy it: he will imagine I have been your mistress, and that humanity, commonly termed honour, now induces you to pity me, and so"—there is an engaging innocence in Augusta's analysis of the thought processes of a royal rake—"and so veil my follies by an honourable marriage. My own beloved Prince, forgive me if I am warm upon this. I wish you to feel that you owe me nothing: and whatever I owe you,

I wish to owe to your love and to your good opinion, but to no other principle. Tell Mr. Gunn," she sweeps on, "my own Augustus, that you love me, that you are resolved to marry me, that you have pledged your sacred word: tell him, if you please, that upon the Bible you have sworn it, that I have done the same, and nothing shall ever divide us; but don't let him imagine that I have been vile. Do this, my only love, but pray take care of the character of your wife, of your Augusta."

Augustus was not only an honourable young man, but he was deeply in love, and with a girl some few years older than himself. This at an age when a very few years, balanced on the woman's side, give an immeasurable degree of command and power. "I am yours, my soul, ever yours," he replied, with promises of obedience.

But all George III's family were affectionate by disposition, and none of them particularly well-balanced. What he wanted, he must have. He was sick for the love of a lady, and she must and should be his. By April 4th he was frantic. He had taken no food for two long days and nights. "I must be married or die," he diagnosed. "You alone can make me: you alone shall, this evening. . . . O Augusta, my soul, let us try; let me come: I am capable of everything"; the royal Habakkuk declared, "I fear nothing. . . ." He ends with the same pronounced certainty on medical points. "I shall go mad, most undoubtedly."

Mr. Gunn fortunately was not obdurate, and Augusta was able to reply, "My treasure, my dearest life and love, how can I refuse you? And yet dare I trust to the happiness your letter promises me? You shall come if you wish it: you shall do as you like; my whole soul rejoices in the assurances of your love, and to your exertions I will trust. I will send to . . . but I fear the badness of the night will prevent his coming. My mother," she gives the firm directive, "has ordered her carriage at half past seven, and will not, I fear, be out before the half hour after. To be yours to-night seems a dream that I cannot make out." She goes on with simple Elizabethan frankness: "The whole day have I been plunged in misery, and now to awake to joy is a felicity that is beyond my ideas of bliss. I doubt its success: but do as you will: I am what you will: your will must be mine, and no will can ever be dearer to me, more mine, than that of my Augustus, my lover, my all."

The victim was willing, Mr. Gunn was ready, the Prince was determined. On April 4th they were married, and from then on, for the soft Italian summer that followed that wild Mediterranean night, Augustus and she managed to keep their secret. At night he would climb into her hotel; there would be a brief ardent interlude, and then an equally secret retreat. Her people were as yet to know nothing, and there could be no establishment. As a matter of fact, he would have had nothing on which to keep an establishment, for he had not yet been promoted to full adult status and given a dukedom and a grant. It was convenient indeed that the Dunmores should continue to feed and clothe his bride and thus, indirectly, to nourish his heir.

For Augusta, after the habit of young matrons, was pregnant. And Augustus was extremely anxious and most attentive. His attachment was patent before, now it was more pronounced than ever.

In the summer, at Florence, Lady Dunmore had to be told everything—about the marriage, their hopes and their fears, the news of the baby coming, the dread of royal displeasure. Some degree of royal displeasure had, in fact, been incurred already. Reports had been carried back to England, and it had been decided that Augustus was obviously *lié* with a young lady to a degree to excite scandal. And, having regard to her parents' position, it would be scandal of a difficult kind.

Augustus was recalled to England and the young couple were separated. Lady Dunmore, who had no wish to see the marriage dissolved, acted with vigour. She brought Augusta and the other daughter whom she was chaperoning back to England. They went to 16 Berkeley Street, and, as autumn advanced, Augusta rounded in discreet comfort, with her Augustus at hand to cherish and encourage.

One problem continually exercised them. The need for secrecy was great, but the need for absolute certainty as to the complete validity of the marriage was even greater. Not only was there Augusta's position and scruples to consider, but there was also the Dunmore family. A purist would probably say that they were, in this case, marrying rather beneath them, but the fact that Augustus was a younger son of a monarch tended to offset much that was unrefinedly Teutonic in his background.

There were precedents for similar marriages, for instance, a Duke of Cumberland and Walpole's fair niece. But to make matters more sure, they decided to marry yet again. Mr. Gunn had united them by Anglican rites, it is true, but in a foreign city and without witnesses. He knew them, who they were, and the reason for the whole procedure. In England, however, under the immediate shadow of the Royal Marriage Act with its pains and penalties, it would be exceedingly hard to find a clergyman willing to take upon himself such a burdensome intelligence and still perform the ceremony. It was decided on this occasion, therefore, to disguise their identity, but to secure witnesses.

St. George's, Hanover Square, was the church chosen. Augusta went to the clergyman and told him that she wished to be, not married, but remarried. It was, she explained, a family custom when a bride over twenty-one took a husband yet a minor; they remarried on the husband's coming of age. In actual fact, Augustus was now twenty-one, so that she was keeping as close to the truth as possible. She gave the name, too, as Frederick, Mr. Augustus Frederick. It was apparently a name common enough to arouse no suspicion.

In order to establish residential qualifications, they took lodgings with a man who kept a coal hole in South Molton Street. On December 5th, seven months and a day from that stormy Roman night, they remarried. Their landlord and landlady were among the witnesses; so was Lady Dunmore, and she brought with her another daughter. A man from Twickenham and the clerk of the parish also were present. It was quiet and soon over, and no rumours spread to trouble Augusta. Even the publication of their banns had created no suspicion.

Augusta at once went down to Essex, to await, in the unencouraging depths of an East Anglian winter, the birth of their son. He made his appearance on January 13th, 1794.

Instantly the bomb burst. Hardly was Augustus *fils* safely in this world, than his parents' secret had reached the King. Lord Loughborough told him, and he took it fairly well. Augustus *père*, alarmed at what the future might hold, left England on the 16th. The very day after the King had learned that there had been a marriage, a writ was applied for to set it aside. That was the immediate reaction.

Away down in Essex, in the gloom of January, Augusta lay abed with the responsibilities of a two-day-old baby, while her husband was en route for exile and her father-in-law was busying himself with attempts to nullify her marriage.

The Privy Council bent its collective mind to an examination of the facts. Lady Dunmore was questioned, Lord Thurlow maintaining that the young lady was considerably older than her spouse and that Lady Dunmore had been *au fait* with the entire romance which was, in fact, no more than a plot to entice and entrap an innocent boy. Lady Dunmore protested that her daughter was but a girl, not more than a year or two older than Augustus; she could not, unfortunately, remember exactly when Augusta had been born.

Lord Eldon records the solemn farce played out when the priest who had remarried them in England came to be questioned as to how he had allowed such a thing to happen, and how he had not been struck by the names when reading out the banns. The rector protested that he could not know that they were not *bona fide* residents in the parish. Frederick was a common name there, and in any case he had two thoroughly respectable curates on whom he had always laid the most solemn injunctions not to marry any parties without the fullest enquiries. "The curates were then examined, and they said theirs was a most respectable parish clerk, who wore a gown, and they had always most solemnly given a like injunction to him." The clerk reported that he was blessed with the most excellent wife, who conducted these matters for him, and on whom he laid the strictest behest to make due and thorough investigation. The lady then made her appearance and pleaded the age-old preoccupations of the housewife. "She must sometimes be about her own and not the parish business: but that she had two female servants, as discreet as any in the parish, and she had always given them a like solemn injunction."

Unfortunately for His Majesty, those who had drafted the Royal Marriage Act had rather over-reached themselves in the matter of sanctions. "Unluckily," pointed out Lord Eldon, with acid delight, "they had made all parties present at the marriage guilty of felony: and as nobody could prove the marriage except a person who had been present at it, there could be no prosecution, because nobody present could be compelled to be a witness."

It was a difficult moment, but the King was undeterred. Before the summer was out, and in spite of every effort on the part of the bride and her family, he managed to get the marriage finally set aside. Augustus, from distant sun-soaked Italy, protested bitterly. He even went so far as to ask to be allowed to resign his rights, to lose his place in the succession, to become merely a private gentleman, if he could keep his charming and virtuous wife and legalise the position of his infant son and heir. George III naturally would hear nothing of this absurd suggestion. He ordered the young man to Berlin, and considered the matter closed.

Neither bride nor groom was so readily defeated as that.

There had been much argument, and would be more later, over the Hanoverian position, to name one point only. Augustus was a Prince of Hanover, in the direct succession, and the Royal Marriage Act of England could not control the marriage of Prince Augustus Frederick of Hanover, or illegitimise his issue by the virtuous Princess Augustus Frederick, formerly Lady Augusta Murray. It might be an even more eccentric marriage there than in England, for German royalty liked to breed from no lesser stock, but surely it was valid.

Meanwhile Augusta, who had had a very bad time in childbed, had recovered, and the baby was well established. The couple decided to be separated no longer. Augusta, unlike her husband, had the solid support of her family, and she was able to procure a false passport and slip over to Berlin with her baby. Certainly she would have been stopped had the King known, but as it was, they made the crossing and jolted across Germany. The family was reunited.

Now at last, nearly two years after their marriage, they could set up an establishment for the first time. It seemed to be the beginning of peace and freedom, and they laid plans reaching far ahead.

England, turbulent and democratic, was having considerable fun at the expense of the Royal Family. A scurrilous pamphlet, on the matrimonial history of "Young Juba," gave a bold and rollicking account of the whole affair. The man's name, Young Juba. The lady's name, "The beautiful and captivating Lady A.M." Where they met, at a ball. He said to her, "Let the sufferings of a lover plead as an excuse for my boldness in thus addressing you, accomplished as you are by every captivating charm. Vouchsafe, therefore, most lovely of your sex, to bless me with an interview, that I may personally convince you of the sincerity and honour of my love. Then all my fortune at your feet I'll lay, and follow you through all the world. AF" She said to him, "The prospect is so high to climb that, should I reach the summit, I might soon fall from it, and dash the bark of ambitious love upon the rock of despair, never, alas! to rise again." And the consequence was summarised with salacious despatch.

Berlin received them more calmly. She was the legal and equal wife of the Electorial Duke, with the title of Princess Augustus Frederick. Their infant was the Prince Augustus. His father expressly and more than once made wills in the baby's favour, and the two parents in the meantime enjoyed the society of Berlin and awaited the passage of time.

For they still had a very strong hope. In 1798, Augustus would be twenty-five, at which age he could on more equal terms take on an encounter with the Royal Marriage Act. For four contentedly wedded years Augusta cherished this hope, and they were, perhaps, the happiest years of her life.

There were, of course, the usual financial difficulties on the horizon. George III, spendthrift himself, was not a generous father, and none of his sons had a real taste for strict economy. Augustus and Adolphus were the two most easily contented, but even they felt that though they must live, their income was quite often insufficient to achieve this purpose.

However, 1798 came in time, and Augusta felt more than encouraged. They were happy, she was acknowledged and received in their own circle, the little boy was alive and well, and Augustus was writing, on advice, a long and correct letter to Lord Erskine. He was not with her at the time, he was writing from Naples, at the end of January. His asthma never allowed him to winter even in England, and made the Mediterranean climate advisable.

He began by setting out in some detail the early history of the Union. "After four months' intimacy, by which I got more fully acquainted with all her endearing qualities, I offered her my hand unknown to the family, being certain beforehand of the objections Lady Dunmore would have made." The one constant on which Augusta could apparently pin her faith was parental disapproval.

He outlined her attitude. "The candour and generosity my wife showed on this occasion, by refusing the proposal, and showing the personal disadvantages I should draw on myself" were eulogised with copious underlining. He expressly ex-culpated Lady Dunmore from any privity, "for she never was informed of it until three months after." He was frank as to the reason for informing her then: "I was forced to make it known to her, for fear she should occasion my wife to miscarry." That had indeed been a fear of Augusta's, that family correct-ness would prefer abortion to a bastard, even if the mother were unwilling.

He explained the second marriage, made to ensure Prince Augustus's legitimacy, and grew indignant over the setting aside of his marriage. The Law Suit was "conducted with great inhumanity, as it was not only not sanctioned by the laws of our own country, but even in strict defiance of them. My wife was prosecuted the second day after she was brought to bed, perfectly defenceless, for her husband was absent."

He went back to Berlin full of hope.

Augusta waited on through the summer, but the outcome was the final crash of their hopes. The marriage was definitely declared to be null. There were left only complicated proced-ures involving an approach to the House, and, at this juncture, funds were running short.

In 1800 he sent her back to England, in the hope that an increase in his grant would follow. It is hard to realise how much hope and fear must have fluctuated in her heart at that time. For the strongest of all weapons, the one most frequently successful in bringing any one of the brothers to heel, was to refuse financial aid. That he loved her, she knew, but if a larger grant were to be given conditional on leaving her, who could tell the outcome? The position was complicated by the fact that at times after the final pronouncement, she had awful doubts as to her status and that of the boy. For six years now

Eighteenth century Berlin. A view of the Prussian Capital

Miniature of a boy, reputed to be that of the Chevalier d'Este,
son of Prince Augustus Frederick (Duke of Sussex) and
Lady Augusta Murray

she had been the Princess Augustus Frederick, mother of young Prince Augustus. It seemed that so little was needed to set the seal on their peace and happiness, and that little had been refused.

The increase in income also was refused, but later in the year Augustus came over and joined her. They were first in Hertford Street, and later at 40 Lower Grosvenor Street, and once again Augusta was pregnant. He could not stay with her, for his chest troubled him again, and he went to Lisbon for sunshine and dry air. Early in 1801 Jane Austen's young brother, Charles, officer in the *Endymion*, had Augustus for shipmate on the homeward voyage. Jane wrote to Cassandra that "They were very well satisfied with their royal passenger, whom they found jolly and affable, who talks of Lady Augusta as his wife, and seems much attached to her."

It was a happy reunion. In August his daughter, Augusta, was born, a little princess to join the little prince.

And then, just when the quartette might have set out once more, might even in time have broken down opposition and brought their designs to success, Augusta suffered the one real and bitter blow in her kind and courageous life. Augustus threw in his hand.

At the end of the year he was created Duke of Sussex and given his grant—and he left Augusta. One wonders which of them thought then of that little document, drawn up together in Rome before Mr. Gunn came on the scene, "On my knees before God our Creator, I, Augustus Frederick, promise thee, Augusta Murray, and swear upon the Bible, as I hope for salvation in the world to come, that I will take thee, Augusta Murray, for my wife, for better, for worse, for richer, for poorer, in sickness and health, to love and to cherish, till death

P

us do part, to love but thee only, and none other: and may God forget me if I ever forget thee!" That paper, with its little heading, "It is a promise neither of us can break, and is made before God our Creator and all merciful Father," was forgotten now.

It was over. Whatever the more personal aspects of the separation, it is to Augustus's credit that he never, in the remaining twenty-nine years of Augusta's life, regarded it as other than a separation from a living wife.

She was not much over thirty and had two small children and an allowance of £4,000 which her husband made her as soon as he got his grant. By no means all the royal family were unfriendly to her. Kent showed kindness to the boy and William IV appointed him equerry when he came to the throne. Augusta was, in fact, far from friendless. And it appears that she too regarded it as a separation, a disagreement, between husband and wife. She called herself Duchess of Sussex. It is hard to see what else she could have called herself, now that Augustus was Duke of Sussex.

Augustus's views were less clear. He was prepared to keep his vow to marry none other in her lifetime, but he was not prepared to admit that she was the wife of the Duke of Sussex. The children were still taught to call themselves Prince and Princess, Augustus and Augusta of Sussex.

She found her grant more illusory than she might have hoped. Three years later she had to apply to the Court of Chancery to obtain aid in getting payment, and they refused to help her. 1805 was a tangled year, with money and other worries on her mind, and the problem of the children's status rankling incessantly.

And then, the year after that, Augustus himself actively

entered the field against her. He brought an action to stop her from using the Royal Arms and calling herself Duchess of Sussex. How far from the day when he had promised to love and to cherish "till death us do part."

The matter had once again to come before the King, and a compromise was found. She was given the King's licence— an unusual way of conferring rank—to call herself Countess d'Armeland, sometimes rendered d'Armaland. The children took the surname of that noble Italian house with whom they were on both sides related—d'Este—Mademoiselle and the Chevalier d'Este. There was a romantic and foreign ring to it. There was also an income, a pension, for her.

Augusta was still obstinate. True, little Augustus had been left in the Hanoverian succession, from which there was no obvious way of winkling him out, but that was the sum total of practical recognition. The little Augusta was also legitimate in Hanover. But their mother could not bring herself to stop impressing upon them that they were the true and legal offspring of their father, as he had himself once so stoutly maintained.

She settled with the children in Kent. She lived at Ramsgate, having an estate on the East Cliff, developed later as the Mont Albion Estate, when she could look down on the sands and on that busy little port, built for the Russian and West Indian trade.

It was not a very cheerful time for her. John Murray, Earl of Dunmore, was home from his Empire making-and-breaking, an old man getting on for eighty. Augusta was devoted to her own family—they indeed supported her loyally throughout— and she nursed her father when he was ailing. His wife, Charlotte, was still alive and with him. She had been tamed a little by the passage of years and was now an exemplary old lady whom virtuous acquaintance could no longer shun; but she was getting on in years, and it was Augusta who tended the aged earl. She did not merely order his comforts; she nursed him with her own hands. In fact, in moving him on one occasion, she injured her spine so seriously that the trouble persisted all her life.

Then, just when young Augustus was fifteen, the age when he needed not only guidance but also a champion, the Earl of Dunmore died. It was in the chill of February, in 1809.

But more trouble was ahead. Augustus objected to the fact that his children were being brought up to consider themselves royal. In spite of the limited nature of the paternal recognition given them, he reserved the right to remove them from their mother, and now he appointed Lord Moira as guardian.

For Augusta it was a cruel blow, and she appealed.

Ramsgate still called her, and would always call her, Duchess of Sussex; she was not deliberately making trouble either for Augustus or for the royal family. Augustus seems to have been quite fond of his children, but he had no intention of stomaching their pretensions. It was courtesy and courtesy alone that preserved them in their comforts, and pure sentiment and honour—Augusta had once dreaded that word—which held him to his vow not to marry in their mother's lifetime.

Augustus d'Este, at any rate, was devoted to his mother. He still saw as much of her as he could, and it is possible that there were occasional stormy passages with his father. His uncles accorded him friendship and protection, and Julie de St. Laurent, still with her Edward, the Duke of Kent, welcomed him at their home when, he records, "all ingress under the Paternal roof, for a time, was denied me."

Augusta saw him enter the Army, and it was a great grief

to her when, in 1815, he was sent across the Atlantic to the American theatre of war. On board he made friends with the dashing Harry Smith of the Light Division, he who had wedded an infant bride in Badajos Camp and carried her campaigning along with him. Augustus was still in the Hanoverian succession, in fact at one time only blind George of Cumberland stood ahead of him, and this was, as could be expected, very much in his mind. The vivid Harry, so little his elder in some ways, and a wary, experienced soldier to boot, took his fancy enormously, and looked for high appointment at Hanover, if the lad ever reigned there.

However, nothing more exciting happened than his ultimate return to England, where his mother was living quietly and tending his grandmother, an old lady indeed now. Her father's death deprived Augusta of a very strong support. Left alone, she ceased to raise any claim for her rights, let alone to fight for them with the courage and zeal that the battle had once brought forth.

Her generosity was still undaunted, however. She would make gifts freely, even when her funds were low. On one occasion, unable to produce cash and unwilling to incur an overdraft, she relieved a friend's need by the loan of a large piece of plate. It could be pledged to raise the funds required.

In 1818 her mother died, and was buried with her father. Augusta, now over forty, mourned her sadly. She could not help wishing that, for the children if not for her, all would one day be well, but now she tried to further her case by quiet acquiescence under the fate befallen her. Recognition, so far as she was concerned, would be too late. Only for their sake were all the papers now locked away—Sir J. J. Dillon's opinion, all the letters, and those self-written "marriage lines."

The young Augusta was growing up now. It was she who, later, gave the site for Trinity Church at Ramsgate. There, when the East Cliff Estate was opened up, the long flight of steps cut from the cliff down to the beach were named Augusta Stairs.

In Kensington Palace, far from the quiet seaside house, Augustus bustled amongst his collections, which, as the years went by, included the friendship of the widowed Lady Cecilia Buggin. How much Augusta was told of the acquaintance, how deeply she resented it, is unrecorded. At any rate, it was not to trouble her for very long.

Early in March of 1830 she died, and the story that began in Rome was ended on the bleak Channel coast in early spring.

Augustus celebrated her death by marrying the Lady Cecilia Buggin, but he had not heard the last of his family and their claims. The young Augustus filed his claim at once, in 1831, demanding recognition of his birth and a royal dukedom. The papers that were locked away by his mother were produced, and his father's love letters put in as evidence, without his father's consent. He was unsuccessful.

On his father's death, in 1843, he and his sister tried once more, their case handled by Sergeant Wilde, later Lord Truro, that obstinate, intelligent man. This time the son claimed succession to the Dukedom of Sussex, and one, at least, of his royal relations gave him no encouragement at all. Ernest of Cumberland, now King of Hanover, took the gravest exception to the idea. On May 29th, 1844, he wrote from Hanover, "last year when in England I used every argument in my power, and every entreaty I could, to Augusta d'Este, to bring her to desist from this mad and indelicate step; I warned her against Sergeant Wilde, who I told her could have no other object but to pick her and her brother's pockets, for he must very well know that no House of Lords could ratify a Marriage contracted contrary to the Law of the Land, and she must excuse me if I told her in plain English that all I had heard of the transaction I was morally convinced that no real Marriage had ever taken place at Rome, and that as to the second marriage which took place at St. George's, Hanover Square, that being in England must be contrary to Law, and therefore void; besides, Mr. Augustus Frederick was a false name, and, therefore, not only would it show up her Mother's character, but what was equally as bad, would be a slur on the character of her Father."

A few years later Augusta married Wilde, malice saying that she did it because they owed him more than they could pay him. Her brother, Colonel Sir Augustus d'Este, did not live so very long after his parents, dying in 1848, still with his claims refused.

Thus by no means whatsoever, either before or after her death, was Augusta Murray to be allowed to realise her dearest wish for a respectable and recognised marriage to the man of her choice. Of all the gallery of "Unsuccessful Ladies" she knew the least happiness and had the saddest years to live out alone.

THE DUCHESS OF INVERNESS

CECILIA LAETITIA, Duchess of Inverness, was a short, stout, bustling, happy little party. She had some success in life, a success all the more definite because it was achieved amongst people who could not help realising that she deserved it. It is only merit that is grudgingly rewarded.

She lived to be an old lady, growing more and more part. of that world into which she had been moved, settling and sheltering in Kensington Palace. She entered it so quietly that she was officially not there at all, and she left it finally with the Prince of Wales as chief mourner at her funeral.

He was not the Prince of Wales who had wooed and won Maria Fitzherbert. Cecilia lived on, like Augusta of Cambridge, from the age of Beau Brummell to that of the bowler hat. It was the future Edward VII who followed her to her grave.

Her childhood, spent in Ireland, was rather tense. Her father was the Earl of Arran and one of the fifteen original knights of the Irish Order of St. Patrick, instituted by George III. Her mother was the Earl's second wife and she acquired at her marriage no less than nine stepchildren. To these she added seven children of her own. Cecilia was the second girl of this new family.

They were not wealthy, but in the years around 1800 to 1810 she and her two full sisters were well enough off in Merrion Square society. Dublin did not demand vast resources. The

Countess was in any case a woman of determination. She lost her husband in 1809, and her stepson duly became third Earl of Arran. Most of her children and stepchildren did well, for they did not lack drive and energy, but the Countess had additional zeal, as was perhaps natural in a widow with many children to establish in a difficult world.

It is reported that even her whist winnings and those of Cecilia and her sisters were important in the family finances, and that one kindly friend always played his worst when against her so that he might help to swell her small takings.

The new Earl had no wish to remain an obscure member of the Irish peerage, nor had his stepmother any intention of allowing her daughters to languish away into the beds of profitless squireens. Times were hard and Elizabeth, Countess of Arran, was said to grow no more gentle in the midst of her perplexities. However, £400 was raised on a *post obit* to equip the girls for a session in Bath, and by 1814 the eldest brother had his London house, in Dover Street, well established.

He had married, extremely successfully, Mary, last of the Tyrells of Heron Hall, in Essex. She had been a leader of the fashionable world and at one time Governess to the Princess Charlotte of Wales, now growing up and so near to her death. Mary Tyrell was also a woman who had many real friends.

From the house in Dover Street, Cecilia was married in 1815. She was already somewhere between twenty-five and thirty, short and plump, cheerful, fond of comfort, gay and ready for a party, but lacking in that touch of elegance and romance that can in itself be a dowry to a portionless daughter.

She married, as his second wife, Sir George Buggin, at one time of Thetford Hall, in Norfolk. They were married by royal licence, properly and becomingly, on May 2nd, and

Cecilia settled down happily enough in her new home in Great Cumberland Place. She could entertain now, go about, and indulge within reason her taste for clothes and jewels.

The marriage lasted for ten years. Sir George was considerably her senior and he died in May of 1825, at the age of sixty-five. She was left a plump, kindly little widow in the quiet lands between thirty-five and forty.

She stayed on at Great Cumberland Place and, after a suitable interval, she continued to entertain and be entertained. She met old friends and made new ones, amongst them a gentleman who resided at Kensington Palace. He was bound, under his own word, not to marry during the lifetime of Lady d'Armeland, then living near Ramsgate. For this gentleman was Augustus, Duke of Sussex.

In 1830, Augusta d'Armeland died. In 1831, Lady Buggin changed her name. The phrase is not facetious. That is literally what she did. She abandoned the somewhat unattractive surname bestowed upon her by the late Sir George and assumed by deed poll her mother's maiden name, Underwood. She was the daughter of an earl. She became now the Lady Cecilia Underwood, and in her own house, the mansion in Great Cumberland Place, she married once more, again by special licence. Augustus had for the second time acquired a wife who could only occasionally and unofficially be called Duchess of Sussex.

He had been attached to Cecilia for a considerable time, had loved this merry little lady, so good-natured and happy and human. It was a highly successful marriage, too. Augustus had a taste for gorgeousness. He loaded his little wife with trinkets, and, in May of 1831, Creevey, meeting them both at dinner, reported her as "Ciss Underwood with such a profusion of

gold bijouterie in all parts that nothing was wanted but something hanging from her nose."

It seems hard that the Dowager Countess could not see the
new establishment, but she had died two years before in Brussels.
However, Cecilia was gaining a new family, for now began the
slow, quiet absorption of Ciss Underwood, until she became
a loved and integral part of the new royal family that was
growing up.

William was on the throne and was ready enough to be civil
to her. She and Augustus received many invitations. Creevey
met them at Lord Grey's in 1832. He even refers to them as the
Duke and Duchess of Sussex. Her favourite phrase of later
years, "Come and dine!" was already on her lips. He records,
in the summer of the following year, that "as I was walking,
Lady Ciss, or Princess Ciss, passed me in her carriage and immediately pulled up. She wished to know if I was disengaged,
as the Duke and she were going to dine quite alone, and they
would be delighted if I would join them. Affable, was it not,
in a r–y–l dame?"

For a time she rented Niddry Lodge on the quiet slope of
Camden Hill, near Kensington Palace, where Augustus had his
apartments and where she would soon join him. For the
moment, however, she was happy amongst the orchards.

There was more than a hint of malice in the comments of
Creevey and some others, but her good-natured kindliness eventually disarmed her critics. She had no advantages of person.
One writer reports her as "very small and common-looking,"
ridiculous in her stiff brocades of gold and silver at the side of
the portly Hanoverian husband. But she loved him dearly, and he
needed her, for his eyes were beginning to fail him. It was cataract,
and he awaited the necessary operation with his sight closing in.

She read aloud to him, injuring her own eyes by peering at the close print in a room heavy with tobacco smoke. But it was a loving service, a pleasure for her to do all she could for him.

She was indeed a part of the family now. When Augustus had the influenza, in the year of the young Queen's accession, Maria Fitzherbert wrote enquiring after him, and Cecilia answered volubly: "I told him of your kind enquiries. He desires me to thank you and give you his love, and say how sorry he is that you have been ill, and we both trust that you will take care of yourself and escape this horrid complaint which seems to spare nobody. I believe the best way is to remain within doors, and I am sure the advice given to you to do so is the best and the only way to avoid it."

That was in the family circle, but the general public had heard little of her. However, in the same year, her husband firmly told Mr. Adolphus that "the world will hear more of her before long," and very soon this came true.

Augustus's niece, Victoria, had fallen in love in her turn with Hanoverian thoroughness. Albert of Saxe-Coburg must be taken into the bosom of the Guelph family, into the British royal house. He would have his place, a difficult and un-comfortable one, as the Queen's husband, and he must also have his precedence.

The reactions of Victoria's uncles when they were asked to step back for this young man were various, but Augustus saw the occasion plainly and simply as one on which one good turn could be bargained for another. He would have no objection to yielding the *pas* to Albert, if Victoria, in her turn, would do something by way of recognition of Lady Cecilia. On those terms, something was quickly, and amicably, arranged.

It was not a complete recognition of marriage. Cecilia did not become Her Royal Highness the Duchess of Sussex, although she was quite often addressed as such. She was made Duchess of Inverness; Inverness being Augustus's second title. It seemed to the two of them a very pleasant and practical way out of a difficulty.

Not all the world was as pleased as they were. The censorious complained that it was no recognition of a respectable connection, but merely a rather shadowy acknowledgment of the fact that a connection might be said to exist. Greville condemned it as "a recognition of the cohabitation . . . it is a very indecent proceeding."

But the two most concerned were happy enough. They went together to a ball at Lansdowne House, were announced as H.R.H. the Duke of Sussex and Her Grace the Duchess of Inverness. Smiling away at his side, in her glory, she received her congratulations. When Victoria arrived at the ball, Augustus went up alone to pay his respects to his niece, and then Cecilia herself was allowed to go to the Queen's table. She must, it was understood, rank as the most junior Duchess, but, a good-humoured little woman of over fifty, she was now received by the Queen as part of the family.

In the same year, at a dinner at Devonshire House, she was given full recognition of her title as Augustus's wife. True, the other principal lady present was the dubious Princess of Capua, who in this case was also accorded full honours.

The couple went on as they had begun, happy amidst Augustus's collection of clocks and Bibles, with the little Duchess inviting their acquaintance to dine. But it was not, for all its happiness, to last much longer.

In April of 1843, Augustus was taken ill with erysipelas. For a time he sought new strength on a diet of turtle soup and orange ices, but there was something more gravely wrong with him. On the morning of April 21st he realised that he was dying, called for his servants, and duly departed this life. He had lived, on the whole, in a blameless and honourable manner, and his widow mourned him sadly.

Some time before his death Augustus had said to Emily Adolphus that she had his full leave to contradict utterly any statement that might be made, after his death, about his papers. He kept none. All letters were destroyed. There was to be no prying and peering. It is impossible not to feel that he was, in part, thinking of his son, Augustus d'Este, whose rights he had once so burned to ensure, whose claims he was now so anxious to quiet, to sweep aside into forgetfulness.

One can be sorry for the shadow of Augusta Murray, and for the "rightful" new Duke of Sussex. But undoubtedly Augustus d'Este's unsuccessful claims made things easier for Cecilia Laetitia. Actually there was no difficulty in recognising both wives as Duchesses of Sussex. Augustus had behaved with great respectability and the young Colonel d'Este could well have been the new Duke of Sussex. However, the refusal of his renewed claims seemed somehow to establish Cecilia the more securely.

The Duchess of Inverness was granted apartments in Kensington Palace; she was now indisputably a member of the circle and was treated as a relative. Adolphus was home from Hanover, and the wicked Ernest with his unwelcome Frederica had gone over for good. The Duchess of Cambridge accepted the stout little Duchess of Inverness, and the former Augusta of Hesse-Cassel had quite decided views on whom she accepted and whom she did not. So far as the royal family were concerned, the days of misdemeanour were over, and a strong almost suburban feeling of family life prevailed.

Little Princess Mary Adelaide of Cambridge, whom Cecilia loved dearly, came up from Kew to see her. When she was older she came sometimes to dine, and to dance afterwards. For the "little Duchess" was a well-known figure in society now. She commanded neither dignity nor sweeping deportment, but there was something about her, something kind and quaint, little and lovable, that drew them all to accept her constant invitation.

Her more intimate parties were a little trying, for the small dining-room was fitted up cosily as a tent, and the cosiness involved an almost total lack of ventilation. The larger room, used for bigger occasions, was far more pleasant.

The FitzClarence family she knew of course, and the other younger ones, but Mary Adelaide seemed to be one of her particular favourites. She gave her a bracelet for a birthday gift one year, went down to Kew, and was tender in her sympathy when her father, Adolphus, died. But if there were fewer of the famous brothers left as the years went by, the family had sprouted new shoots. It was a long time since there had been so many cousins, so much coming and going; one Cambridge princess married, another grew up, the Crown Prince of Hanover was coming over, there was George of Cambridge to be seen, and Victoria was filling her nursery. But still the older leaves fell. In 1857 she went to visit the dying Duchess of Gloucester.

Social life was her great pleasure. She watched the procession of those known to her world as it filed through the tent dining-room or entered in state when the proper reception of royalty demanded all the pomp at her command. The Duc d'Aumale came, Lord Chelsea, and the Duchess of Sutherland, who gracelessly turned one of her balls into a romp. One Christmas Eve, Cecilia dined at Kew with the widowed Duchess of Cambridge. Dr. Quin, Augusta's rather unorthodox physician, was there, and he was the life and soul of the party. Cecilia Laetitia let herself go, for she always found laughter infectious, and they were merry that night, the old and young together.

Mary Adelaide took her time, but in the end she married the Duke of Teck. This was no arranged marriage for they were genuinely in love. It was a great pleasure to Cecilia that Mary Adelaide was given apartments at Kensington adjoining her own. Soon there were little Teck children to visit and to watch coming in and out. Victoria's son, Edward, had married, and there were his children too. It was so nice to see them all, so nice to feel oneself useful, for Mary Adelaide could always send her family in for lunch if she were going down to Kew. It helped the kitchen. There was always "my *kind* neighbour, the dear little Duchess, to rely upon."

So it went on as the seventies turned into the eighties, and the dear little Duchess into a little old woman, doing perhaps a little less, but still twinkling with the good humour that had won Augustus half a century before.

She was between eighty and ninety when, in the winter of 1873, she had a bad stroke. It was mid-February. They all came quickly, exchanged bulletins, asked for news of her. "A very bad account of the dear Duchess of Inverness," wrote the Duke of Cambridge. "She has had a paralytic stroke on the left side. Drove to Kensington, where I saw the dear Duchess, who was perfectly conscious and seemed pleased to see me. Stayed with her but a few minutes. Her mind was quite clear. She gave me all the rings of the late Duke of

Cecilia Laetitia, Duchess of Inverness
From a miniature in the possession of Col. F. J. M. and Miss I. Gore

Augusta of Hesse Cassel, Duchess of Cambridge (1797-1889)
The maternal grandmother of H.M. Queen Mary

Sussex." And he ended, as though it were the most natural thing in the world, "She has seen the Queen twice."

His own mother had suffered the same complaint, away in Germany, not so long before. Now Victoria had this second aunt to worry about. She wrote, in Windsor Castle, "I ran up to Kensington this morning to see our poor, kind old Duchess, whom I found very feeble, but she just knew me and blessed me and all my children. She is stronger again this evening, I hear!"

Indeed, although the Queen herself had said good-bye, the little Duchess was by no means beaten yet. Augusta of Cambridge recovered and managed to return to Kew, and Cecilia Laetitia also struggled against the inertia of partial paralysis. For six months she fought it, and then the heat of August came and she could struggle no more.

She died and was buried at Kensal Green with her husband. Edward, Prince of Wales, was chief mourner, Augusta sent her carriage, Cambridge was there, Lord Camoys represented the Queen, and Mary Adelaide followed her friend. There were no ambassadors' carriages; it was tactfully decided that the little Duchess herself had desired a private, royal family, funeral. Thus she, who had entered a palace almost by the side door, was followed to her last rest by an assembly almost entirely royal.

When the last rites were over they lingered in the vault before returning to the blazing August sunshine. They inspected the Duke's coffin, which had not decayed during the thirty years it had waited there alone, and perhaps they looked again on the plate freshly graven for that day's ceremony: "Cecilia Laetitia, Duchess of Inverness, relict of his late Royal Highness the Duke of Sussex."

The word "widow" would perhaps have taken things a little too far.

Q

THE DUCHESS OF CAMBRIDGE

AUGUSTA WILHELMINA LOUISA was born in July of 1797, born to the troubled, if outwardly prosperous, state of Hesse-Cassel.

Magnificently did the Landgraf, Duke Frederick, drive out every day, still dressed in the attire of the days of Great Frederick. His white pigtail was severely plaited, two liveried footmen ran before his carriage. Twice a year he moved in state between his summer residence, Wilhelmshoehe, and the Belvedere Palace.

In actual fact he was a slave-owner, as were his fathers before him. The prosperity of the country had largely been built up on the hire of her mercenaries, and the tall Hessian levies often marched away to die for a cause which had no interest for them and only a financial one for their Duke. The English hired some of his warriors to help them in their struggle against rebellious colonists on the far side of the Atlantic.

Consequently the little princess and her five brothers and sisters grew up against the splendour of cascades and waterfalls, fine pictures, music, all that culture and civilisation could lavish. They had an adoring mother, daughter of the reigning family of Nassau, and a great deal of affection from the old gentleman, their father.

In 1803, the Landgraf assumed the title of Elector, the Elector of Hesse-Cassel. Napoleon assumed in his turn the imperial title, and became the tyrant lion, crouched to leap. Duke

Frederick thought it wise to recall the sixty or so of his subjects who had commissions in the Prussian army. The spring reviews were cancelled, as an act of balance, to avoid offending the marching French.

Merely to avoid giving offence, however, did not seem to be enough. The Elector asked the Emperor's support for the union of German princes which he was trying to establish. Before Augusta was ten years old she probably heard of her father's peace-loving attempts to butter his bread on both sides. To conciliate him, the Allies gave him unfettered command of the Westphalian army. To conciliate Napoleon, he replaced on the peace establishment a corps held ready for field service. By 1806, when the English withdrew from the Continent to spend six fortress years on the other side of the Channel, a French army of 100,000 menaced his land, and the all-powerful Emperor had lost his cordiality. Indeed, he created a Kingdom of Westphalia for his brother, and Duke Frederick thought it wise to flee, "to avoid useless bloodshed." When "liberation" restored him and his mistress and favourites to the arms of his subjects, he appears to have lost much of his popularity. He drove by unapplauded in his carriage; on his face the dark, cancerous growth that eventually was to kill him.

It was in those years of marching and occupations, battles and forays, requisitionings and pillage, that Augusta grew up. She was the youngest daughter, tall, with dark eyes and eyebrows, her features fining down to a striking beauty. Her expression was tranquil, almost severe as she matured, but it was lightened with a quick charm when she spoke. Her hands were lovely. They were capable also and could tend a flower-bed or pattern fine embroidery, but they remained always lovely, just as her beautiful soprano voice stayed with her on into old age.

When Adolphus, Duke of Cambridge, a high-minded if not overbright bachelor of forty-three, saw her, he decided that "the Princess Augusta would make an ideal Queen for England!"

All his life Adolphus had been put more than a little into the shade. His father approved of him, however; he was the son "who had yet to commit his first fault." Brother Frederick, Duke of York, whom he would one day succeed as Commander-in-Chief, was sorry for him when he was sent in 1813 to a "liberated" Hanover. "Poor fellow! I hope he will succeed in all his undertakings, as it is a great sacrifice. . . ." Even Adolphus's triumphal entry was a little clouded by the fact that brother Ernest, Duke of Cumberland, had hurried there first and rode in as the rescuing hero. It was not clear then, as it became later, that Ernest would succeed to the Hanoverian throne. Even if it had been realised, that saturnine individual had a dangerous reputation, and it was safer to install the unexciting Adolphus as Viceroy.

He did his best. Sir James Milles Riddell says firmly that his manners and address were most prepossessing, his air fine and manly. "Officers of the household copy him and are the most gentlemanlike men as well as the pleasantest set of fellows that you can imagine."

Brother William, Duke of Clarence, separated from Dora Jordan and urged on by Charlotte's death to marriage, trusted Adolphus's judgment enough to ask him to look out for a possible Duchess of Clarence. Adolphus did as he was asked, and his eye lighted on Augusta. It was hard, in the face of so much loveliness, dignity and amiability, to resign her to William, but he was nevertheless prepared to stand aside. William was the more likely to reign, and here was the "ideal

Queen." His own admiration shone through his praise of her, and William, it is reported, decided that the younger brother should at least have his opportunity, and stepped aside. "So Adolphus has her—if she will have *him*," he comments.

There was no hesitation. Before the end of January of 1818 Adolphus was writing to Lady Harcourt, "I really believe that on the surface of the globe there does not exist so happy a being as myself. Every hour I feel that my esteem and attachment for my bride increases; and she is really everything both as to heart, mind and person that I can wish."

They were married in May at the Belvedere Palace in Cassel, and Augusta was whisked off to England almost at once, accompanied by both husband and father, to be married yet again in the presence of the Queen.

Augusta suffered from sea-sickness all her life. How incessantly in the years ahead was the Channel to lay her low, how often was she to face the narrow seas with the old foreboding! When the ship drew in, all she could contrive, hanging in her husband's arms, was a faint nod of greeting to those who welcomed her. But all her life, too, she was a wonderfully sound sleeper, falling quickly into long deep slumber. To this she probably owed the great old age to which she lived and the alert brain that stayed so much younger than her body. By eight the next morning she was recovered, strolling on the pier on Adolphus's arm, dressed in white, with a purple pelisse and scarf. It was early summer and she wore a small straw bonnet with white ostrich feathers.

After the long familiarities of Cassel, the taciturn citizens and deep German passivity, these demonstrative rough English were alarming. Adolphus promenaded her in the park on the Sunday after their arrival, and Augusta, for all her tall dignity, was so alarmed by the milling crowd that she almost fainted. For she was popular with the crowd as well as with the royal family. On one occasion, when she was taken down to Rundle and Bridges, the jewellers in the City, she was recognised in her carriage, and could not move for twenty minutes through the shouting mob.

Augusta and Adolphus were not long in England. Before the winter, he took her back to Hanover, to the Palais, renamed Cambridge House, to the dignities and duties of a Vicereine. It was viceroyalty with all the trappings of royalty itself, a hereditary prince filling by mandate the second throne of his House.

The Duke of Clarence crossed over too, bringing with him his own bride, later Queen Adelaide.

Already Augusta was with child, and her adoring husband, his eyes on the succession, took every possible precaution. Special witnesses were brought to the Palais for the birth, in view of the babe's nearness to the throne. Special couriers were rushed to England to tell the King that there was a child, a boy, little Prince George of Cambridge.

Within a few months two more infants, Victoria of Kent and George of Cumberland, had taken from little George of Cambridge the distant promise of two crowns. But nothing and no one could ever lessen him in Augusta's love. For with the babies came her special genius. She was a clever woman, unusually well-informed, politically interested, and widely read. She was cultivated in the narrower sense too, her soprano voice was trained, her musical knowledge was sound, she read aloud beautifully. But from 1819 on until 1889, for seventy years, her real being was with the children and grandchildren.

They were a handsome family, of an appealing Saxon beauty.

Even the over-idealised Court portraits leave them a deal of charm.

While George was still a baby, his uncle the Prince Regent came to the throne, and in 1821 he visited Hanover. Augusta was not displaced, even if her husband the Viceroy had to step down, for no Queen came with George IV. On October 10th the new monarch made his grand horseback entry into the capital, a coronation was hastily arranged. It was to be one of many for Augusta, and none of them her own, for the "ideal Queen" never reigned.

In 1822 her elder daughter, Princess Augusta Caroline, was born, at Hanover as the brother had been. Augusta Caroline was to live long too, on into the new century, and die as Duchess of Mecklenburg-Strelitz in the old home of Frederica of Cumberland and of her own aunt-mother-in-law Marie, during yet another world war. She did not die until 1916.

That was nearly a century ahead. In quiet Hanover, under the new and liberal constitution given to it by the broad-minded Adolphus, the children throve. Young George nearly died of the scarlet fever, and Augusta always believed that he owed his life to his father who, hastily summoned, came straight from table with his glass of wine still in his hand. The boy begged for it, drank, and turned the corner. He had to be rescued too from a demented assistant teacher, toiling in Freudian entanglements which made him believe that he was condemned to kill the child by whose bedside he nightly, at Augusta's command, read the Bible. For she was vehemently Protestant, proud of an ancestor who had supported Luther, strong in the Reformed faith. Fortunately the assassin was lured safely away.

Between Cambridge House and Monbrilliant, their summer

residence, life went on. Adolphus dutifully imitated his father's domestic manners, resolved, in his own words, not "to forfeit his happiness by any misconduct." Augusta, however, was by no means a copy of her rather limited mother-in-law. Apart from her looks, her sweeping liberal mind and her charm, the was fond of entertaining. Hanover was ready to be summoned, and there were countless visitors from farther afield. Her brother Frederick came, and sister Marie.

It was well for Augusta that her husband remained devoted, for she was too intelligent to have prospered unsupported at that time. Because she was the youngest of the Ladies, and lived longer than any of the others, her life spans an indigestible compass of time. She had her girlhood darkened by the wars of the tyrant Napoleon. Waterloo was fought when she was eighteen and yet she lived to send a message to Victoria on her Jubilee; death did not take her till after her ninety-second birthday. Her daughter, Augusta, died, an enemy alien princess, in Germany during the First World War. Her grandchild Mary, then Queen Dowager of England, was to see her London palace damaged by weapons undreamed of in the eighteenth century, when the madman from Berchtesgaden unleashed the Second World War.

Yet with Augusta of Cambridge all the stages of her life were gradual, ruled and controlled. She moved on now, the lovely young Vicereine and mother, offering hospitality to her widowed sister-in-law, the Dowager Landgravine of Hesse Homburg, who wrote back to her brother, the King, of "the dear Duchess of Cambridge, who has been all goodness to me and considers me in everything. She improves upon one the more one knows her. Her conduct as both wife and mother is very delightful." Sister Elizabeth, commenting on

Adolphus's amiable and devoted attachment and affection, apparently considered that such qualities alone laid an obligation of delight on the wife. If the husband loved and was faithful it would be inexcusable in the wife to be other than happy—a fortunate simplification of emotion in which Augusta was wise enough to concur. At least she was sensible of the treasure she possessed in owning one of George III's more virtuous if less intelligent offspring.

The children progressed well. In the icy winter of 1828–29 they contrived to have chickenpox, but recovered. Adolphus had decided now that George must soon go to England to be educated. He could go to Adelaide, tenderest of aunts, but Augusta suffered in advance for every hour of the separation. Adolphus bought Cholmondeley House as a *pied-à-terre* in England, and hoped to take her over in the summer or autumn of 1829 to arrange it to her liking. In her housekeeping Augusta was meticulous and decided.

The year 1830 brought Louis Philippe to France and a wave of high-minded revolutionary zeal to Europe in general. Belgium fought for national entity, the Duke of Brunswick was forced to flee from his devoted subjects, there were outbreaks at Dresden and at Cassel. But for Augusta the worst struggle of the year was the parting with George. In August he went away and she was left behind with his sister, writing "My Precious George," pathetically, "These are the first words I have to address you by the help of pen and paper, since it is the first time we have ever been separated." He obviously was like other boys, before and since, in ten-year-old horror of maternal demonstrations, for she adds, "Did I not, my angel boy, keep my promise to you to make the parting quick and short? . . ." Next morning she was wishing him well over the voyage. In

May of 1831 she tells him that "Since I love you so unutterably, my good George, I do not like a single day to pass without my having written you at least a few words, otherwise in the evening it seems to me to have been a lost day. . . ."

She saw him again in the summer, taking his sister with her to London. They were nearer the throne now, for William reigned and Adelaide was childless. Certainly there was young Victoria (and always Ernest), but perhaps Victoria could be woven into the pattern of things. She and George were of an age. True she appeared to prefer her other cousin George, the handsome prince of Cumberland, and people were mentioning his elder half-brother, Frederica's son, the Prince of Solms-Braunfels, but nothing could be settled for some time yet.

Augusta had both her children with her when the anniversary of the accession of the House of Hanover was celebrated in August and thirty state barges swept the royal procession down to the opening of the new London Bridge, to watch a balloon ascent, and to lunch with the Corporation. There was something touch-and-go in the atmosphere; the pinions of Europe's left wing were in contagious fine feather, but nevertheless the populace obliged with its countenance and received the tremendous display with affability.

This was more than happened in Cassel, and Augusta, always devoted to her brothers and sisters, thought of them with anxiety. The Duke of Hesse-Cassel, away with his mistress at a watering-place, returned on the murmur of insurrection. The lady was persuaded by frontier demonstrations not to re-enter the country. The Duchess and the young heir returned from exile, to which they had gone when the murder of a valet had looked like an attempt on the life of the young master. There was an official reconciliation fête. But the nominally discarded mistress rumoured a return. Life was hard on reactionary Dukes, and in the end he preferred to bestow a liberal constitution on his people, appoint his son Regent and leave the land, to die a wanderer.

In England there was a coronation once again. The procession formed on Constitution Hill with a squadron of the Life Guards as escort. In Augusta's carriage was the Lady Elizabeth Murray. William was established on the throne now, the devilish Ernest was at one remove only, there was but the life of the little Princess Victoria. And she could not reign in Hanover.

Augusta returned home. Soon she was with child again, and this time it was a shock to her. She was "comfortably happy," as a sister-in-law had said, "and full of my brother's amiable and devoted attachment and affection for her," but she was very much afraid for herself. Her distress alarmed him. He adored her and her fears affected his own health.

Early in December Mary Adelaide—named for the beloved aunt—was born, and Augusta was very ill indeed. The Rabbi of Hanover, Dr. Adler, offered public prayers for the wife of the liberal and gracious Viceroy, and after some anxious days she recovered. Adolphus ordered for her, from Paris, a magnificent toilette, white crêpe and *blonde* over pink, and in it she attended the christening. Her blood ran chilly that winter, the rooms were heated to fainting point, and she left the ceremony to go back to the comforting warmth by the fireside.

Baby Mary Adelaide, heavy in Aunt Mary's arms, owed her alarming weight to a long dress of drap d'argent, pink bows, an enormous train, much Brussels lace, and two supporting pillows.

1834 came, Augusta's health returned, and with the spring she was as strong as before, able to return to society, to visiting, to the opera, and, with devotion, to the theatre. She gave a gay and magnificent masquerade for Adolphus's birthday that year—it was a day she would never cease to celebrate—attiring herself as a fine lady of the seventeenth century. There were quadrilles. After the quadrilles the guests patronised a "Fair" where the noble stall-holders gifted their acquaintance as expensively as they could afford.

It was the habit of Adolphus and Augusta to allow Hanover to see the family unity that prevailed on the viceregal throne, and they would promenade daily in Herrnhausen Avenue, followed by the two elder children. It was just as Adolphus's father had done at Kew, so many years before, with his more ample train. And later, at Kew again, people were to "notice" the little Mary Adelaide, grown to sturdy childhood, and Augusta would insist to the governess that the child must never let a greeting pass unacknowledged. Certainly it would not spoil her to know herself observed, insisted Augusta vigorously, born herself to the semi-publicity of royalty. She would soon get used to it.

Meantime, Augusta did not go over very often to see the beloved son. She had her duties and she was also a consistently bad sailor. However, she made the crossing in 1835 and took both the little sisters with her to stay at Windsor. On August 8th, George was confirmed, and this was an occasion which the whole family took very seriously indeed. They were deeply and sincerely religious, devoutly Protestant. He even felt that he must formally write to his grandfather in his own hand on the occasion. On the 11th, Augusta wrote to her father that "as George felt it to be his affectionate duty to

announce to you his confirmation, I left it to him. . . . It has
been a real great happiness to me, I confess." She added, sadly,
"But I am afraid I shall not be allowed to bring him away with
me; the King, alas, will not yet part with him, and it is so
important now to give him a military education." It was important, too, that he should remain as intimate as possible
with young cousin Victoria. At the moment she had a decided
preference for him over their cousin of Cumberland. They did
not, it is true, see very much of each other. The Duchess of
Kent kept her single chick in strict quarantine. But Adelaide
had, after all, the rights of aunt and queen, and she loved young
George like a child of her own. For the matter of that, she
loved the other George too, Frederica's tall, blind, handsome
son. And Augusta, even if there was a little rivalry, loved her
nephew tenderly.

A week after the confirmation both boys were invested
with the Order of the Garter, and Augusta returned to Hanover.

Her health failed again in the following year, and she lay
there ill, wondering all the time about the son still separated
from her. In July, however, he returned, the first part of his
education completed although he was still under the care of his
military tutor. George had grown up well. He was a rather
impulsive, not over-sophisticated, rather good-looking young
man, full of animal vigour, mamma-ish repressions, good
resolutions and high courage. Augusta recovered and, with
his sisters, could watch him when he drilled his men in the
avenue, at a spot especially chosen so that she could see him.

A good deal was happening in Hanover then. William
obviously could not last for ever and the succession seemed
clear at last. Victoria would succeed in England, and Ernest
would be King of Hanover. He was already making himself a

backstairs influence in Hanoverian politics. It was not, of course, a matter which Augusta could discuss with Frederica at their meetings, for they were very friendly indeed. Was not Augusta's sister, Marie, married to Frederica's brother at Mecklenburg-Strelitz? And would not their son, not so many years later, marry Augusta's elder daughter, "Gussy"? Charles Solms, too, was one of George's friends. It was certain at any rate that Frederica would reign as Queen in Hanover, and Augusta could see that Adolphus was now extremely unlikely to reign anywhere. But for George her ambition was strong and hopeful. Victoria liked him. If that liking led to a marriage, surely it would be necessary for the cousins to reign as equals, joint sovereigns?

When the inevitable happened and the couriers brought word of William's death, George was hurried over at once to England for the funeral. Adelaide's brother crossed with him. George must do his best. And Augusta must pack and go. Ernest had hastened to Hanover to take possession. The Duchess of Gloucester wrote in July that Adolphus lamented his inability to pay his last respects to King William. He could not leave Hanover. "It was necessary for him to wind up the business there as soon as possible."

The Cambridges were returning to England. George had remained there and had not rejoined them. First, Augusta planned a tour—Dusseldorf, Bonn, Wiesbaden. From there Adolphus wrote thanking a friend for "the interest you take in dear George, and very much obliged, therefore, for the suggestions concerning his travelling. In many respects I agree with you and indeed I have more than once talked with the Duchess of the propriety of his making a tour through the different parts of Europe." But, whatever anyone might suggest, young

George would begin no tour just at the moment when an affectionate girl cousin had come to the throne, discarded her overshadowing mamma and was showing him attention. Now was not the moment for continental excursions. His father ends sagely, "he is not yet sufficiently prepared for such a journey, which I fear he would now make without deriving much benefit from it." In a year's time, when the education interrupted in Hanover had been completed in England, it might be a sound idea.

The tour ended up at Rumpenheim, that family centre where the Landgraf's children gathered so often in his lifetime and afterwards. He left it as a joint legacy, asking only that they should all forgather there every other year. It was a stipulation that was happily kept, and at one time it could almost be said that all Europe's gossip and half her forthcoming engagements were discussed there before they were known elsewhere.

In August, however, the visiting came to an end. Adolphus wrote that he proposed leaving early in the following month and journeying down the Rhine. He would cross to England, spend a week in London and then go on to Dover for some sea-bathing and to await Augusta. She would spend another month with her relations and then join him.

In the autumn Augusta came to London, to another Cambridge House, in Piccadilly. She decided also to enlarge Cambridge Cottage at Kew, the gift of her father-in-law, which she and Adolphus had not visited since their honeymoon. They waited in town until the work was completed, and she walked in Kensington Gardens with little Mary Adelaide, who had the royal privilege of being allowed to pick the flowers. George and Gussy she took with her to the Guildhall, accompanying the young Victoria who was paying her first state visit to the City of London. They dined there and the young cousins were friendly and cordial.

This period was perhaps the most difficult of her life. There was first of all the problem of George and Victoria. Then the news from Hanover was not exactly a compliment to their work there. At Cambridge Cottage, the drawing-room chairs and ottoman covers and the centre carpet were worked for her by loyal ladies of the Viceregal Court, but as soon as Ernest was installed he set himself against the policy of liberal enlightenment followed by Adolphus. In fact, he was establishing a one-man right-wing reaction, and it was apparently, and gallingly, successful. The still handsome Frederica made an excellent Queen, and he was later to be called the Good King Ernest. But it was not by any means easy for Augusta, relegated to Piccadilly and Kew Gardens.

However, time went on. The baby daughter, who was to be her loving prop when "dearest mamma" was an old lady in a bathchair, played among the flowers at Kew. There was another coronation, and this time Adolphus was in the carriage with her. In the Abbey, George and his sister sat in the royal box, while she and their father paced in the procession, she in purple robe and golden circlet, her train borne by Lady Caroline Campbell, her coronet by Lord Villiers.

George was nineteen now. On his birthday his father gave him forty pounds and Augusta gave him twenty. Victoria was friendly with both him and his elder sister, who went to a Court ball and sat with the young Queen and other royal females on an elevated sofa to watch the waltzing.

Then the whole picture changed. George was not the cousin who would share Victoria's throne. He was posted to Gibraltar, for no one wanted him to remain hanging round

London. He left in September, and a grey autumn and winter settled in.

Augusta entertained a considerable amount. She went down frequently to the House of Lords to listen to debates, for she was strongly interested in politics, less liberal than Adolphus, but nothing if not enlightened.

In March the young Augusta—Gussy—was confirmed by the Archbishop at the Chapel Royal. George was still in Gibraltar, but by the end of the year he was attached to the 12th Lancers and in Ireland. It was good to have him nearer. She could remember with revived grief that day, in the previous year, when he had driven out with her after breakfast, as collected as usual, and all the while she had known that before the day ended he would be on his way overseas. For the "ideal Queen" never became anything else, in her innermost heart, than the completely adoring mother. And with George, the adoration was to be taxed to the utmost, for all his constant devotion to her.

In the following year, Prince Albert dawned on England's consciousness. It was vexatious enough to see another intrusive member of the Saxe-Coburg family in the place where George should have sat, but even more annoying when Victoria calmly announced that he should have precedence over the Princes of the Blood. Adolphus was invited to discuss the matter, and was advised to yield. The advice did not come from his wife. She wanted him to be firm. The *pas* was yielded, Adelaide smoothing the way. But Augusta was indignant. At a dinner, though Victoria and Adelaide rose for Albert's health, she remained seated. Vengeful Victoria refrained from asking any Cambridges to her ball.

People were more than a little shocked to know of these

R

domestic palace squabbles. Greville outlined the precedence question in a pamphlet and again Augusta was angry, this time because she thought the definition he gave of George's position might make it difficult for the boy if he went to Germany.

She decided to take both girls travelling, and set out for Italy. Gussy, now of an age to travel intelligently, must be launched on the world. Little Mary Adelaide was, perhaps, better kept out of germ-laden and damp churches, but she could be allowed to run up and down outside in the sunshine until her mother and sister reappeared. Home news followed them and it was not good. Between Augusta and her niece on the throne there was now a fairly strong antipathy that faded only slowly with the years. And George was at the feet of an actress, after an amatory career composed mainly of impressing country belles. Louisa Farebrother was all that was amiable and virtuous; she was to make him for fifty years the most devoted wife, would bring up his sons and make the house in Queen Street a home for him, but she was on the stage. George insisted upon marriage, or yielded to her insistence, or never dreamed of suggesting anything else to a virtuous young woman.

Victoria was furious. It was not altogether clear which of them, she or George, had dropped the glove such a short time before, and which declined to pick it up. To cap it, George made little secret of his dislike for Albert, although he always admitted the honest fellow's good points.

One cold January morning, while his mother was taking his sisters round Roman churches, George took Louisa into a London church, with quite a different object in mind. They came out man and wife.

Society boycotted Louisa; she made no attempt to enter it.

The Queen was inarticulate with rage; yet the Queen lived to ask to meet her. Augusta stayed on in Rome; Louisa's son was to stand, with his wife, by Augusta's deathbed.

When Augusta did return she went to Kew. The young Lady Augusta Somerset came to stay, for the Somersets were friends of the family. She was a spirited, headstrong girl, but her father was abroad and she was good company for Gussy, who saw little of her brother these days. Not that Gussy would for much longer require company at home. Little Mary Adelaide was growing into a great girl, but Gussy was a marriageable princess. The family were to be bound yet closer in their network of relationships, for the plan discussed with Aunt Marie at Mecklenburg-Strelitz was to succeed. If Augusta's son were not to marry an eligible cousin, her daughter would, and be happy in the life. Duke Frederick of Mecklenburg-Strelitz, Cousin Fritz, was an agreeable young man. Alas, like Gussy's cousin George, he was eventually to lose his sight.

On the surface, in spite of the drama of George's marriage and the approach of Gussy's, Augusta's life went on much as usual. She visited Lady Jersey, saw Lady Wilton. Baron Knesebeck, that invaluable and unvarying member of the Cambridge household, was in evidence and as busy as ever. Adolphus was often in the public eye, fulfilling a string of engagements. George alternated between Ireland and Queen Street; and in Queen Street a baby was expected. Louisa FitzGeorge—that was the name the family had selected—was already with child by George, and in 1843 Augusta had her first grandchild, named for both his father and grandfather. It was not the only event in her circle at the time, for she had also to console the little Duchess of Inverness when the Duke of Sussex died.

Then, in June, Gussy was duly married at the Chapel Royal, in the presence of Victoria and Albert. All was smoothed over, and Adolphus bestowed his daughter upon Duke Frederick. She wore three tiaras, Brussels lace over white satin, and orange flowers and myrtle in the German fashion. (Gussy was as German as Mary Adelaide was English.) The diamonds at her neck, and one of the tiaras, were Adelaide's gift.

So Gussy left for Strelitz and the sheltering wing of her aunt-mother-in-law.

The difficult and troubled days seemed now to have passed. The next eight years were to be a quieter platform from which Augusta could survey life. The dramatic had had its day. She could entertain now, garden at Kew, keep her punctual appointments, adore the children, and the increasing arrival of grandchildren, in greater tranquillity.

In 1845, she took Mary over to Strelitz for Christmas, a real German Christmas such as the whole family were always to celebrate, with table-loads of presents, singing and feasting and enormous spoiling of any babies who happened to be there.

The following year her brother Frederick came over to pass the winter with her. George presented the world with another son, and with yet another in the year to follow. A fire at the Kew cottage necessitated repairs, in which alterations were included.

George was in Ireland over "the trouble," and from his window saw O'Connell's long funeral in the rain. Adolphus was growing deaf. In 1847 they visited Hanover again, and went on to Rumpenheim to join the vast family party.

In the following year the Princess Sophia died, with her hand in Augusta's. It was a worrying time, for Augusta would have liked to go over to Strelitz for Gussy's confinement. However, under sister Marie's care it passed off well. More anxious yet was the news of the revival of riots and unrest in Strelitz, which made Fritz send his young wife to shelter for a short time away from the Castle. Gussy even wrote gaily of the possibility of refuge in England, that so-solidly-established isle.

Quiet came back, and in the following year Gussy was again with her mother in England, attending the Birthday drawing-room in white and pink, with sapphires. Augusta wore blue, with pearls and diamonds.

Poor Adolphus had the gout rather badly, and Augusta began cancelling engagements in order to remain with him, for to be deaf and gouty at the same time, and not overbright at any time, was hardly cheerful for so worthy a man. Augusta was very fond of him indeed. There is no denying that she had the brains. Was she not "the ideal Queen"? She was no cloistered princess either; she had lived in the world. She was on terms of friendship with the "old" royal family, as was right and natural, she visited the houses of the established aristocracy and knew the world of diplomacy as one containing old and valued friends. But the real core of her life was the family of three children: George, who might have shared Victoria's throne, but was obviously happy in Queen Street; Gussy, married and settled down, with Augusta's beloved sister Marie to watch and ward; and Mary Adelaide, growing into strong young womanhood. All were part of her, but none had the full glow of her personality. Mary Adelaide had her home-loving heart, her unbounded charity; she loved gardening, sewing and crochet; Gussy was more of the world of fashion and affairs, better looking, better dressed, more "aware." George, success-ful in his career, determined, upright, honest, the servant of the country, was the descendant of the Vicereine of Hanover. And

Adolphus, who had loved her so long and so well, and who now sat tied by the gout and hearing only with difficulty, he had his place in that core of affection.

They lost Adelaide. Sadly Augusta read George's letter, " . . . the thousands who depended upon her kindness . . . she was a remembrance of the dear, good old times, which, alas! are past and gone." Already the vitality of the eighteenth century had waned on to the romanticism of the nineteenth. The good old days became the thing, the present had ceased to be the fashion. Not until nearly the end of the century would "to-day" become the mode once more.

Frederick came over again to pass the winter with her. He went back, leaving her at the end of yet another period of her life, for in 1850 she lost Adolphus.

He lay ill in the great curtained bed, in the room with books lining the wall facing the tall windows. The great square overmantel mirror looked down on Augusta and Mary Adelaide. The little statuettes on the desk watched them as they fanned him and damped his forehead with eau-de-Cologne. He pressed their hands and murmured the little names of affection. Augusta hardly left the bedside, nursing him devotedly. Gussy had been sent for and was coming as fast as she could. But death came faster. One brief moment, when Augusta was out of the room, was enough for the abrupt ending. A few hours later the elder daughter arrived, to fling herself down by the bed and cry "Too late!" She was fated to use those words again.

He was buried at Kew, in the church they had attended so often. Then, with Mary Adelaide, Augusta went down to Wales, to Plas Newydd, where she had stayed before with Adolphus, to rest and recover.

When she came back there was much to do. Cambridge House, where he had died, was to be given up. She was to have apartments in St. James's Palace, where Gussy would also always have her rooms. Cambridge Cottage would remain her home; she would still sit under the familiar Persian lilac, doing her needlework or reading aloud in her lovely, clear voice with its perfect modulations. It was necessary to make plans, readjustments, but once her path was clear, there would be no faltering. There never had been.

She brought Mary Adelaide back to Kew and firmly refused to be hurried over the preparations at St. James's Palace.

George, now Duke of Cambridge (Parliament gave him an income of £12,000 a year and £3,000 to each sister), had to leave for the Crimean War. He behaved during the campaign with credit, was slightly wounded at Inkerman, met Florence Nightingale, and was eventually invalided home.

Augusta and Mary lived on letters. So often in the history of the world have mothers and sisters lived on letters—always the same ones—the note that implies its writer's life and health, the news so ill-expressed that it is unintelligible, the scrawl at the end more intelligible than sunlight itself. George's mother and little sister sat up to all hours, copying the letters for the various relations; they carried them round to read aloud and passed on the news to every one interested. Augusta thanked God without reserve when her son came home safely.

There was another child to think of too. In the spring of the following year she launched Mary Adelaide on the world, at a Drawing-room. From then on they remained as inseparable as any two friends could be. Augusta took her abroad in the summer, first to a family gathering at Rumpenheim, and then on a tour that served the double purpose of beginning her career in the world and distracting her after the tragic death of her father. *Via* Nuremberg, Salzburg and Munich, they went to gay Ischl, where Vienna came to play. They visited Vienna, lovely old Prague, Dresden and best of all—Strelitz, the second home, in time to spend Christmas with the family.

Augusta came home by way of Hanover and went to live at Kew. Through the winter she paid long visits to her apartments in London, but she preferred Cambridge Cottage and loved to entertain her friends there. The jovial Dr. Quin was a frequent guest. He was a homœopathic physician in whom Augusta had such confidence that she made him a member of her household. It was when visiting his apartments near Victoria Station that she first used a hydraulic lift. To be hauled up a narrow London house in a glorified bucket was indeed a far cry from the sweeping elegance of the grand staircase of the Belvedere Palace, down which this princess of Hesse-Cassel had passed to the pageantry of her wedding nearly half a century before.

During the following summer Augusta and Mary Adelaide went to the Isle of Wight for a prolonged visit while workmen were busy on some alterations to the Cottage. Mary Adelaide had by now grown into a buxom, sensible girl, one of those solid, cheerful, healthy daughters-at-home, who are the delight of their parents' heart. George's letters continued to arrive regularly, and it was at this time that the devoted Major Purves came as an Equerry to Augusta's household, to remain for so many years. Few members of her household ever left for any reason but death and extreme old age.

In the summer of 1855 there was a big family party for Augusta's birthday. They went to Prince Albert's own special project, the wonder of the age, the Crystal Palace. For time was running on indeed. No other of the Ladies was to live so long or see so much.

Next year came peace and she could go abroad again. She wanted to go to Strelitz where Gussy's husband, Fritz, was now nearly blind. Lady Geraldine Somerset joined her as lady-in-waiting and remained with her to the end. "Geraldo" swam with her, walked, enjoyed her company. But the year had in store an even greater pleasure than the visit to Baden and to Rumpenheim. George, the beloved son, was appointed Commander-in-Chief of the Army.

It was a joy and a triumph, for many thought that the appointment would go to Albert. But George carried battle honours, he had seen service. He was the only royal duke of his generation, now that his blind cousin lived in Hanover. The appointment was popular with the country and a cheerful ballad announced that "For Commander-in-Chief the brave Duke is the man," under the title "Gallant Cambridge jumping over Prince Albert."

In 1857 Augusta went to Rumpenheim again and enjoyed the gathering there as much as ever, but when she came back it seemed as if another phase of life were over. She felt older now. Still lovely, the austere face still shapely, the sensitive hands slender and firm, she began to know the approach of age. Lady Wilton, her oldest friend in England, died, also Baron Knesebeck who had been such a close link with the past. The Duchess of Gloucester died too and Augusta was at her death-bed.

She decided now that she could not attend the Queen's Drawing-rooms and she spent more and more of her time at Kew. Gussy came over on frequent visits and she could chaperon her young sister, for Mary Adelaide showed no disposition to marry. Certainly Augusta was not failing. She was well and strong and her gift of deep sound sleep remained with her. She even slept through a fire at Kew when every one else was awakened. The visits to Rumpenheim continued and she saw Cassel again, the Belvedere Palace where she had been married, the prim façade opposite, the cleanly, quiet streets. But she was beginning to feel old and her bones ached. Her daughter, Gussy, became reigning Duchess; poor Fritz, entirely blind by now, had succeeded to the dukedom.

At Brighton each year, at Rumpenheim and Strelitz, life followed its pattern. At Kew, where Augusta still drove herself, there were perhaps fewer visitors now, although George came constantly, often bringing senior army men. His position as head of the British Army was a source of great joy to her. His massive figure and whiskered Hanoverian face was the delight of her dark eyes.

In 1866 Augusta gave a dinner-party which was to have a lasting effect on affairs. It was at St. James's Palace and was given for her old friends the Duc and Duchesse d'Aumale. It was on this occasion that Mary Adelaide met Francis, Duke of Teck. He was in fact in no better position than the unfortunate Augustus, Chevalier d'Este, or Mary Adelaide's own little nephews in Queen Street, for his mother, Claudine, Countess de Rhe'dey was morganatically married to Duke Alexander of Württemberg. The unhappy lady was trampled to death when her horse threw her at a review, and he was the only son. The Prince and Princess of Wales had met him at Hanover, liked him, and invited him to England. He came, met Mary Adelaide, fell in love with her, and they were married in the little church at Kew, and lived happily ever after.

It was as sudden as that, but perhaps not altogether as smooth.

Barely were they married when war broke out again on the Continent. This time it brought Augusta even greater tragedy, for her daughters were in opposite camps. Francis hurried back to his post in the Austrian army. "Alas!" she wrote, as the marching started again, "all the dearest countries that my heart loved have been stolen (I can't give it any other name). Hanover, which is the cradle of our English family, Hesse is mine, and Nassau was my dearest own mother's. . . ." But Francis came home safely, and in 1867 Mary Adelaide's first child was born.

The Duchesse d'Aumale brought Augusta the news. It was a little girl, Mary. Here at last was the one who would be Queen, for this was little Princess May, destined to become Duchess of York, Princess of Wales, and Queen Mary.

Before the year was over, Augusta was at Rumpenheim again for the funeral of her brother, the Landgraf. She returned to England to a cheerful Christmas, kept up in the lavish family style, although in English version, by Mary Adelaide. She was now in her apartments in Kensington Palace, next door to the Duchess of Inverness. George was there too. In the summer Augusta's elder daughter and the blind Duke Fritz visited England.

In the summer, too, Mary bore a son who was named for her father, another Adolphus. That was a delight to Augusta. And it was pleasant to pay country house visits, to meet George's friends, to go to the theatre, and above all to have baby Princess May at Kew and to watch her play under the chestnut tree.

Victoria gave White Lodge to the Tecks, to use as a country residence. It was near Kew, and Augusta was delighted.

It was unnecessary sorrow that she had to lose the good

Colonel Purves, her Equerry. He had been driving with her down the Kew Road when a dashing hansom cab overturned her more sedate brougham. She was shaken, but unhurt. The Colonel was injured in the leg and two months later he died of lockjaw. The Royal Cambridge Asylum, the peaceful refuge of many soldiers' widows, benefited by an annual gift, "Augusta's bounty," which Gussy presented to commemorate her mother's escape on this occasion.

The fiftieth anniversary of her wedding came, with lilies-of-the-valley from the Teck babies, and from Mary and Francis a small, myrtle-leaved orange tree. And then, quite suddenly, she came to the beginning of the long end.

She had been really distressed over the Prince of Wales's illness. Alexandra was her great-niece and the Wales children were nursery friends of Mary Adelaide's little ones. But all that was over now, and she went happily on to Strelitz after a visit to Rumpenheim. There, driving on a November day in an open carriage, she got a chill. It brought on a stroke.

Augusta was strong and Dr. Gotz was wonderful. A bed was made up on the ground floor and she fought her way back to consciousness, but never back to her full strength.

In the first week of December, Mary Adelaide arrived from Vienna with the children. Augusta was resolutely cheerful, patient and plucky. She saw the adored grandchildren, insisted on having them with her now and then. She was not strong enough for the full festivities of Christmas, but she could move about again, slowly and with a stick.

It was impossible to go back to Kew until midsummer, and even then Mary Adelaide and George anxiously devised every safeguard in their power. The ship was to be the steadiest, the train and platform made as convenient as possible. Lady Geraldine Somerset would be with her.

Augusta managed the journey, for the last time, and got down to Kew. "The old, wonderful power of sleep," Mary Adelaide wrote, "has returned." She and her brother paid constant visits. Victoria presented her aunt with a wheeled chair, to make the open air more accessible, and Augusta spent long hours out under the lilac tree, although there could be no more gardening.

Not even needlework remained now, for the use of the left hand never returned. Sister Marie, old too, and widowed like herself, came venturing over from Strelitz to visit her, and the two sisters rejoiced in each other as they had done so often before. Marie, who had not been in England for so long, wanted to see London, to go about, and Augusta grudged every minute of her absences, but it was a pleasant and successful visit and the old vigour streamed back into Augusta's mind, although it was never again to reach her limbs.

Reluctant as she always was to haunt the doctors, she had to go up to town at times; soon even that small journey became a burden and Kew was another of the pleasures that must be renounced. She moved up to St. James's Palace for the remainder of her life.

She was seldom lonely. She still entertained, invariably there was a party on her birthday, and on that of Adolphus. Mary came daily, George would drop in when in town, bringing senior officers with him. Her brain was active and talk was nearly all that was left to her now, talk and music and the babies. All the little ones were brought to her, although perhaps she saw more of the little Tecks than of the others. They would come round her chair and sing with her simple songs and hymns,

English and French, including a little ditty she loved dearly, "Trois Anges."

Alexandra was at Marlborough House, near to her great-aunt, and she came over constantly. The Prince of Wales sent bouquets and bonbons. No one forgot her. And nearly every evening, if he were in London, Signor Tosti would come in and sing. Or, if Augusta were not equal to that, they would talk music a while. The Empress Eugenie came, and many others.

Her blind nephew, now the King of Hanover, came over in 1876, and in that warm summer spent many afternoons by her chair in the gardens of Buckingham Palace. Perhaps she trusted the weather too long, for in November, while Mary Adelaide was abroad, she had pleurisy. She recovered, however, enough for a great family party on Christmas evening.

King George of Hanover died, it seemed too soon. Princess Frederica came over to her great-aunt. She was perhaps the favourite amongst the younger ones.

There were still compensations, even when Mary Adelaide had to give up the apartments at Kensington Palace, which she could no longer afford, and go abroad for a long trip, taking her growing daughter with her.

Augusta was still an excellent correspondent. She wrote, as always, just as she spoke and felt. To Lady Dalrymple she sent thanks for " . . . better accounts of your so beloved mother—my excellent friend—may she be spared to you for many years to come, if," she went on with the sad exactitude of experience, "if *without* suffering. . . ."

Her Will had been made long since, but there were many little things she wanted remembered, tokens, special gifts. She could not face a lawyer again, it was beyond her, but she wrote little slips of paper, her sentences full of the vehemence that was so like her speech, " . . . to my precious, beloved son, George, the large topaz seal which the beloved late Duke gave me at our marriage, the ring that I always wore with the small ruby, the repeating watch which I have always at my bedside, Augusta's miniature painted at Rome, and that of Mary in enamel after Winterhalter, and the photograph of Alix in her bride's dress." She asked her children to honour these little requests, tried to assure them that there was no favourite amongst the three. "Should my dear George wish for anything else of my things, my dear daughters will leave him his choice— it is not from any want of love that I leave him so little, but he has so much in his own house I hardly know what else to name!" Then, suddenly, "I *love* you *all* equally, warmly, and intensely—that you know. God bless you, my precious George, that is the best thing I can leave behind for you; your loving mother until death, Augusta."

Death was not very far away now.

Victoria's Jubilee came, and the old aunt sent across to her aged niece a little note of enquiry, which brought back the quick reply, "Very tired but very happy." It was a just summary too of Augusta's life. She was a little deaf now and memory was fading. The long ago seemed clear and vivid, the cascades and gardens of Wilhelmshoehe, the first landing in England, the babies, the gentle years of their Viceroyalty in Hanover. She had now come to her ninety-second year, but she would still command guests to dinner when her husband's birthday came round again.

Then, in the spring of 1889, her strength began to fail. She was ill, rallied and seemed to recover. Augusta was always difficult about seeing doctors, and perhaps would not have

Sir Oscar Clayton summoned as often as the family would have liked; but she was so old the great silence had come very close and probably her health and doctors seemed unimportant to her.

Early in April she failed again, and in a few days she was dead. Alexandra, the beloved great-niece, was at her bedside, but not one of her own children could come in time. Her son was in Ireland, her elder daughter arrived again too late, and even Mary Adelaide was not there to say farewell. "Dear precious darling," George wrote in his diary, "May God have mercy on her dear soul."

Three hundred callers came to the Palace, for a figure had gone from the world. George's son, Admiral Sir Adolphus FitzGeorge, came with his wife to the service held at the bedside immediately after death. The Prince of Wales was there, and Alexandra. And then Augusta journeyed down for the last time to Kew and Victoria came to see her laid beside her dear Duke and to hear the singing of Augusta's favourite 90th Psalm:

"For a thousand years in thy sight are but as yesterday, seeing that is past as a watch in the night. . . ."

INDEX